FLANNERY
O'CONNOR

A Study of the Short Fiction

Also Available in Twayne's Studies in Short Fiction Series

Andre Dubus: A Study of the Short Fiction
  by Thomas E. Kennedy
John Steinbeck: A Study of the Short Fiction
  by R. S. Hughes
Peter Taylor: A Study of the Short Fiction
  by James Curry Robison
Tennessee Williams: A Study of the Short Fiction
  by Dennis Vannatta

Twayne's Studies in Short Fiction

Gordon Weaver, General Editor
Oklahoma State University

Flannery O'Connor, 1952, at a Reception celebrating the publication of *Wise Blood*. Photograph courtesy of Robert Giroux, Flannery O'Connor's literary executor.

FLANNERY O'CONNOR

A Study of the Short Fiction

Suzanne Morrow Paulson
Minot State University, North Dakota

TWAYNE PUBLISHERS • BOSTON
A Division of G. K. Hall & Co.

/

Twayne's Studies in Short Fiction Series No. 2
Editorial Assistant to Gordon Weaver: Stephanie Corcoran

Copyright © 1988 by G. K. Hall & Co.
All rights reserved.
Published by Twayne Publishers
A Division of G. K. Hall & Co.
70 Lincoln Street, Boston, Massachusetts 02111

Excerpts from *Mystery and Manners* by Flannery O'Connor copyright © 1957,
1961, 1963, 1964, 1966, 1967, 1969 by Flannery O'Connor; reprinted by
permission of Farrar, Straus and Giroux, Inc.
Excerpts from *The Habit of Being* by Flannery O'Connor copyright © 1979 by
Regina O'Connor; reprinted by permission of Farrar, Straus and Giroux, Inc.
Excerpts from "The Lame Shall Enter First," "Revelation," "Judgement
Day," and "Parker's Back" from *The Complete Stories* by Flannery O'Connor
copyright © 1971 by Flannery O'Connor; reprinted by permission of Farrar,
Straus and Giroux, Inc.

Copyediting supervised by Barbara Sutton.
Book design by Janet Zietowski.
Book production by Gabrielle B. McDonald.
Typeset in 10/12 Caslon by Compset, Inc.

Printed on permanent/durable acid-free paper
and bound in the United States of America.

Library of Congress Cataloging-in-Publication Data

Paulson, Suzanne Morrow.
    Flannery O'Connor : a study of the short fiction / Suzanne Morrow
Paulson.
       p.   cm. — (Twayne's studies in short fiction ; TSSF2)
    Bibliography: p.
    Includes index.
    ISBN 0-8057-8301-6 (alk. paper)
    1. O'Connor, Flannery—Criticism and interpretation. I. Title.
II. Series.
PS3565.C57Z83   1988
   813'.54—dc19

                             88-14681
                                CIP

Contents

Preface   ix
Acknowledgments   xv

PART 1. THE SHORT FICTION: A CRITICAL ANALYSIS
    Introduction   3
    Death-Haunted Questers   13
    Male/Female Conflicts   28
    "The Mystery of Personality" and Society   46
    Good/Evil Conflicts   85

PART 2. THE WRITER: SELECTED COMMENTS BY O'CONNOR, HER
    FRIENDS, HER MENTORS, HER EDITORS, AND HER CRITICS
    Introduction   121
    The Author's Art, Her Reader, and Her Community   123
    The Critics and O'Connor's Responses   139

PART 3. THE CRITICS
    Introduction   151
    • Sister M. Bernetta Quinn • Maurice Lévy
    • Dan Curley • Robert Fitzgerald • David
    Eggenschwiler • David A. Myers • J. M. G.
    Le Clézio • Arno Heller • M. A. Klug
    • Michel Gresset • Sarah Gordon • Louis D.
    Rubin, Jr. • Leon V. Driskell and Joan T.
    Brittain • André Bleikasten • Bartlett C.
    Jones • Claire Katz [Kahane] • Louise
    Westling • Preston M. Browning, Jr. • Mary L.
    Morton • Frederick Asals • Sheldon Currie
    • Edward Kessler • Claude Richard • Robert
    Drake • Dorothy Walters

Chronology   225
Bibliography   229
Index   234

Preface

> The storyteller has managed to maintain a status as a kind of third-rate celebrity, where he ranks somewhat below Miss Gum Spirits of Turpentine and a little above the Lone Ranger's horse, but he attains this distinction as an oddity, and not as an artist.[1]

> It is the way of drama that with one stroke the writer has both to mirror and to judge. When such a writer has a freak for his hero, he is not simply showing us what we are, but what we have been and what we could become. His prophet-freak is an image of himself.[2]

One possible response to Flannery O'Connor's work is to consider it "odd" because it blends, as she puts it, "the Comic and the Terrible." It is also "odd" that whatever version of O'Connor critics adopt, there is some evidence of a contrary version. Sometimes critics see O'Connor as, for example, a Roman Catholic satirist of Protestant Georgia, while others identify her with the nihilist Hulga, a character O'Connor called her "heroine." Such contradictions in the criticism and the tragicomic mix of her work may seem different, but she still did not consider herself or her work "odd"—even though both critics and members of her own community emphasized her "peculiarity."[3]

Flannery O'Connor simply called herself "a Catholic peculiarly possessed of the modern consciousness" (*Letters*, 90). I will develop the version of O'Connor emphasizing her Catholicism in the last section of this book, but I will first focus primarily on O'Connor's "modern consciousness" to explain why her work at first glance seems "different" and to suggest a more balanced approach than the strictly theological one that dominates most criticism on O'Connor today. In fact, many of O'Connor's characters, like others in the modern tradition, are primitive and grotesque. They struggle for a sense of significance in a scientific/industrial world that undermines the human capacity for meaningful relationships and defines humanity not in terms of spirituality but as animals, or worse, machines. Almost half of O'Connor's published stories end with a shocking death: a young boy hangs himself, an escaped convict exterminates an entire family, a grandfather murders his granddaughter.

O'Connor's emphasis on murder, madness, and alienation may not be so "odd" given the works of other modern writers. Certain nineteenth-century authors—whom O'Connor studied as she explored early modernist short fiction—also present shocking events and grotesque characters struggling with modern dilemmas. In *The Metamorphosis*, Kafka's protagonist turns into an insect with "a brown fluid [issuing] from his mouth." In *The Double*, Dostoyevski's hero goes mad, driven by an imagined antagonist who is an exact duplicate of himself. Conrad's *Secret Sharer* harbors a murderer and identifies with the criminal impulses at issue. The grotesque elements in O'Connor's work are even more understandable considering that she went through an "Edgar Allan Poe period" lasting "for years" (*Letters*, 98).

An elderly acquaintance once chided O'Connor for writing "horror tales," and she responded, "Mine is actually a *comic* art. Not that that fact detracts from its seriousness."[4] Her unusual brand of "comedy" does not appeal to everyone. And yet in spite of first impressions, her work encourages readers to laugh at themselves and thus to sympathize with her "prophet-freaks" by identifying with them. Not every reader can manage this feat initially, but the unsympathetic reader should try to keep in mind that these "freaks" are symbolic of human nature generally. Even though O'Connor's stories present grim occurrences in human life, portions of them all—including the most grim—abound in humor. Almost nostalgically, O'Connor comments: "I like [my stories] better than anybody and read them over and over and laugh and laugh" (*Letters*, 249).

O'Connor's stories are, however, not merely funny and not simply grotesque. They are philosophical, complex, intricately crafted, and symbolic. This Catholic writer of the South says that she writes "tragicomedy," just as Faulkner and others writing in the modern tradition do. O'Connor's portraits of women are especially complex and sometimes misunderstood because readers miss the author's sympathy for her tragicomic female intellectuals, widowed farm managers, "sluts," "sibyls," grandmothers, mothers, aunts, daughters, and sisters. Laughter does distance the reader from its object, but if we also recognize ourselves as participants in the human comedy, laughter encourages sympathy. O'Connor's work challenges us to identify with human vulnerability and to develop self-awareness.

Readers embarking on a study of O'Connor's short fiction should expect eventually to "laugh and laugh" but only after understanding that her stories cannot be read as simple realism superficially understood. Nor should they be read simply as Southern regionalism. O'Connor warns that "If you are a Southern writer, the danger that you will remain just that is very great and to the serious writer, it is also rather terrifying."[5] Her work is demanding and should be read and reread as one reads poetry. Approaches to reading her stories will be explained later, but here we should note that the rewards for a careful reading are many—not least as they provide insights into Catholic values, modern philosophy, and human psychology.

What I wish to emphasize is the fact that we should first of all consider the traditions in which O'Connor wrote rather than explain the tragicomic mix of her work by pointing to her presumably stern Catholicism, her Southern background, her ill health most of her short life, her allegedly overbearing mother, and the early death of her father from disseminated lupus erythematosus, the same disease that took her life. While it may be true that O'Connor's disease and the personal tragedies she suffered led her to develop her comic impulses as a defense, what is more important is that her suffering led her to identify with human frailty. She both judged and loved her characters. Her capacity for love and sympathy was expanded by daily experience of physical weakness. She herself mourned "for the world," as did Thomas's mother in "The Comforts of Home."[6] She contemplated her characters and their place in the larger modern world, not just as representatives of her region. She should be placed with the best twentieth-century American, British, and European modernists obsessed with alienation, the dark side of human nature, and death. She should also be counted among the greatest comic writers of all time.

In part 1 of this text, I identify a variety of O'Connor's themes and clarify important literary techniques through detailed readings of all her stories except "The Crop," "The Train," "The Peeler," "The Heart of the Park," "Enoch and the Gorilla," "You Can't Be Any Poorer than Dead," "Why Do the Heathen Rage?," and "The Barber," which are preliminary fragments or were rewritten as parts of the major novels better studied in their final form.

I have arranged the readings in four chapter groupings to highlight certain themes. My groupings are meant to establish O'Connor's diverse concerns. I do not believe, as Robert Drake first suggested, that this Catholic writer has only "one story" to tell.[7]

"Death-Haunted Questers" focuses on the alienated self struggling for security in a modern world devoid of spiritual reassurances. "A Stroke of Good Fortune," "Wildcat," "The Geranium," and "The Capture" develop a single character and imply existentialist concerns. In "The Lame Shall Enter First" and "A View of the Woods," a death-haunted parent remakes a child into a mirror image of himself, thereby achieving the secular man's substitute for immortality. Interactions with the community (social or racial groups) are not fully developed in any of the above stories.

"Male/Female Conflicts" focuses on sex-related differences. The masculinization of culture and a revulsion for femininity are important motifs in the unpublished manuscripts and in "The Comforts of Home," "The Enduring Chill," and "Greenleaf."

"'The Mystery of Personality' and Society" differs from previous groups because death-haunted questers and parent/child or male/female pairs refer the reader to the community. These stories present class conflicts, racial differences, and the mindless conformity of groups marching in processions or parades and basing their sense of identity on such status symbols as uniforms, possessions, skin color, and the Christian faith. Establishing the right relation to community is the primary focus of "Good Country People," "The Partridge Festival," "A Late Encounter with the Enemy," "The Displaced Person," "Judgement Day," "The Artificial Nigger," and "Everything That Rises Must Converge."

The largest and last category of stories, "Good/Evil Conflicts," discusses how the protagonist grappling with such conflicts subconsciously perceives them as conflicts between spirit and body. Sadistic impulses (a major concern of O'Connor's) dominate these characters who want to repress unpleasant reminders of man's corporeal nature. The stories in this group are related to the stories involving male/female conflicts and in a way return us to the early death-haunted stories. These stories about good/evil conflicts are different, however, in that they refer the reader to theological issues. The various facets of evil are defined in traditional Catholic terms. For the most part, evil results from man's perverse will—for example, the active will of The Misfit in "A Good Man is Hard to Find" or the passive will of Mr. Shiftlet in "The Life You Save May Be Your Own." Mrs. Cope in "A Circle in the Fire" suffers a paranoia for natural disasters—what Catholics call "metaphysical evils" (a minor category when contemplating the workings of evil in the world). Three other stories—"The River," "A Temple of the Holy Ghost," and "Parker's Back"—focus on the human tendency to see the physical world itself as evil. In these latter stories, O'Connor means to affirm the Incarnation.

Part 2 presents a selection of O'Connor's own comments on her art, her reader, and her community. The authorial commentary alternates with criticisms of others—thus developing some interesting interrelationships. I have also selected brief views of O'Connor by those who knew her well. The most important excerpt in this section is O'Connor's introduction to a book outlining the tragic case of a child afflicted with cancer (*A Memoir to Mary Ann*).

Part 3 presents a sampling of critical essays revealing that a variety of themes and approaches have been identified by critics with diverse interests—theological, philosophical, psychological, sociological, historical, New Critical, stylistic, and/or structuralist. I have included translations from French and German articles, demonstrating that O'Connor's works transcend time and place. Critics writing in Canada, England, France, Germany, and Austria are represented.

The bibliography includes carefully selected entries in the hope that those who are fairly new to O'Connor studies will find sources representing a variety of approaches from various parts of the world. Readers should consult Robert E. Golden and Mary C. Sullivan's reference guide for a comprehensive list of early sources.[8] Neither this bibliographic list nor the selection of criticism is meant to be comprehensive, although the bibliography and the footnotes to this book do mention most of the major commentators on O'Connor's work. In addition, the bibliography includes some voices consistently missed and deserving attention.

I am grateful to those who helped me to develop my ideas and to produce this book on modernism and Flannery O'Connor. The University of Minnesota provided a grant for my research in Georgia. The College of St. Thomas provided superb secretarial help in the person of Linda Halverson. The University of Minnesota, Morris, and the University of Illinois assigned research assistants to my project. Carol Pagliara, graduate student and expert typist, patiently met the challenge of working with a complex manuscript.Mary Pat Paulson Byrnes proofread with an eagle eye. Kent R. Bales, Lonnie J. Durham, Archie I. Leyasmeyer, Ed Griffin, and Arthur I. Geffen of the University of Minnesota; Lynn Altenbernd and Mary Loeffelholz of the University of Illinois freely offered criticisms and corrections. Robert D. Wirt expanded my understanding of Freud, and George T. Wright enlarged my capacity to analyze O'Connor's work in terms of its poetic elements. Gordon Weaver, Liz Traynor, and Anne M. Jones were supportive, thoughtful, and thought-provoking editors. Many years ago, Chester G. Anderson first encouraged my study of Flannery O'Connor and the double figure. His wisdom and knowledge of psychoanalytic approaches to literature have been major factors in my scholarly endeavors. Finally, my husband, James, and my sons, Mark and Craig, shared the doldrums of the writing process—and love.

Suzanne Morrow Paulson

Notes

1. Flannery O'Connor, unpublished document, Ina Dillard Russell Library, Georgia College, file no. 258; hereafter abbreviated FO followed by the Georgia College file number. These quotations are copyright © 1988 by the Estate of Flannery O'Connor and are used with their permission and that of the author's literary executor, Robert Giroux.

2. Sally Fitzgerald and Robert Fitzgerald, eds., *Flannery O'Connor: Mystery and Manners* (New York: Farrar, Straus & Giroux, 1969), 117–18; hereafter abbreviated *MM* followed by page number.

3. Sally Fitzgerald, ed., *Letters of Flannery O'Connor: The Habit of Being* (New York: Random House, 1979), 105, 106; hereafter cited as *Letters* followed by page number. Algene Ballif, an early reviewer of *The Violent Bear It Away*, complains that O'Connor's characters are too odd—"Strangers from a foreign land" who "come to us too abruptly, too nakedly, too literally from the realm of the unconscious" (review in *Commentary*, October 1960, 358–62). Martha Stephens says that: "It is difficult to imagine any childhood for a person so odd and eccentric as O'Connor" (*The Question of Flannery O'Connor* [Baton Rouge: Louisiana State University Press, 1973], 155).

4. Margaret Inman Meaders, "Flannery O'Connor: 'Literary Witch,'" *Colorado Quarterly* 10 (1962):382.

5. This quote was taken from a typescript of O'Connor's and reprinted by Louise Westling in *Sacred Groves and Ravaged Gardens: The Fiction of Eudora Welty, Carson McCullers, and Flannery O'Connor* (Athens: University of Georgia Press, 1985), 136.

6. *The Complete Stories* (New York: Farrar, Straus & Giroux, 1971), 397.

7. Robert Drake, *Flannery O'Connor: A Critical Essay* (Grand Rapids, Mich.: William B. Eerdmans, 1966), 17.

8. Robert E. Golden and Mary C. Sullivan, *Flannery O'Connor and Caroline Gordon* (Boston: G. K. Hall, 1977).

Acknowledgments

I am especially grateful for the work of Edith and Fred Farrell, whose research and translations made accessible fine examples of French criticism. I only regret that their enthusiastic efforts unearthed more essays than I was able to include. Robert Giroux and the publishers of the excerpts reprinted in parts 2 and 3 were prompt and generous in granting permissions, and for this I also express my thanks. Finally, Sarah Gordon, who teaches in the Department of English at Georgia College and who edits the *Flannery O'Connor Bulletin,* and Gerald Becham, the former curator for the Flannery O'Connor collection housed in the Ina Dillard Russell Library of Georgia College, devoted considerable time in support of my research when I visited Milledgeville to investigate the manuscript files. They deserve special recognition for encouraging O'Connor scholarship and for sharing both materials and insights related to the O'Connor canon.

Part 1

THE SHORT FICTION:
A CRITICAL ANALYSIS

Introduction

Blessed are the smilers; their teeth shall show.

(*Letters*, 114)

The charge that O'Connor writes horror and not humor is made most
often by those who use *Mystery and Manners* exclusively as a touchstone
to her work. This collection of essays—based on lectures delivered to
Southern, conservative, and/or Catholic audiences—was compiled after the author's death and suggests that her work is written from a
strictly theological perspective. In many cases, O'Connor was speaking
to an audience containing individuals who subsequently visited the
O'Connor home and thus discussed her lectures with her mother, a
devout Catholic. Totally dependent on her mother most of her life,
O'Connor joked about her mother's response to her work ("She hasn't
learned to love Mrs. Watts" [*Letters*, 35]). Sally Fitzgerald, her official
biographer, explains that "she had, in fact, only one great fear—that
her mother would die before she did" (*Letters*, xii). In sum, O'Connor's
essays to some degree are affected by her mother's Catholicism and her
community's conservatism.

Since the publication of O'Connor's letters, critics have noticed
basic contradictions between authorial suggestions in *Mystery and Manners* and statements found elsewhere.[1] In one case, for example, a *Mystery and Manners* quote reads: "all my own experience has been that of
the writer who believes, in Pascal's words, in the 'God of Abraham,
Isaac, and Jacob and not of the philosophers and scholars'" (*MM*, 161).
But O'Connor's stories and novels do develop philosophical themes,
especially themes related to existentialism. In fact, one of O'Connor's
most common character types is the modern intellectual struggling for
significance and permanence in a world of alienation, fragmentation,
and transience. Hazel, Rayber, Sheppard, Hulga, Asbury, Calhoun,
Walter, and Old Dudley all suffer existential encounters with nothingness as the philosophers of her day defined them. *Mystery and Manners*,
then, fails to represent O'Connor's "modern consciousness" and intellectual interests.

O'Connor of course satirizes modern life; her "modernism" needs to be qualified and carefully defined. This issue will be developed throughout my readings of the stories, the final basis for my judgments. And at times, O'Connor denies being an "interleckchul" (*Letters*, 574), but there is much to suggest that she did indeed recognize herself as such.[2] She once wrote a revealing letter to "A":[3] "If I were to live long enough and develop as an artist to the proper extent, I would like to write a comic novel about a woman . . . the angular intellectual proud woman approaching God inch by inch with ground teeth" (*Letters*, 105–6). And a later letter reveals that the intellectual woman she would satirize is herself. She discusses an essay on Saint Thomas and Freud and says that it "has the answer in it to what you call my struggle to submit, which is not a struggle to submit but a struggle to accept and with passion. I mean, possibly, with joy. Picture me with my ground teeth stalking joy" (*Letters*, 126). The similarities between this portrait of herself and the plan to portray the intellectual woman cannot be missed here. In spite of her claims to being a simple storyteller, O'Connor's intellectual gifts must be recognized in order to understand her work.

It is difficult to believe that nothing except Catholicism is important when reading O'Connor because so many alternatives to this exclusive attitude can be found in sources other than *Mystery and Manners*. O'Connor declares that "One of the great disadvantages of being known as a Catholic writer is that no one thinks you can lift the pen without trying to show somebody redeemed" (*Letters*, 434). She also says that "To write for a Catholic audience would mean that the writer would either (1) have to write down, or (2) starve to death. Neither is advisable." Variation of the idea that art takes precedence over theology is found in many different sources. Most emphatically, O'Connor says, "I don't think theology should be scaffolding" for art.[4]

This Catholic writer does in fact contradict herself, like Walter, a character in her unfinished novel. Walter projects a variety of different personalities when he writes letters that communicate what a particular correspondent wants to hear. Likewise, O'Connor confesses, "People are always asking me if I am a Catholic writer and I am afraid that I sometimes say no and sometimes say yes, depending on who the visitor is" (*Letters*, 353). O'Connor is more serious-minded than this fickleness suggests, and she was indeed writing from a Catholic perspective. But readers should give some thought to the context of authorial statements and should not rely too much on statements of intention found in *Mys-*

tery and Manners—statements emphasizing her Catholicism and apparently leading some to assume that her theology requires a stern view of humanity and a lack of compassion.

I do not want to contradict Sister Bernetta Quinn's statement that in order to understand Flannery O'Connor "one must read and meditate upon the Bible."[5] Many stories, however, cannot be understood unless readers also consider other contexts, especially those related to modernist thought.

Psychoanalytic Approaches

According to O'Connor, modern fiction explores "the mystery of personality," which she conceives as "the general mystery of incompleteness" (*MM*, 167). The divided self in literature refers to characters with an uncertain sense of identity—a sense of incompleteness. When the boundaries of a character's self are unclear, he or she depends on the identity of someone else, usually the parent, to establish self-worth. In the forties, fifties, and sixties when O'Connor was writing, Freud's theories of the divided self were widely discussed by academics and writers alike. Psychoanalytic approaches are essential to any basic understanding of Flannery O'Connor's stories.

Madness is the central issue in only one work (her best novel, *The Violent Bear It Away*), but neurosis, as Freudian psychology defines it, is an issue throughout the canon. O'Connor admonishes Cecil Dawkins, a fellow writer, for neglecting "psychological and metaphysical realities" (*Letters*, 104)—this at a time (the fifties) when many critics still viewed Freudian psychology with reserve. O'Connor renders human primitive instincts unflinchingly and considers both "psychological and metaphysical" factors. She did express the inadequacies of Freud's psychology due to his view that religion is "wish fulfillment" and his alleged acceptance of psychic determinism (which excuses "sin"). She did object to the tendency of many Freudians to rationalize murderers and rapists as merely "sick" and not "responsible." She made no excuses for bad behavior and wanted to be certain that "the Devil gets identified as the Devil and not taken for this or that psychological tendency" (*Letters*, 360). Still, O'Connor says that she is "ready to admit certain uses for [Freud]" (*Letters*, 110) and even saw Aquinas and Freud as "rowing in the same boat" (*Letters*, 491). O'Connor declares that she had "quite a respect for Freud when he isn't made into a philosopher" (*Letters*, 491). In her personal copy of Jung's *Modern*

Man in Search of a Soul, she marked the passage: "Only a great idealist like Freud could devote a lifetime to the unclean work." The dark, narcissistic, and aggressive side of human nature is more easily repressed than tidied up.

O'Connor's letters vacillate between disdain and respect for Freudian principles applied to literature, depending on who is applying them and how. She was angered by readers who used psychology to label her characters "pathological" freaks rather than symbols of human weaknesses we all experience to some degree. And she also disapproved of an egg hunt for Freudian symbols. In her letters, she imagines two participants in the Writers Workshop at the University of Iowa "chained together by mutual hate on one of the less important circles of the inferno, eternally arguing if church steeples are phallic symbols" (*Letters*, 128).

When Cecil Dawkins pointed out that though behind her idiot priests the edifice of Catholicism stands unscathed, she lets her idiot sociologist "stand for Freud," O'Connor reacted with: "In heaven's name where do you get the idea that Sheppard represents Freud? . . . Freud was a great one, wasn't he, for bringing home to people the fact that they weren't what they thought they were, son if Freud were in this, which he is not, he would certainly be on the other side of the fence from Shepp" (*Letters*, 491). It is dangerous to generalize too much from isolated statements of O'Connor's without considering their context. Considering that she sometimes justifiably discouraged Freudian readings, one should not conclude that she therefore rejected Freudian thought wholesale. The stories themselves suggest otherwise. She knew that many of her readers had studied Freudian theory. O'Connor's characters frequently exhibit symptoms that are unmistakably Freudian: they suffer internal conflicts because of their own narcissism and regressive behavior. O'Connor might substitute the word "pride" for narcissism and think of regressive behavior as the sign of a spiritually underdeveloped soul, but O'Connor's and Freud's basic judgments regarding human nature are similar. O'Connor was attracted by Freud's emphasis on self-knowledge regarding aggressive and libidinous instincts as a first step toward gaining self-control and maturity. To declare that psychology is not relevant to O'Connor studies is tantamount to declaring her stupid and unable to predict that Freudian suggestiveness would be identified by her readers. O'Connor does say that Freud is inadequate to understanding "the religious encounter"

(*MM*, 165). She does not say he is inadequate to understanding human nature.

The New Critics

Besides considering the philosophical and psychological currents of O'Connor's time, readers need some background in the major theories of the then-fashionable New Critical creed—especially as shaped by Cleanth Brooks and Robert Penn Warren, the critics O'Connor studied. Brooks and Warren were Southern critics at the forefront of the New Critical movement that overwhelmed the literary world in the forties, fifties, and sixties. My summary here can barely hint at the complexities of New Criticism as it developed from such critics as T. S. Eliot, I. A. Richards, William Empson, John Crowe Ransom, and Yvor Winters. I will try, however, to delineate some basic principles, focusing on those O'Connor seemed to appropriate for her own purposes.

O'Connor in fact defines herself as belonging "to that literary generation whose education was in the hands of the New Critics. . . . With these people the emphasis was on seeing that your thoughts and feelings—whatever they were—were aptly contained within your elected image."[6] Brooks and Warren recommend techniques of "showing" and not "telling," which require an extremely alert reader. As O'Connor explains it: "Modern fiction often looks simpler than the fiction that preceded it, but in reality it is more complex. . . . The author has for the most part absented himself from direct participation in the work and has left the reader to make his own way amid experiences dramatically rendered and symbolically ordered" (*MM*, 139).

The New Critics directed the reader's attention to a close reading of the work itself, its overall structure, its dynamic form, its style, the relation of parts to one another, tensions between the literal sense of the work and its implications—between that which is denoted and that which is connoted; between the concrete level and the abstract. They focused their attention on describing the rhythms and pace of the work's language; the appropriateness of metaphor, imagery, and symbolism; patterns of repetition; the intricacies of point of view; the strategies of juxtapositions; chapter beginnings and endings; titles and naming; the precision of descriptive detail, incident, dialogue; tone used to define character and to suggest theme; allusions to other literary works; the management of plot, flashback, foreshadowing, suspense—all of the literary elements that should, in a superior work, achieve a unity of effect.

The New Critic usually does not consider the writer's biography, the reader's emotional response to the work, the work's historical setting, or its significance as it relates to such disciplines as psychology, philosophy, or sociology—although many critics do consider such contexts after first focusing on the structure of the work itself. The only valid means of understanding the work is to study its formal aspects, according to these critics.

The major task of any critical approach is to explain how form relates to meaning and how meaning relates to the concrete experience depicted by a particular poem or fictional work. The New Critics felt defensive in a technological age that seemed to reduce art to the didactum of its moral message or to useless decoration. They affirmed, then, its importance in providing "an experiential grasp of our world which eludes the systematized abstractions of the Knowledge-giving disciplines," as Murray Krieger puts it.[7] O'Connor's scorn for the sciences and for direct statement of abstract "truth" is partly due to the New Critical movement. The experience rendered in all of its concrete particularity in a work of art is unique and therefore valuable. Form and content are organically unified—inseparable. The work offers the complexity and fullness of experience without the confusion of a transient, constantly changing world, because the experience is clarified, crystallized, by its form, which is controlled by the individual writer or poet. The more complex and dense is the depiction of concrete reality, the more valuable. The particulars of life are our only means of glimpsing "truth." Although critics argue about whether there is a timeless, unchanging, disembodied "truth" to be found in the greatest works that transcend time and place, most New Critics emphasized that each fictional work or poem represents a totally unique depiction of reality, and further, each reader's reexperience of the work is a kind of recreation. The experience of poetry and fiction humanizes us—allows us to share the writer's unique perspective, his or her ability to see beyond the general, beyond the stereotype, to the essential "truth."

In sum, the New Critics, especially Brooks and Warren, the critics O'Connor admired most, asserted the value of particularity, the concrete level of the work. The work's value resides in the aesthetic structure that captures concrete experience, not in its "moral," or message. On the other hand, Yvor Winters emphasized the ethical purpose of the work, which he saw as a necessary consideration when judging a literary piece. Still, the moral sense should be expressed indirectly. Thus, the New Critics demanded a great deal of the reader and paid special attention to understatement, irony, ambiguity, paradox, form, style, and "strange skips and gaps" (*MM*, 40), as O'Connor puts it—gaps that imply meaning rather than stating it directly. They valued the work as it rendered concrete experience with a certain intensity: the abstract is expressed indirectly through the concrete life of the work. The Southern critic and friend of O'Connor, Allen Tate (whose writer wife, Caroline Gordon, offered early encouragement to O'Connor), judged a literary work by its controlled complexity—its ability to form a coherent order that connotes a complex configuration of meaning. Each word, image, or metaphor truly belongs to the whole, suggests ideas that also belong, and logically leads to the central idea of the whole. He too admires a suggestive density of connotation as opposed to authorial intrusion.[8]

Many critics have cited James Joyce's work as an example of an author's gift for "showing"; Stephen Dedalus in *The Portrait of the Artist as a Young Man* proclaims that the artist should be "like the God of creation . . . within or behind or beyond or above his handiwork, invisible."[9] Ideally, an author does not address his or her readers (explaining whether or not a character is moral or immoral, foolish or wise) but rather presents the character's situation "dramatically" so the readers can make judgments indirectly. O'Connor offers advice of this sort to a writer friend: "When you present a pathetic situation, you have to let it speak entirely for itself . . . let the things in the story do the talking . . . paint with words. . . . Do you know Joyce's story 'The Dead'? . . . Show these things and you don't have to say them" (*Letters*, 83–84). In sum, the New Critics admired complex literature that dramatically rendered concrete experience in all its particulars, suggestively arranged to convey indirectly the author's experience and ideas. They assumed a reader willing and able to grapple with the complexities of the work—willing to contemplate subtle implications, complicated structures, and multiple levels of meaning.

The Author's Voice

Because "The modern novelist merges the reader in the experience" (*MM*, 139), as O'Connor explains it, the reader must analyze carefully whether or not the protagonist expresses the author's sentiments. More often than not, subtle ironies are at play, and O'Connor's characters express ideas that the author would condemn. She uses a limited, third-person perspective that at times expresses the authorial voice but at other times (in the same story) reveals only the protagonist's views, not to be confused with the author's. In fact, this special kind of dramatic irony is one of O'Connor's most common techniques and was developed by Joyce, among other modern writers.[10]

Sometimes critics, such as Josephine Hendin, Claire Katz [Kahane], Carol Shloss, Martha Stephens, and Ruth Van der Kieft, charge O'Connor with sadistic impulses because they confuse a sadistic character's viewpoint with the author's.[11] Readers therefore must be on the lookout for subtle signals that we are viewing the world through a particular character's perspective. When a character is shown as looking at something, contemplating another character or scene, and/or relating his past or participating in a dramatic exchange of dialogue with another character, then the sentiments expressed usually belong to the character and not to O'Connor herself. They express a distorted view, the nasty lens of a particular character's perspective. This requires an alert reader able to pinpoint whose eyes are temporarily being used as windows to O'Connor's fictional world.

For example, Thomas in "The Comforts of Home" is shown looking out of the window at his mother who is driving up with a juvenile-delinquent woman and planning to offer their home as a mission of charity, against her son's will. We are presented with Thomas peering down at this woman, and we are told that "the little slut" (CS, 383) got out of the car.[12] The judgment that the girl is a "slut" is surely the jealous Thomas's thought and not O'Connor's authorial judgment. In fact, Thomas's mother keeps reminding her son that this woman is not so different from himself. In "A Circle in the Fire," we are told that Mrs. Cope "saw that [the Negro, Culver] had not gone through the gate because he was too lazy to get off and open it" (CS, 176). This communicates Mrs. Cope's own prejudice regarding Negroes, not O'Connor's. Tanner, not O'Connor, sees his daughter as "stupid" (CS, 543). Other examples of this technique will be developed as we analyze the stories more particularly, but for now, we should simply remember that point of view is extremely complicated in O'Connor's works because the author aims to disappear but at the same time wants to reveal the inner landscape of her characters.

In the O'Connor canon, then, overt authorial intrusion rarely occurs—and then only in the later works. Discouraged because her more subtle methods were misunderstood, she seemed to plan explicit authorial intrusion, for example, at the end of "The Enduring Chill." Rather than indirectly suggesting that Asbury gains self-knowledge by some specific action on his own part, the author intrudes, telling us that "the last film of illusion was torn as if by a whirlwind from [Asbury's] eyes" (*CS*, 382). Critics have cited this authorial intrusion as a weak moment in an otherwise controlled canon. Considering O'Connor's ideals regarding an extremely objective narrative voice, we might guess that she would concur.

The New Critics admired not only an objective narrative voice but also richly symbolic textures in both poetry and fiction. But dense symbolism must also achieve a unified effect through the underlying structure that results in a harmonious relation of parts to each other and to the whole. This unity, harmony, or coherence is the primary distinguishing characteristic of great art. O'Connor, a painstaking and compulsive rewriter, crafts her art with New Critical ideals in mind. She controls the associations of literary elements contained within each work by developing unified, underlying, symbolic structures. Images repeat throughout a particular story and throughout the entire canon so as to accrue significance as the reader considers the interrelationships of these patterns. The number of different images that form a consistent line of thought and feeling throughout the canon is remarkable. The sun, the woods, the pig, the panama hat, Girl Scout shoes, and spectacles are examples of recurring images. The hunt (or the pursuer and the pursued, a motif common to doubling fictions), the deformed body, the idea of displacement, the divided self, the act of devouring or eating, and the procession/parade are more abstract concepts variously presented in different symbolic contexts. The suggestiveness and complexity of O'Connor's methods account for some of the difficulties readers experience when they fail to see the relationship of consistent patterns or to take the time to reconstruct meaning. O'Connor's fiction achieves this density of pattern and implication or what Brooks calls "the sharpness of selected detail" as seen in a larger degree in poetry: the careful patterning, repetition of images, concentration of figurative language, richly suggestive texture of connotative diction, ironic tone, and exploitation of sound and sense (alliteration, assonance).[13] Indeed, although they admired Joyce, the New Critics more often were focused on the poets.

In this matter of symbolic patterning and unity, O'Connor explicitly posits recommendations that sound like Brooks. In "The Uses of Formal Analysis," Brooks says: "The primary concern of criticism is with the problem of unity—the kind of whole which the literary work forms or fails to form, and the relation of the various parts in building up this "whole." O'Connor says that "the whole story is the meaning" (*MM*, 73). Brooks asserts that "form is meaning" and "the general and the universal are not seized upon by abstraction, but got at through the concrete and the particular." O'Connor says that "the form of the story gives it meaning." Finally, Brooks emphasizes that "literature is ultimately metaphorical and symbolic." O'Connor says that the good novelist expresses feeling in symbols (*MM*, 156).[14] As her view of the symbolic and ethical function of art develops, she does seem at odds with Brooks and Warren (sounding more like Yvor Winters) when she asserts that "Many contend that the job of the novelist is to show us how man feels, and they say that this is an operation in which his own commitment intrudes not at all. . . . The good novelist not only finds a symbol for feeling, he finds a symbol and a way of lodging it which tells the intelligent reader whether this feeling is adequate or inadequate, whether it is moral or immoral" (*MM*, 156). Still, she echoes Brooks and Warren again when she emphasizes that the novelist must not "lack moral vision" but must first of all attend to his art.

It is difficult to determine conscious sources for O'Connor's fiction. Indeed, O'Connor asserts that "You don't begin a story with a system . . . [but it] may affect your writing unconsciously." So when she says, "I don't have any theory of literature," we should be wary given the contradictions in authorial statements mentioned above and the fact that much of her own "theorizing" does sound like Brooks and Warren or other New Critical theorists.[15]

Finally, then, readers should take a complex view of O'Connor's art—allowing for the influence of New Criticism and considering the intellectual, cultural, and social context of the modern period. Theological perspectives are important, but so are modernist traditions and the American romance tradition that prefigured modernism. Identifying ideas many Catholic and modern thinkers share (an obsession with death, for example) may help to reconcile critical perspectives and to clarify O'Connor's art. I begin that process with an analysis of stories that most emphatically relate to the modern dilemma of feeling orphaned by God and suffering a terrible conflict between the biological and intellectual sides of the self.

Death-Haunted Questers

Many critics and teachers have identified the importance of existentialism to O'Connor's art. The existentialist and the Catholic share certain important concerns and values: the acceptance of despair and an awareness of human mortality as a means of heightening one's moral sense, the emphasis on the developing individual, the ideal of responsibility for one's actions, the importance of freedom and choice, and the assertion that individuals must establish a proper relation to their community, thereby overcoming alienation and psychic fragmentation. With the Christian existentialist, the Catholic shares a belief in the importance of making "the leap of faith," as Kierkegaard puts it, or "the wager of faith," as Pascal would say. Kierkegaard sees despair due to an awareness of the soul/body dichotomy as "man's advantage over the beast." The sense of despair paradoxically enables Kierkegaard to make this "leap."[16]

Despair and a hyperawareness of death may result in the desire to establish one's sense of identity as entirely independent from others, thus denying that one exists as a link in a long chain of human life. The body is the most obvious reminder of our connection to others. O'Connor characters who suffer a fear of death and are alienated from self and society are divided against themselves. The Jekyll/Hyde figure in literature refers to this kind of dividedness and psychic fragmentation. There are many different kinds of conflicts within the human psyche (conflicts between masculine and feminine, between self and society, or between good and evil), but the conflict between mind and body is fundamental.

The double figure reflects the sense of dividedness suffered as humankind becomes more and more aware of the disparity between spiritual aspirations and animal instincts, between the quest for immortality and the reality of physical decay. Being tied to what most human beings feel is a decaying (and in O'Connor's case, diseased) animal or body naturally leads to an acute awareness of physical processes and a desire to be more than mere flesh. Alienation from the physical self leads to alienation from the human community. The fate to be avoided is the fate we all share—mortality. And yet a communal sense is necessary in order to face the inscrutability of the universe. O'Connor felt that ideally the individual functions as a part of the larger religious community as well as a part of the social community.

The stories that most suggest these kinds of concerns focus on a single character—death-haunted questers alienated from self, family, and any form of community. The character sometimes dreads following the fate of another character earlier in time. For example, Ruby Hill in "A Stroke of Good Fortune" is subconsciously aware that she is pregnant but fears following the fate of her mother, who died in child-birth. She denies her pregnancy, prefers to think she has cancer, and tries to escape becoming "something all dried and puckered up" like her mother, who is a sharp contrast to "somebody as alive as her[self]" (*CS*, 99). She associates pregnancy with mortality.

A fear of death results in an inability to love, an incapacity to give oneself to family or community. Ruby suffers a profound sense of alien-ation—from the whole human community, from her husband, and from her own body—because she does not want to participate in the generative process, a process prefiguring her own death and requiring self-sacrifice for others rather than independence from others and affir-mation of her personal significance. She is ironically presented as "a whole thing climbing the stairs" (*CS*, 99). She is divided rather than "whole" because she is obsessed with her own mortality. Her body is "shaped nearly like a funeral urn," signifying the threat of generation—of sexuality, which requires that the parent give up the self for the sake of the child and participate in a chain of events leading to the parent's death. A collard green stuck to her cheek seems to her "a poisonous seed" (*CS*, 95).

O'Connor declares that this story is "in its way, Catholic" because it presents "the rejection of life at the source" (*Letters*, 85), especially the rejection of the physical body. Ruby is threatened by her husband who reminds her of her own physicality and sexuality. She blames him for her pregnancy and imagines that his resistance to buying a house in the suburbs is an attempt to "kill her" (*CS*, 96). She wonders if she should "kill herself" (*CS*, 97). The opposite sex is in fact envisioned as a mortal threat. Ruby believes that her baby brother had "killed" her mother and made her mother "into an old woman" by making her suffer childbirth, the "misery" that made her that much "deader" (*CS*, 97).

Her neighbor, Professor Jerger, refers Ruby to what she most fears. It is significant that Jerger teaches history—a linear process reminding us of our progress in time toward death and decay, not life. Ruby seeks "the fountain of youth" that Professor Jerger locates in the heart (*CS*, 100), but her quest for life everlasting is doomed to fail because she ignores "heart." She fails to love and fears not only death, but life itself. O'Connor explains that quests for immortality need guidance: "our salvation is worked out on earth according as how we love one another, see Christ in one another" (*Letters*, 102).

Nathan A. Scott, Jr., sees Ruby as "disgustedly fighting off knowledge of her own pregnancy with disgusted recollections from childhood of her mother's various pregnancies."[17] But Ruby deserves some measure of sympathy since she suffers from the same insecurities that plague many different characters in O'Connor's works. Freud's lecture on "Archaic and Infantile Features in Dreams" discusses the death wishes of parents for their children.[18] Ruby's death wish for her unborn child can be better understood in this context. Freud explains that these death wishes owe to the "unbounded egoism" of the infantile mind—egoism all human beings suffer to some degree at some time in their lives. Ruby regresses to an infantile mindset because of the traumas she has experienced with the death of her mother and siblings. Her struggle with the facts of her own mortality is worthy of sympathy, however much we may condemn her inability to accept motherhood.

A blind, old Negro, Gabriel in "Wildcat," is another O'Connor character obsessed with mortality and afraid he will follow the fate of someone earlier in time, that is, "Ole Hezah," another old man apparently mauled to death because he was left behind by the hunters. Gabriel thinks of himself as fair game for the present wildcat that has been terrorizing the neighborhood. He associates himself with the previous victim of another wildcat rampage that occurred when he was a boy. Gabriel wonders "was he Hezuh" but reassures himself that "He was Gabrul" (*CS*, 30).

Suffering blindness and the infirmity of body due to old age, Gabriel wishes to establish control over his mortality by being in control of the hunt. He fantasizes himself in the role of master hunter, a role that also confirms his masculinity and differentiates himself from femininity, which he associates with powerlessness and death. As a child, he resented being "Shut up wit these women like he one too" (*CS*, 27). As an old man, he asserts that the wildcat "won't gonna git him like he

15

was a woman" (*CS*, 30). In an early draft, Gabriel clearly associates woman with "evil" and the wildcat. His son's woman is a "high-yeller," "arched up" woman with "hair that stood up like the feel of dry thistle"—suggesting the image of an alarmed wildcat. In this draft, the reader cannot always sort out the object of Gabriel's hatred and fear as O'Connor alternates descriptions of the wildcat with descriptions of the woman and allows no transition to clarify the case (*FO* 14a and 14b).[19] To Gabriel, the wildcat seems deadly and feminine.

But Gabriel is denied his chance to capture a dangerous wildcat. He wishes to assume the power and control of being the hunter rather than the hunted but is left behind, even by his grandchildren and their friends as they pass him on their way to join the hunt. At the end, he panics and imagines how "the [wildcat's] teeth would cut sharp an' scrape his bones inside" (*CS*, 30), and he frantically pulls down a shelf in his effort to escape. The old man's animal panic then causes him to become a double for the wildcat itself: "He turned wildly . . . caught hold of the shelf and . . . sprang up" (*CS*, 31). That Gabriel fears he will repeat the fate of Hezuh suggests a fatal repetition no human or animal can escape. The wildcat in this story serves as a symbol for mortality.

Nowhere in O'Connor's works is the theme of alienation and the fear of death more evident than in "The Geranium." The struggle to overcome mortality by establishing one's significance apart from others is clear; Dudley refuses to relate constructively to his daughter and his neighbors. This sedentary and alienated old man spends his last days staring out the window at his neighbor's geranium, which is perched on a windowledge high above the abyss of a multi-storied apartment complex in New York (cf. T. S. Eliot's poem, "Gerontion," which presents an "old man . . . waiting"). The precarious position of the geranium refers us to Dudley's own situation—and to the image of "dangling man" as the existentialists have defined it or to the image of man as "a rope over an abyss," as Nietzsche has envisioned the human predicament.[20]

This suggestion of Dudley as emblematic of modern man is more obvious in an early manuscript. In this version of the story, Dudley actually does commit suicide by leaping off the ledge of his window. Prior to his leap, "Old Dudley lifted his feet over the ledge and let them dangle out the window" (*FO* 126). In the published version, Dudley migrates to New York because it seemed "an important place

. . . it had room for him" (*CS*, 4), and he expects it to affirm his self-importance. He longs for significance and wants to distinguish himself from the crowd—the mass of humanity that drains his sense of individuality. But the city instead reminds him of his own mortality: "New York was swishing and jamming one minute and dirty and dead the next" (*CS*, 6).

At the start of the story, Dudley's alienation and the problem of time's progress are emphasized. A flashback to his earlier life shows that he did maintain a sense of community at his boarding house. O'Connor juxtaposes his memories of his neighbor's geranium with the geranium of the present. Dudley stares at the actual flower in front of him while he recalls the flower "cared" for by "Mrs. Carson back home" (*CS*, 3). This old man longs for the security of the past represented by Mrs. Carson's geranium, which was "better-looking" (*CS*, 3) than the faded flower of the present about to fall off the ledge. The city geranium's roots are only tenuously secured in the flowerpot so near the edge of the alley precipice. When Dudley recalls how Lutish, his former servant, "could root anything," his own uprootedness seems worsened (*CS*, 3). It is only when stripped of community because he moves to New York that the old man suffers an identity crisis. Then he struggles for meaning in a meaningless world where the streets lead "nowhere" (*CS*, 6).

In New York, Dudley avoids others because he fears the overwhelming mass of humanity he sees everywhere and also because he fears being defined in a negative way, as when, for example, the black neighbor calls him an "old timer" (*CS*, 12)—time being the less obvious antagonist here. This identity represents the powerlessness of old age in contrast to the masculinity he envisions in his past when he could assume superiority in his community. Then he assumed superior knowledge, for example, when he explains the mechanism of his gun to his black servant, Rabie. And the boarding house ladies bolstered his male ego by praising his abilities as a fisherman ("It took a man to get those fish," they tell him). His sense of self depended on masculine stereotypes—playing the role of "protector," owning a gun, being the "man in the house," and being the provider of fish (*CS*, 5). Dudley depends on others for self-definition. He seems fond of his servant, Rabie, but he cannot relate to him as a separate and significant human being. Rabie merely supports Dudley's ego by playing the role of black servant to white master. The black man's ability to serve Dudley selflessly suggests a certain connection to life and community that Dudley lacks. The red river of life, loved by Rabie, means nothing to Old Dudley.

It is by his own choice that Dudley isolates himself from those in his former community, from his daughter by resenting her care, and from his black neighbor by resenting his help. Despite his spurious independence from other personalities, Dudley cannot define himself independently, but instead assumes stereotypical roles, such as masculine head of household or white master—roles that support his need for power over others. Thus, he cannot form meaningful relationships with others when he moves to New York. He cannot consider himself one with the community because this requires an acknowledgment of mortality: sameness, not difference.

Because he does not recognize that he shares the same fate as all of humanity, Dudley feels a revulsion for life and for others. His daughter takes him shopping downtown, and he panics at the crowds, the "people rushing . . . under him" (CS, 7). In the subway, she pulls him back from the edge of the train platform where he almost falls because the scene overwhelms him: "People boiled out of trains and up steps and over into the streets. . . . black and white and yellow all mixed up like vegetables in soup" (CS, 7). Dudley is terrified because he cannot differentiate the different races of people and thereby establish himself apart from the mass of others.

Claire Kahane notes about "Judgement Day" that for many whites "the epitome of chaos" is integration—requiring an acknowledgment of sameness and depriving them of their superior white identity.[21] Fearing dependence on blacks is a peculiarly Southern fear. Dudley asserts his superiority over and independence from Rabie and from his black neighbor. This theme will be more rigorously pursued in those stories addressing racial conflicts, but we should notice here that being helped up the stairs by his black neighbor amounts to a surrender of self from Dudley's perspective—a loss of power. At the end of this story, the geranium of life falls to the alley below, but Dudley refuses to retrieve it because, in order to receive this life, he must risk encountering the black neighbor again. He would accept the Negro as a servant helping him up but not as a neighbor whose hand he might shake. Finally, Dudley is very much like the owner of the geranium who complains about Dudley's habit of staring at his window. He tells the old man that he does not "like people looking at what I do." He is also like his uncommunicative daughter who "never listened the second time" (CS,

6) to her father. This story defines what many thinkers have identified as a major problem of modern life—alienation from self, family, and community.

In O'Connor's earliest stories, characters suffer alienation, despair, and loss of identity and thereby engage the reader's sympathies. The reader identifies much more with Old Dudley than with, say, Tanner, the protagonist of a later reworking of the "geranium" tale, "Judgement Day." A brief comparison of "The Geranium" and "Judgement Day" reveals O'Connor's tendency as she developed to move away from depicting the despair of individuals to depicting social contexts and focusing on interactions between several individuals, often referring to class or race lines. "The Geranium" and "Judgement Day" use the same basic situation of the Southerner displaced in the North, stripped of identity, and desiring to return home. The similarities, however, stop there. The differences in tone and philosophical perspective are marked. The latter story more rigorously satirizes the racist, whereas the former explores the alienated quester struggling in a meaningless world.

We can easily understand the obsession with death and the quest for significance when mature characters are depicted, but O'Connor even portrays a child (Ruller McFarney in "The Capture")[22] as feeling a vague sense of being pursued by "Something Awful . . . tearing behind him with its arms rigid and its fingers ready to clutch" (*CS*, 53). The story begins and ends with this image. At the start the boy is himself that ominous figure "edging nearer [to a turkey he intends to bag] with his arms rigid and his fingers ready to clutch" (*CS*, 43). In this story about a young boy's frustration because neither his family, his community, nor God affirm his sense of significance, O'Connor again focuses on a single alienated character wishing for self-definition and uneasy about life. This theme does not work so well when the protagonist is a child, and this experiment prefigures the next category of stories depicting death-haunted parents wishing to overcome mortality by remaking a child into an image of themselves. The motif of sibling rivalry developed in "The Capture" also relates it to the next group of stories. Still, the basic issues of "The Capture" are more similar to those found in the stories above than to those found in the next section.

"The Capture" is narrated in the third person and told through the limited perspective of the boy hunter, who at the start imagines himself as a powerful figure, a sheriff capturing a rustler. When the "sheriff" is startled by an actual (rather than imaginary) prey, a wild turkey, he takes up the pursuit. During this initially fruitless hunt in which the turkey escapes, Ruller suffers the powerlessness of childhood, epitomized in his sense of someone playing "a dirty trick on him" (*CS*, 45) by tempting him with a turkey he cannot catch. Then when he reasons that God is the one playing the trick, it is clear that no divine will intervenes to affirm his self-importance. He seems to learn in the course of the story that circumstances are ruled by chance. "Capturing" in this story amounts to controlling fate. Neither the boy's wish for divine guidance nor his wish for control of his own destiny is satisfied.

Ruller's need for recognition and his sense of alienation from his family are partly due to the fact that his parents are engrossed with his older brother Hane's problems. After being put to bed at night, Ruller listens to his parents comparing their sons as they talk in bed before going to sleep. His parents consider Hane "unusual." Hane appears to be more "significant" or "unusual" exactly because his parents worry more about him than about their younger son. Ruller's need for attention prevents him from perceiving the negative side of his parents' worry that Hane will end up in the penitentiary. Ruller wishes to "rule" his own destiny and to establish a sense of self independent of Hane. After the first fruitless encounter with the turkey, the boy attempts to prove his significance by imitating his elder brother's habit of swearing (*CS*, 46). As he models his behavior after his brother's, he begins to feel a loss of self. He feels that "his white ankles sticking out of his pants legs . . . didn't belong to him" (*CS*, 46).

Through no efforts of his own but by chance, Ruller then happens upon the place of the turkey's collapse, and he imagines that this "capture" will finally make him "more unusual than Hane" (*CS*, 49), who "hadn't ever caught anything" (*CS*, 44). He will win his parents' notice and establish his self-importance. Ruller's wish to be noticed by his parents is ultimately a wish to return to infancy, to the stage of development when the mother's gaze reassures the child as she attends exclusively to his personal needs. This young exhibitionist imagines his parents saying, "Look at Ruller with that wild turkey" (*CS*, 43; repeated *CS*, 45 and *CS*, 48). The need for attention from the parents relates to a deeper need for religious reassurances. Ruller's ultimate satisfaction occurs when he imagines God watching him (*CS*, 49) for the second time. He imagines his self-importance confirmed by the fact that God seems to have provided him with the turkey.

But O'Connor acknowledges that we must live in a world without easy reassurances of our individual significance. Ruller's newfound confidence is destroyed when a group of "country boys" steals his turkey, leaving him again feeling insignificant, impotent, and pursued by "Something Awful" (*CS*, 53). O'Connor once said that "death has always been a brother to my imagination"[23] and "When I was twelve I made up my mind absolutely that I would not get any older. . . . I was a very ancient twelve; my views at that age would have done credit to a Civil War veteran. . . . The weight of centuries lies on children, I'm sure of it" (*Letters*, 136–37). This early story of course cannot finally bear the weight of its philosophical and theological implications, but it belongs with those stories addressing alienation and a fear of death.

In the stories above, the death-haunted protagonists are elderly, adolescent, or female. When the death-haunted protagonist is a male parent, human aggression caused by fear of death, a major theme of O'Connor's, determines plot. Two such stories, "The Lame Shall Enter First" and "A View of the Woods," like the stories discussed above presenting death-haunted questers, focus on quests for significance, struggles with despair, and alienation from family and community. They differ, however, in that they are better understood in light of Freudian theories defining aggressive and primitive behavior.

The father figures presented exhibit aggression against a child. The death-haunted parent seeks to remake a child into a mirror image of himself. Developing a crippling interdependence of the parent/child pair, the plot progresses according to whether or not the death-haunted parent is successful in remaking the child to satisfy his own needs, thereby extending his will in time. Suspense is created as the reader identifies with the child who seeks a sense of self independent from the parent.[24]

These death-haunted parents are obsessed with self-love; they feel threatened if the child refuses to obey their will. In "The Lame Shall Enter First" (modeled after *The Violent Bear It Away*), Sheppard, a city recreational director and volunteer counselor for a local reformatory, overdisciplines his son, Norton, who hampers his efforts to reconstruct an intelligent—thus more worthy of his own self—juvenile delinquent boy, Rufus, into a replica of himself. Sheppard misdirects his energy toward someone else's child and adopts Rufus. He fails to acknowledge his own son's grief over his mother's recent death and forces his son to accept the intruder, Rufus. The neglected son commits suicide.

The Short Fiction: A Critical Analysis

In an early draft, O'Connor depicts Sheppard's rage at his own guilt when he severely reprimands Norton for what the father sees as selfishness. Sheppard then experiences an "uncanny" feeling, "as if he [Norton] had some peculiar power to bring on his father's fate" (*FO* 171, 30). The sense of fate derives from repressed aggressive and narcissistic impulses, according to Freud. The irony here is the fact that Sheppard, not Norton, serves as an overpowering fatality. No other parent figure in the O'Connor canon is quite so insensitive to his offspring.

When we first meet this father/son pair, Norton seems a faded version of his father, like the "shadow" of the cowboy printed on his shirt. His eyes are "a paler blue than his father's" (*CS*, 445), his shirt faded. These images suggest the powerlessness of childhood and Norton's vulnerability, which intensifies our criticism of Sheppard's failure. Sheppard's "pink sensitive face" (*CS*, 445) does not reflect sensitivity but rather reveals a certain childishness to match his son's. The father's immaturity, unlike the son's, does not abrogate his responsibility. Ironically, Sheppard's self-centered stance of the do-gooder rescuer of Rufus Johnson matches the selfishness he complains characterizes his son. We blame Sheppard for being unable to overcome his narcissism, whereas by comparison, Norton seems blameless and only normally narcissistic for a child of ten grieving for his dead mother. The boy's despair is so great, he vomits his breakfast—an event his father concludes is due to overeating and greed. The boy's habit of sorting out his money, of "arranging packages of flower seeds in rows around himself" (*CS*, 452), and of trussing himself up in a rope (*CS*, 460) is compensation for the loss of his mother.

Sheppard chastizes his son for weeping, for insensitivity to the "suffering" of the criminal Rufus, and for not appreciating his "family" (*CS*, 447)—this latter criticism ignoring the lack of a mother that so disturbs the child. It is Sheppard who is insensitive to suffering—the suffering of his only son whom he criticizes for "moping" (*CS*, 448). When Rufus invades his mother's bedroom and tries on her corset in jest, Norton withdraws. Sheppard later finds him hiding in a closet, wrapped in her coat, "his face swollen and pale, with a drugged look of misery on it" (*CS*, 457), but the father still demands that his son and only child accept the intruder. Sheppard even allows Rufus to sleep in Norton's mother's bed, and he beats his son when he objects. This father asks too much, wanting his son to reinforce his own narcissistic "sacrifice" by sharing skimpily apportioned parental love before the son has adjusted to the loss of his mother.

This is not to say that Sheppard does not also feel grief. Sheppard's way of hiding his grief is to keep "busy helping other people" (*CS*, 448), that is, to repress it by a plunge into the finite world and to aggrandize his own self as a martyred do-gooder. He considers his office as "a confessional," his "credentials . . . [not much] less dubious than a priest's" because "he had been trained for what he was doing" (*CS*, 449). O'Connor tells us that Sheppard is an "empty man who fills up his emptiness with good works" (*Letters*, 491). He boasts that he is "beyond simple pettiness" (*CS*, 458), but the delinquent boy demonstrates more insight than the counselor himself when he expresses his "outrage" at the do-gooder's pretense with the snide comment, "He thinks he's Jesus Christ" (*CS*, 459). The terrible gap between Sheppard's limited, this-worldly shortsightedness and the religious perspective is evident in the dramatic irony here—the gap between Sheppard's pretense to goodness and his failure to extend charity to his own son.

In the relationship that Sheppard tries to develop with Rufus, we see O'Connor's most explicit rebuttal of the notion that upbringing and environment ought to excuse bad behavior. Sheppard excuses Rufus because he suffers a club foot ("His mischief was compensation for the foot," *CS*, 450). But Rufus is a striking version of a character type common to O'Connor's stories: the vicious child. Like the children who lure Bevel into the path of a dangerous shoat in "The River" or the destructive boys who burn Mrs. Cope's woods in "A Circle in the Fire," or the young girl who attacks her grandfather in "A View of the Woods," Flannery O'Connor acknowledges the primitive nature of children. In her letters, she notes how "children . . . are quite capable . . . of committing the most monstrous crimes out of the urge to destroy and humiliate" (*Letters*, 120). Of all her portraits of children, Rufus seems most to represent motiveless malignity.

Since Norton cannot accept his father's explanations that his mother "doesn't exist" (*CS*, 462), he eagerly accepts Rufus's interpretations of death—that she lives on in heaven. In spite of his satanic tendencies, Rufus has a clearer grasp of the truth than Sheppard. It is Rufus who sees through Sheppard when the counselor projects a veneer of his own good intentions on the boy, totally misreading the boy to suit his own version. Rufus, able to perceive how Sheppard threatens his sense of identity, refuses his new shoe to remedy his club foot—a self-defensive act and a declaration that he will preserve his own identity, however evil.

Ironically, when Sheppard purchases a telescope in order to stimulate Rufus intellectually, Norton takes an interest in it because he reasons that he might see his mother in heaven through it. Rufus tells him, "You got to be dead to get there" (*CS*, 462), and so Norton commits suicide. The story ends with Sheppard suffering an awareness of his error—all too late: "His heart constricted with a repulsion for himself so clear and intense that he gasped for breath. He had stuffed his own emptiness with good works like a glutton. He had ignored his own child to feed his vision of himself" (*CS*, 481). Sheppard's failure appalls us, but the effect is shock at the grotesque event of Norton's body swinging from the attic beams, not the deep understanding of human frailty we see in O'Connor's best work. O'Connor regretted the fact that she could not "know" or "sympathize" with Mr. Sheppard like most of her other characters (*Letters*, 491). What seems most intensely wrought in this story is the moral lesson to face the shadow within, the pride and aggressiveness that cause parents to inhibit the development of their children: a major theme clearly present when O'Connor presents death-haunted parents who destroy their own offspring.

O'Connor calls "A View of the Woods" "a little morality play" (*Letters*, 186). In this story, grandfather Mark Fortune murders his granddaughter, Mary Fortune Pitts, because she rebels against him. In the stories that present a parent's efforts to remake a child, the child invariably suffers a terrible sense of being a divided self—split between conforming to what parents demand and asserting his or her own self-image felt to be more real and less mortal. In spite of the child's efforts to be *unlike* the parent, the child is destroyed. In each case, a parent figure fails to nurture his child and instead generates so much narcissistic energy that the child is destroyed. In the prototype for these stories, *The Violent Bear It Away*, the child, Francis Tarwater, adopts the behavior of his crazy uncle who believes himself a prophet of God. Whenever a child adopts the behavior of a domineering parent, the point is that he has lost himself.

In "A View of the Woods," Mary Fortune Pitts reflects the narcissistic will of her grandfather—his primitive aggressive drives—but we cannot identify with his viciousness or hers. Nor do we lament her loss of self as she ends up explicitly revealing in an actual physical attack the meanness Fortune hides in underhanded ways. She begins as "a small replica" (*CS*, 336) of the old man and ends up miming his aggressive willfulness. We sense little struggle on her part to seek an independent self, although we identify with her desire to preserve the woods, what O'Connor says is a "Christ symbol" (*Letters*, 190). Mary Pitts and Mark Fortune lose sympathy because the reader does not understand their struggle as an existential plight.

This is an inferior work because it is weak in philosophical and psychological richness. Characters lack depth. Mark Fortune might be seen to suffer the powerlessness of old age, like Dudley in "The Geranium," but what Old Dudley suffers more passively Mark Fortune suffers aggressively. Human vulnerability does not seem represented as much as human viciousness. Fortune merely notes in passing that "Anyone over sixty years of age is in an uneasy position" (*CS*, 337). He more than compensates for old age by exerting his power over others. The point is that he worships material things.

Grandfather Fortune denies his existential plight so completely by asserting his power over others that the reader even wishes for his downfall. Completely embedded in this world, Fortune lacks any spiritual impulses—being so involved in petty material pursuits that lead him to destructiveness and destruction. His tractor is the primary symbol for the human destructiveness that results when human will becomes cold and mechanical. The tractor appears in a "red pit" as a "disembodied gullet [which] gorge[s] itself on the clay" (*CS*, 335), suggesting flesh. Mark Fortune essentially "gorges" himself on Mary Pitts's self by expecting her to conform to his will because he considers her "thoroughly of his clay" (*CS*, 338). He denies her independence.

When Mary Pitts positions herself half on her grandfather's Cadillac and half on her grandfather "as if he were no more than a part of the automobile" (*CS*, 339), the point is that Fortune's materialism and cold-heartedness reduce him to being like a mechanism. He and his granddaughter watch his "construction" projects that destroy both nature and his son-in-law's inheritance. The construction occurs because the old man is selling off the land his son-in-law wants to preserve for himself. The tractor and the Cadillac represent power in the material world—power Mark Fortune loves to wield. He also values his automobile over human life; it provides him with a sense of his own identity.

Mark Fortune does not suffer an identity crisis as more sympathetic characters do. He is secure in the fact that he is "PURE Fortune" (*CS*, 351), but his security depends on his granddaughter carrying out his will. And she rebels against him by allowing her father to beat her.

When this happens, Mark Fortune sees her as "completely foreign" and becomes "infuriated" (*CS*, 340). He feels her surrender to her father as a personal failure. Mr. Pitts beats his youngest daughter as revenge against the grandfather-in-law, treating her as the one possession he can still control even if he cannot control his father-in-law's sale of the land. "She's mine to whip" (*CS*, 341), he declares, thereby treating the human as property. In this way, he reflects the materialism of the man he would overcome.

This rivalry between the grandfather and the son-in-law suggests Oedipal conflicts and the regressive behavior of death-haunted parents. The old man no longer can compete with his own father for the love of his mother and therefore turns to his daughter's love and competes with the son-in-law. Rejection by the daughter amounts to rejection by the mother and is intolerable. The daughter's love for the father is encouraged by the father in order to retain her as a child under his control, to satisfy his own need for maternal love, and to prevent her from growing up and marrying the man who will replace him. Unable to overcome infantile possessiveness, Mark Fortune disinherits his daughter when she does marry because he feels that she prefers "Pitts to home" (*CS*, 336), as the jealous father puts it.

Mark Fortune maintains his power over his daughter and her family by treating them as tenants, not family, and selling off tracts of land whenever they displease him. Like Old Dudley, he also in fact denies his daughter, who considers herself dutifully caring for him. He feels threatened by her care and by her pretense of duty, which, in his view, conceals a desire to "put him in a hole eight feet deep" (*CS*, 337). Mark Fortune then turns to his granddaughter to satisfy his narcissistic need to possess a single love object like himself and to seek revenge against his daughter because of her "rejection."

This family system of rivalry, crippling interdependence, jealousy, and revenge finally fails when Mary Fortune rebels more emphatically against her grandfather because he threatens to obscure the family's view of the woods by selling off the front lawn for the construction of a gas station. The patriarch rationalizes this attack on his son-in-law by idealizing "progress." He wants to destroy the natural scenery and replace it with automobiles and corrugated steel, thereby expanding his self and imposing his "view" on Pitts's pasture. Mark Fortune expects his look-alike granddaughter, Mary, to value things over people and nature exactly as he does.

But Mary has learned from her grandfather how to exert her own will. When her grandfather chastizes her for not supporting him, he speaks as if he were "a suitor trying to reinstate himself" (*CS*, 347). Nonetheless, his strategy to win her back fails. Eventually, he sees her not as a satisfying mirror image of himself but as an ominous "other." Ironically, Mary's willfulness (which Fortune now calls "Pitts") actually does reflect his own self—his own willfulness, only this time not directed by him. He perceives her to be veering away from his image, but actually she is imitating his egoistic, destructive, and willful behavior. She attacks her grandfather when he tries to beat her for throwing bottles at him and Tilman as they sign an agreement that ensures the construction of a gas station on Pitts's front lawn. Mark Fortune then murders his own offspring to preserve himself—to rid himself of what he now perceives as a reflection of the son-in-law's will.

Mary Pitts's shift from support of her grandfather to support of her father signifies a growing awareness of the grandfather's waning power as well as a desire to preserve her view of the woods. The old man suffers a heart attack after his struggle with his other self, and his last view is ironically of the woods or "the gaunt trees" and the "monster . . . gorging itself on clay" (*CS*, 356)—that is, the parent devouring the child, a common motif in myth.

The next group of stories retains the theme of parent/child conflicts but develops it in a context that focuses on a less obvious but important motif in the O'Connor canon having to do with gender and male/female conflicts.

Male/Female Conflicts

"The Comforts of Home," "The Enduring Chill," and "Greenleaf" subtly develop some of the same ideas about male/female conflicts that were posited by the psychoanalytic theorists writing in the 1950s and early 1960s, especially Carl Jung and Erich Neumann—modern thinkers O'Connor read and respected. Jung defines the psyche as being divided between masculine and feminine impulses, the animus and the anima. He further asserts that an integrated and mature self should achieve a balance between these impulses—as does a constructive society. Neumann worries that the dominance of masculine aggressive values in the modern world threatens the hope for a peaceful and civilized future of humankind. Femininity stereotypically is thought to contribute tenderness in human relations.[25]

I do not wish to establish, as Freud tried to do, that anatomy is destiny or to deal with whether sexual stereotypes are culturally acquired or biologically determined. What is important to see is simply that certain of O'Connor's stories represent qualities stereotypically associated with masculinity and femininity, sometimes inverting these stereotypes. Mrs. McIntyre in "The Displaced Person" aggressively manages her farm hands, Hulga in "Good Country People" adopts the views of Nietzsche, and Mary Grace throws a book at Mrs. Turpin, a symbolic act of aggression against the mother in "Revelation."

And yet sex-related differences are not the primary focus of the above stories as in the three stories to be discussed next. These latter stories represent sex-related differences stereotypically defined but also imply the dominance of masculine forces in society—what Otto Rank laments as "The gradual masculinization of human civilization" because "woman-psychology has been misinterpreted . . . [to designate] wickedness."[26] Thomas in "Comforts of Home" and Asbury in "The Enduring Chill" both feel rage toward their mothers. Mr. Greenleaf, although appearing subservient, still competes aggressively with Mrs. May and is partly responsible for her death. These male characters express revulsion for and rage against the mother figure who serves to thwart their sense of power and control.

According to those concerned with the paucity of feminine perspectives in modern life, the degree to which both males and females relate to the opposite sex with love rather than hatred measures human development or the degree of spiritual evolution. O'Connor's interest in Jung and Neumann relates to her interest in Teilhard de Chardin's ideas of human "evolution," measured by the degree to which a particular society overcomes revulsion for others as a result of egoism. O'Connor compares "Jung and Teilhard . . . [who] both [have] the evolutionary view" (*Letters*, 383).[27]

Masculine forces in modern life encourage women to conform to roles demanding that they project an image of purity, passivity, obedience, and dependence—a role that limits how women contribute to culture and society. Sometimes, women remain like children, unable to develop and to participate in the evolutionary process. The South has always been sensitive to male/female dichotomies—the Southern belle being a model of feminine purity and the Southern Confederate soldier a model of masculine potency in spite of the reality of defeat. The idea of woman in a male-dominated society is divided—gardenia or whore. The Southern lady affirms the purity of the Southern gentleman. The need for power and independence is great for the Southerner tormented by a long history of suffering related to the Civil War.

Beyond the local consideration, however, O'Connor defines the masculine tendency to isolate the self and the need for independence more generally. Rank points out that "Man from time immemorial has tried to avoid his role as the bearer of the procreative life-principle of which his self is but an ephemeral manifestation."[28] Establishing a family requires that one give up the self to the human community and accept one's own physicality/mortality.

Several O'Connor stories (and both novels) are in fact distinguished by male protagonists who are antagonistic toward family, express an aversion for femininity, and try to repress all reminders of their own physicality (sometimes represented by a particular woman character). Joseph Campbell's insights about male perceptions of femininity are relevant in these cases: "When it suddenly dawns on us . . . that everything we think or do is necessarily tainted with the odor of the flesh, then, not uncommonly, there is experienced a moment of revulsion: life, the acts of life, the organs of life, woman in particular as the great symbol of life, becomes intolerable to the pure, pure soul."[29]

Not that the revulsion for woman is a new idea. Neumann tells us that in myth "the winged horse symbolizes . . . the freeing of libido from the Great Mother, in other words, its spiritualization." In Plato's *Symposium* love is defined in such a way as to suggest the desire of the male "to get rid of" repulsive female fecundity: "The Love who is the offspring of the common Aphrodite is . . . apt to be of woman as well as of youths, and is of the body rather than of the soul. . . . [This love] born of the union of the male and female . . . partakes of both." On the other hand, "the offspring of the heavenly Aphrodite is derived from a mother in whose birth the female has no part—she is from the male only. . . . Those who are inspired by this love turn to the male, and delight in him who is the more valiant and intelligent nature." The theme of separation from the mother is very ancient, but it is only in recent times that philosophers and psychologists have recognized its significance as it expresses a profound revulsion for femininity.[30]

In O'Connor's stories dealing with this issue, male characters exhibit aggressive behavior, sometimes explicitly based on male prerogative. In "Greenleaf," Mrs. May complains that Mr. Greenleaf takes advantage of her because she is a woman. Mrs. May's sons indulge in angry tirades against their mother and at one point attack each other. In "The Enduring Chill," Asbury verbally attacks his sister and mother. In "The Comforts of Home," Thomas feels revulsion for Sarah Ham and ends up accidentally killing his mother. These three stories in the canon share a special focus on symbolic contexts related to sex. Male potency (procreative and creative power) is represented by images of twins, horns, bull, walking stick, gun, and/or even artist. Female purity is represented by Thomas's mother, depicted as a "sibyl," but otherwise femininity is related to the reproductive process symbolically represented by images of cows (the herd), milk, and the female container (cow's "bag," purse). Various negative images of women are projected by aggressive males: Thomas sees the delinquent girl as a "slut" in "The Comforts of Home"; Asbury sees his sister as a "sleeping dog" in "The Enduring Chill"; and Mrs. May is presented as a kind of Medusa with her "Green rubber curlers [that] sprouted neatly over her forehead and her face . . . smooth as concrete" (*CS*, 311).

The male characters in these stories are uncomfortable with their own physicality. They feel revulsion for women representing physicality, and they assert their need for "control" sometimes in brutal ways. Being independent of woman—that is, not subject to physical birth and not being a participant in the procreative process—amounts to immortality. Claire Kahane has accused O'Connor of "a repugnance toward femaleness," but her charge is a misunderstanding. The "repugnance" in the stories does not express the author's view but is felt by the male characters (males like Thomas toward females like Sarah Ham). In one case ("A Stroke of Good Fortune"), a female, Ruby Hill, feels repugnance for a threatening male, her husband, Bill B. Hill.[31]

In the stories analyzed below, then, male characters feel an aversion for female characters—thus suggesting the need to counter the masculinization of culture, not least to encourage tenderness in human life and to accept the body self and the facts of human mortality. These themes connect with O'Connor's Catholic concerns. Frederick Asals notes the relevance to O'Connor's work of the biblical idea that "there is neither male nor female: for ye are all one in Christ Jesus" (Galatians 3:38).[32] Only when sex-related differences are harmoniously integrated can spiritual development take place. Revulsion for femininity and the body self provides a measure of alienation from the community and signifies a lack of evolutionary progress toward unity within the family and within God's community.

Passive Caretakers

In "The Comforts of Home," Thomas tries to control his mother, who infuriates him by offering her home to Sarah Ham, a delinquent young woman she wishes to help. Unlike his mother, Thomas does not consider the suffering of others, but seeks his own creature "comforts"—an interesting choice of words given the Rheims-Douai Catholic Bible, which refers to the Holy Ghost as "comforter" and explains God's "many rooms," a sharp contrast to Thomas's unwillingness to have *his* rooms invaded by what his mother calls a pathetic "nimpermaniac" (*CS*, 385).

Thomas is his mother's opposite, the antithesis of the nurturing mother and a compendium of the worst masculine traits of his father. But to complicate matters, he also represents an inversion of his masculine sex (the worst of the stereotypically defined feminine traits). He is passive and dependent when, for example, he seeks the "comforts" of his womby room, his electric blanket, and his Morris chair. All will be lost, he feels, if his mother brings a voluptuous but needy delinquent girl into their home with the idea of reforming her. At the age of thirty-five, Thomas still depends on his mother to feed and care for him. He considers his home "as personal as the shell of a turtle" (*CS*, 395), because he has not differentiated himself from his mother at the level of basic physical needs. The fact that Thomas still lives at home and switches from exhibiting the worst of the feminine characteristics to the worst of the masculine characteristics suggests a divided self unable to integrate the anima and the animus.

Neumann says that as long as human beings exist in a state of drowsiness or delicious passivity, they have not yet discovered their own reality and are ruled by the Uroboros (as if still in the womb and ruled by "the great whirling wheel of life, where everything is not yet individual and is submerged in the union of opposites, passing away and willing to pass away"). Moreover, "Detachment from the Uroboros, entry into the world, and the encounter with the universal principle of opposites are the essential tasks of human and individual development." By this he seems to mean something similar to what Jung calls "individuation," establishing one's independent identity but also integrating the anima and the animus within.[33]

Related to the problem of separation from the mother, Oedipal conflicts clarify this story. As mentioned above, certain of O'Connor's comments, quoted out of context, imply that Freudian theories are not helpful when thinking about literature. Especially with this story, we should consider the context of authorial statements. She answered Cecil Dawkins's comments about Freudian symbols in the story: "Maybe you *are* hearing too much Freudian talk. [Thomas's father's] animosity is directed at the mother because she's his opposite as far as virtue goes. . . . if the Oedipus business is visible in it, it is so because it is in nature, not because I worked with that in mind. I don't think any good writer would do such a thing" (*Letters*, 375). It is a common disclaimer of authors that their art does not *consciously* advocate philosophical systems. O'Connor's angry response reveals her New Critical bias and antagonism to Freudian interpreters who reduce art to its Oedipal components alone, rather than understanding the work's complexity. In this story, part of that complexity derives from the fact that Thomas's possessiveness at some level suggest an Oedipal conflict—an attachment to the parent and an inability to expand the horizons of one's love. Whereas his mother would share her home, Thomas can only declare possessively that it is, as he puts it, "mine" (*CS*, 394). He conflates "home" and "mother" subconsciously. In other words, when he is "overcome by rage" (*CS*, 383) at the idea of having to share his mother's love, he sees the girl as a rival he cannot tolerate, rather than as another human being of the opposite sex he might love.

Thomas sees the girl as a rival threatening his wish to possess the mother and as a reminder of his own physicality so that he responds with aggressive rationality, repressing not only his own instinctual nature but also his ambivalence toward his mother and his father. He denies his more tender feelings, which might have allowed him to express compassion for the suicidal jailbird. What seems especially important is the idea that men should develop nurturing qualities—exactly the qualities Thomas's mother exhibits when she wishes to share her home with the delinquent girl. Thomas presents his mother with the childish ultimatum, "her or me" (*CS*, 383, repeated *CS*, 398), but she means to assert "her *and* you." The mother wants to expand the horizons of her love, while Thomas wants to narrow his. When Star Drake, alias Sarah Ham, appears naked in Thomas's room, he treats her as a threatening animal by "holding the chair in front of him like an animal trainer driving out a dangerous cat" (*CS*, 384).

Sarah Ham represents for Thomas the beast of his own body self. Changing her name from "Ham" (which may be read to refer to the Bible or to physiology) to "Star Drake" (spirituality/masculinity) does not ease Thomas's fears. When in her presence, he feels like "a man trapped by insufferable odors" (*CS*, 395–96). That he differentiates himself from the body is shown when he formulates his own identity in terms of his father's aggressiveness and conniving rationality (mind, not body) and when he considers the relative virtues of the sheriff, "another edition of Thomas's father" (*CS*, 395): a man "at least intelligent and not simply a mound of sweating flesh" (*CS*, 399). This intellectual young man, then, feels "a deep unbearable loathing for himself as if he were turning slowly into the girl" (*CS*, 385) and fears the anima within. Asals in fact says that Sarah "seems an almost comically literal embodiment of Jung's 'anima.' "[34]

Because Thomas resists "becoming" the girl, he instead "becomes" his father, whom he dislikes but still imitates. The commands of his inner "voice" motivate him to actions that perpetuate the old man's will. Thomas views his father as "Untouched by useless [feminine] compassion" and capable only of masculine "enraged action," "reason," and "ruthlessness" (*CS*, 387–88). In short, Thomas's father represents the stereotype of the modern male—a terrible, egoistic, aggressive willfulness that enables males to defend their own superiority in a competitive world—a superiority that amounts to mastery over death.

Thomas, then, depends on his father's traits in his battle against his mother and against the threatening woman who suggests his lack of control because she is a projection of his own physicality and stimulates his own lust. Thomas's violent aggression leads him to hope that the girl will "cut her throat" (*CS*, 396). Later, he declares, "If she shoots herself, so much the better!" (*CS*, 397). That he has a gun ("an inheritance from the old man," *CS*, 397) in his drawer (drawers) suggests that his father represents phallic power. Asals points out that when Thomas places the gun in Sarah Ham's " 'red pocket-book' which has a 'skin-like feel to his touch' and gives off 'an unmistakable odor of the girl,' " he reveals "the sexual fantasy his consciousness so violently denies."[35]

The father's influence causes Thomas to transfer his rage from the girl to his mother as the story progresses. When the mother feels deepest compassion for the girl because she tries to commit suicide, the reader is told that Thomas's "fury was directed not at the little slut but at his mother" (*CS*, 397), perhaps indicating an Oedipal attachment to the father. Thomas's rage matches what his father felt toward women (and his wife). Sheriff Farebrother (notice the importance of gender in this name) belittles the young man and reminds him that his father "never let anything grow under his feet. Particularly nothing a woman planted" (*CS*, 400).

The influence of the regressive father intensifies as the story progresses. In an early portion of the story, Thomas, "like a bull" (*CS*, 392), confronts his mother because he feels his masculinity threatened. The inner voice of his father then accuses him of being "Not enough . . . a man" (*CS*, 393). The father becomes a "squatter" (*CS*, 393) on Thomas's own ground of identity. Thomas finally listens to what seems his father's order to plant the gun in the girl's purse—thus distancing himself from his own responsibility for what happens to her. He most surely becomes like his father when he goes to the sheriff to arrange for the girl's arrest for stealing his gun, an apparently trumped-up charge. Considering that his mother had declared, "I wouldn't turn a dog over to that man [the sheriff]" (*CS*, 394), Thomas's decisive act here seems particularly reprehensible. He sees the girl as a dog ("her hair was cut like a dog's," *CS*, 388), but the reader sees the beast within Thomas's own self more vividly than the feminine "beast."

It is too late when Thomas begins to question his masculine viewpoint and to gain self-knowledge. The sheriff refers to "them two women" (*CS*, 401) as if Thomas's mother and the girl were a pair. When the story ends with Thomas accidentally shooting his mother "as if his arm were guided by his father" (*CS*, 403), Farebrother concludes that the girl and Thomas are a pair: both criminals plotting the murder of Thomas's mother, thus establishing the sameness Thomas's mother asserts throughout the story. Thomas complains that her "hazy charity no longer made distinctions" (*CS*, 388), but the point is that the young man and the young woman share in human culpability.

Like the sheriff, Thomas has been thinking all along in terms of kinds ("her kind" would not commit suicide, *CS*, 397), rather than in terms of differentiated individuals. For Thomas, the world consists of "sluts" (Devouring Mothers) or "sibyls" (Great Mothers). Thomas depends too much on male stereotypes that reinforce his sense of power. He passively conforms to mass values and uses them to differentiate himself from others, thus establishing a sense of self-importance. He also fails to differentiate others when appropriate. He fails to acknowledge his connectedness with others—his own responsibility for developing particular relationships with particular people of his family and community. In O'Connor's view, denying human resemblances is an irresponsible act—a failure to recognize the dark side of the self, which underlies all of human nature. O'Connor constantly draws attention to the fact that Sarah Ham and Thomas are indeed the same: human, physical, morally deficient. The girl's deficiencies are evident to everyone, but only Thomas's mother (and the reader) can distinguish Thomas's deficiencies clearly. Thomas himself certainly cannot.

Thomas belittles his mother for not being "intellectual" (*CS*, 385) and for her conversation, which he says moves "from cliché to cliché" (*CS*, 387). Again, Thomas's reliability is being questioned. In fact, we cannot find the litany of commonplace expressions that characterize O'Connor's other stories undercutting mother figures. Thomas's mother is the best of O'Connor's Great Mothers: independent (she disregards her son's complaints because she rightly judges them to be deficient) and yet responsible to others. She takes candy to newcomers in town, to new mothers, the ailing elderly, or anyone else with a special occasion to share. She is capable of an "omniscient look" (*CS*, 392) because she is capable of "mourning for the world" (*CS*, 397). That she sees the suffering girl's likeness to her own son is the same insight that the grandmother achieves when she sees the resemblance between her son and The Misfit in "A Good Man Is Hard to Find." She honestly worries both about the disadvantaged girl and about her son's inability to recognize his own advantages. She takes responsibility for herself and for others less fortunate. On the other hand, Thomas blames his mother/"comforter," the "slut," his dead father, and "the entire order of the universe" (*CS*, 403) for his misdeeds. Thomas suffers from moral "blindness," a charge he directs at Sarah Ham, who ironically requites him by calling him "Tomsee."

In "The Enduring Chill," Asbury Fox also directs his aggressions toward his mother. He tortures her with the idea that he is about to die and formulates his pronouncement so that "each word [seems] like a hammer blow on top of her head" (*CS*, 372). Like Thomas, he seeks passivity, which inhibits his development. He instructs his mother to "Close the blinds and let me sleep" (*CS*, 365)—wishing to be "blinded" to his own responsibilities. He fails to develop a constructive relationship with his mother and to live a productive life. A would-be writer who left home to gain his independence in New York, Asbury returns to his mother and is convinced he is dying because he has been suffering for several months from vague symptoms of physical distress.

Both Thomas and Asbury suffer from an inability to reconcile the female and male sides of the self. Thomas feels revulsion for Sarah Ham; Asbury gives his sister Mary George "a revolted look" (*CS*, 359) when he first sees her after a long absence in New York. Both of these misogynists blame their nurturing mothers for their failures. A conventional woman, Asbury's mother advocates plain work and sunshine as a cure for his ills. Suspicious of higher education, she extols her husband as successful even though limited to an eighth-grade education. And like the child who identifies with the more powerful parent, she sees him as able to "do anything" (*CS*, 361). She is also conventional in that she wants her son to do "real work, not writing" (*CS*, 361). Mrs. Fox and her intellectual son are thus opposites. He represents aggressive masculinity, isolation, and cold rationality; she represents the feminine caretaker, conventional attitudes of the community, and tenderness. When his mother worries over her herd, especially over a particular cow's "bag" (a comic repetition of her concern for Asbury's more general ailment), Asbury responds to her "in an agonized voice" (*CS*, 362).

Asbury's immaturity is evident when he returns to his hometown with the idea of assisting his mother "in the process of growing up." He is "pleased" (*CS*, 357) to see his mother's grief over his obvious ill health. Suffering delusions of martyrdom, Asbury considers suicide, the ultimate punishment for his mother, but he decides to "spare her," to refrain from suicide and from causing her the "public embarrassment" of failing as a mother (*CS*, 370). He does not refrain from tormenting her in little ways, though, even by asking this Protestant lady to secure a priest for what he figures is his deathbed ordeal.

Ironically, Asbury's rebellion against his mother is the cause of his disease. He breaks his mother's rule of not drinking unpasteurized milk, which causes undulant fever, thus proving this young pseudo-intellectual's immaturity and regressiveness. That is, drinking the forbidden milk is a victory over the mother—revenge against being weaned. Asbury wishes to control his mother, and breaking this particular rule (he insists the black milkers break it, too) reinforces his fantasy of absolute control.

That Asbury's aggressions toward his mother are based on Oedipal conflicts is suggested when he considers his father's death "a great blessing" (CS, 364). He moves to New York but does not really establish independence from his need for his mother. His sister represents a rival for the mother's love, and the competitive relationship of Asbury and Mary George is inadequately mediated by Mrs. Fox. Just as Thomas loathes Sarah, so Asbury loathes his sister Mary George. His animosity toward his sister is likewise self-loathing. She stands for the physicality he would ignore and also for his own viciousness. Unlike Sarah, Mary George is worse in terms of the antagonism she herself feels for her male counterpart. O'Connor tells us that Mary George (notice the mixed gender implied here) and Asbury "had the same features except that hers were bigger" (CS, 359). Mary George's aggression against her brother matches what Asbury levels against his sister. Asbury and Mary George are like the two fields of "bitterweed" framing the road home—both unable to appreciate the members of their family and their community and therefore choking out connecting roads of the self that reach out to people beyond.

Asbury's narcissism, then, is indicated by his aggression toward both his mother and his sister and by his inflated idea of his own literary gifts. Driven toward fame (stereotypically considered, creativity is a masculine gift), he errs by denying human ties (to his mother and sister). The feminine is seen as a limited, limiting factor in his life. In his letter to his mother, he blames her for his lack of creativity: "Woman, why did you pinion me?" (CS, 364). He only wants to establish "difference," which translates into "superiority" defined by intellectual pursuit—an escape from body through mind. He muses that "He had failed his god, Art, but he had been a faithful servant and Art was sending him Death" (CS, 373).

Ernest Becker's insights about how our "projects" enable us to feel that we achieve immortality is important here. Asbury wants freedom from libido and the body self—the sort of flight offered by the esoteric priest in New York, Father Vogle (bird). Asbury pretentiously writes a letter to his mother, thinking that "It was such a letter as Kafka had addressed to his father," and misquotes Yeats in the process (*CS*, 364). That is, he writes of his desire to "find freedom . . . to take [his imagination] like a hawk from its cage and set it 'whirling off into the widening gyre'" [the line actually reads "Turning and turning in the widening gyre"]. Freud tells us that culture derives from a need for immortality, but achievement eats up the hours of our life. The fruits of culture, such as those left by the artist, are enjoyed by the whole tribe but confirm the death of the individual.[36] Asbury, however, ironically feels his art will enable him to transcend death. But he is never shown actually producing anything, actually participating in life. He suffers from an unconscious terror of life, more powerful than a terror of death. The paradox in Asbury's case is seen in his feeling that somehow dying a unique death will enable him to overcome death by escaping the common fate. Above all, Asbury feels that *his* fate cannot be the common one of the earthbound (a progress toward death).

Even the topic of Asbury's unwritten play shows this drive to validate his superiority and to differentiate himself from his community. He plans to write a play about Negroes, or, as he thinks of it, "the Negro" (*CS*. 368)—the abstraction he can tolerate. The superficiality of his intentions is revealed when he encourages the Negro Morgan to drink milk with him: "Here *boy*, have a drink of this" (*CS*, 369), he says (emphasis mine). He is unable to relate to the black workers as individual human beings also striving for significance. His stance allows him to maintain his superiority and to differentiate himself from humanity as a whole. That the Negroes do not warn him of the dangers of contracting undulant fever from drinking raw milk is evidence of their ability to see through his pretense.

Interested in Eastern religion, Goetz, Asbury's New York friend, seeks Nirvana—the loss of individual identity. In contrast, Asbury views his own live as leading to "the *unique* tragedy of . . . a death whose meaning had been far beyond the twittering group" (*CS*, 360). Ironically, death is not what affirms our uniqueness. Asbury rejects his friend Goetz's interest in Eastern philosophy just as he rejects Dr. Block, the community doctor. He uses his illness to differentiate himself from the crowd and from the body self represented by woman. The irony rests in the fact that Asbury's disease is a disease that originates with the herd (usually thought to be female). Asbury's disease reveals the inadequacies of his thinking when O'Connor presents the "small, walleyed Guernsey . . . watching him steadily as if she sensed some bond between them" (*CS*, 362). It is "bonding" that Asbury avoids— especially bonding to the physical body that reveals our connectedness to others. When Asbury's mother suggests that he go to the hospital, he refuses, "turning his thudding head from side to side as if he wanted to work it loose from his body" (*CS*, 377), a striking image of the mind/body split.

Unfortunately, Asbury fails to see that his quest for some last significant, culminating experience that he plans to "make for himself out of his own intelligence" (*CS*, 378) will not come to fruition unless he follows the advice of Father Finn to seek Christ through prayer, to seek family unity also through prayer. Asbury needs to accept "Mind, heart *and* body," as the priest puts it (emphasis mine; *CS*, 375). Unlike the ascetic Father Vogle, Father Finn has "a grease spot on his vest" and is a "massive old man who plowed straight across the room," his "eye . . . focused sharply on Asbury" (*CS*, 375). Asbury tells the priest that "The myth of the dying god has always fascinated me," but he retorts, "pray with your family." The priest represents both community and salvation of the individual, but Asbury is attracted to him only for what he offers the individual, not for any notion of self-sacrifice for the community. This story ends with Asbury's realization that his disease will not kill him; he must face "The Enduring Chill" of accepting life and living in a community of others who do not validate individual self-importance. This requires that he learn to admit the feminine side of his nature and become more like his mother by attending to others rather than being obsessed with self.

Assertive Widows

Asbury's and Thomas's mothers are relatively unassertive caretakers. More often in O'Connor's work, assertive widows assume their dead husband's power and take on stereotypically male characteristics. They are aggressive and unwilling to nurture anything but their own egos. In the first collection of stories, the earliest version of this kind of mother might be the "ravenous" Mrs. Crater, described as being "about the size of a cedar fence post" (woodenly unfeeling and phallic) and wearing "a man's gray hat" (*CS*, 146). But Mrs. Crater appears in a story ("The Life You Save May Be Your Own") that does not focus primarily on parent/child relationships as much as on the problem of evil in the world represented by Mr. Shiftlet. Moreover, in some primitive way, Mrs. Crater is also a nurturing mother: she wants her retarded daughter to secure a husband. Likewise, Mrs. Cope (in "A Circle in the Fire") does seem protective of her daughter, but she aggressively denies the destructive elements of her own psyche and finally becomes a "destroyer" as surely as Powell, the aggressive boy with a faded "destroyer" on his shirt. And this story also focuses on problems of evil in the world (Powell burns Mrs. Cope's woods). Mrs. McIntyre in "The Displaced Person" is as aggressive as any mother in the O'Connor canon, but that story deals with the individual's relation to society, an issue treated later.

There is only one other story that *primarily* focuses on male/female antagonisms, sex-related differences, and mother figures affected by the dominant male culture. One of the most aggressive of the widowed mothers in O'Connor's canon is Mrs. May, the protagonist of "Greenleaf"; this story draws on sex-related stereotypes as they appear in myth. Thus, before pursuing this line of the author's thought as it relates to myth, we need to address the author's comments about the influence of myth in her work. Asals notes that O'Connor once said, "I never think in terms of fable or myth. Those things are far removed from anything that I know when I write." And yet in a 1962 interview, she refers to the Bible as our "sacred history and our mythic background," and in her essays she declares that "It takes a story to make a story. It takes a story of mythic dimensions, one which belongs to everybody" (*MM*, 202). Asals points out that Eliot and Joyce, authors O'Connor admired and studied, brought myth to literature.[37] And we learn from the letters that, as the author puts it, "The only good things I read when I was a child were the Greek and Roman myths" (*Letters*, 98).

The plot of "Greenleaf" exploits the mythical male/female dichotomy by presenting the rivalry between Mrs. May and Mr. Greenleaf—and the rivalry between Mrs. May and her sons. Mr. Greenleaf appears to represent male potency: his phallic nature is emphasized in the figure of his sons' bull, which he allows to run loose in Mrs. May's herd—his way of asserting power over his female employer and of establishing his own territory. The bull is described as "squirrel-colored, with jutting hips and long light horns . . . a Greenleaf bull if I ever saw one"

(*CS*, 323), as Mrs. May puts it. The sexual connotations of Greenleaf's phallic bull is further reinforced when the hired hand looks "with approval at the bull's rump." Moreover, Greenleaf has five daughters and twin sons (representing self-procreative power, as previously mentioned). Greenleaf's sons married French wives and produced three children each. On the other hand, Mrs. May has only two unmarried sons who still live with their mother. Mr. Greenleaf's sons represent male power; Mrs. May's sons represent female impotence and passivity as they function in the world—male aggression when they attack their mother at home.

But Mrs. May herself matches Mr. Greenleaf in her masculine characteristics. When challenged by her sons, she holds "her back stiff as a rake handle" (*CS*, 315)—a phallic image also suggesting her abrasive nature. She carries "a long stick" when walking in the woods "in case she saw a snake" (*CS*, 316). In fact, this unfeminine but female farm manager ironically uses her femininity as an excuse for not being more successful in exacting obedience from her hired male hand: she complains to Mr. Greenleaf that his sons do not comply with her wishes because she is a woman ("They didn't come because I'm a woman. . . . You can get away with anything when you're dealing with a woman," *CS*, 329).[38] The competition between Mrs. May and Mr. Greenleaf results in a power struggle that reveals the violence of the male, materialistic world suggested by both characters—perhaps especially by Mrs. May as she takes over the powerful male role of her dead husband.

In the first incident of the story, the Greenleaf boys' bull appears in the middle of the night beneath Mrs. May's bedroom window and disturbs her sleep. The release of a bull and the construction of the temple at the place of his slaughter was a common ritual of ancient times. The sociologist Mircea Eliade explains this ritual as an attempt to eliminate chaos, discover the real, and organize space by centering himself in the world—choosing a place and then constructing a city in order to found the world. The release of a bull, then, represents a means of staking out a territory, sanctifying space, and creating cosmos.

Mr. Greenleaf operates on such a primitive level in his aim to organize his world in Mrs. May's space.[39] Repeatedly, he is depicted as walking "on the perimeter of some invisible circle" (*CS*, 313; *CS*, 330); he is primitive and confined to the circle of self. This circle implies his narcissism; "circling" also connotes the hunter's attitude toward his prey. Greenleaf strives to increase his power, to enlarge his "territory," and to center himself in the world—thus ritualistically eliminating chaos by superimposing his own order on reality. The pursuit of material territory and the inability to transcend self indicate primitive natures in O'Connor's view. Both Mr. Greenleaf and Mrs. May's ambitions are regressive and profane. In fact, Mrs. May's fear of being eaten—which is suggested in a dream caused by the bull's munching on the hedge outside her window—suggests a regression to the oral stage of infancy, when the infant compulsively takes in the world through the mouth. Mrs. May dreams that something was "eating her and the boys, and . . . eating everything until nothing was left but the Greenleafs on a little island all their own in the middle of what had been her place" (*CS*, 312). The relevance here of territorial claims, possessiveness, and competitiveness coincides with what one expects of the narcissistic self—both Mrs. May and Mr. Greenleaf. That the bull intrudes "like some patient god come down to woo her" and "to tear at the hedge" (*CS*, 311) again suggests myth (violence to women; for example, the rape of Europa) as well as the conflict between male and female forces, the spiritual and the bestial.

Some critics see Christ in the image of "the hedge-wreath" that the "god" wears, and this reference is perhaps suggested elsewhere in the story when Mrs. May perceives Mrs. Greenleaf's shrieks of "Jesus" as "some violent unleashed force . . . charging toward her" (*CS*, 316). But what is clear is the primitive nature of both Mr. and Mrs. Greenleaf's behavior—their distance from the Catholic world. Likewise, Mrs. May wants to become her own God, to be self-creative rather than God's creature. Her "primitive" fear of being eaten by the bull reverses what occurs in Dionysian rites wherein the worshippers rend and devour a live bull.

What at first seems a simple contest of wills between a male farm hand and a female farm manager takes on a complex of allusions relating to primitive ritual and to life-death/male-female iconography found in myth. "Greenleaf" and "May" ironically suggest regeneration. "Green" is the color of the resurrection; spring is the season of regeneration. And yet Greenleaf's character is paradoxical (essentially, he murders Mrs. May), suggesting the death-life oxymoron of Picasso's *Minotaur,* the surrealist depiction of a mythical god holding a knife formed as a leaf.

Without Christianity's promise of the resurrection, human beings regress to self-destructive, primitive practices. Mrs. Greenleaf's peculiar ritual of burying tragic newspaper clippings enables her to believe she controls death. The self-preservation instinct is prominent in the competition between Mr. Greenleaf and Mrs. May—competition that intensifies when they vie for superiority in terms of their offspring. Constantly critical of Wesley and Scofield (Mrs. May's unassertive, bachelor sons), Mr. Greenleaf accuses them of being lazy, and he asserts that his own sons are superior to them. Similarly, Mrs. May accuses O.T. and E.T. (eat/devouring) of lacking pride, when in fact she herself represents prideful self-assertion. She even presumes to control death and says, "I'll die when I get good and ready" (CS, 321). The replacement of religious faith by American ideals of resourcefulness, hard work, and possessiveness causes Mrs. May to be "near-sighted" (CS, 313), obsessed with acquisitive struggles for material success measured by the success of her offspring and the size of her property.

Mrs. May's other self in fact becomes her property. Thinking of the praise bestowed by her friends who admire her success at managing a farm, she identifies with what she has achieved in the material world: "When she looked out any window in her house, she saw the reflection of her own character" (CS, 321). This is the portrait of an egoistic self projecting an identity on the whole world to extend the boundaries of the self (cf. Mrs. Shortley's character in "The Displaced Person"). Mrs. May prides herself on marrying a businessman, and she berates Greenleaf for not having "the initiative to steal" (CS, 313). Jealous that both of Greenleaf's sons managed to gain the rank of sergeant in the service, Mrs. May laments the fact that Scofield was only a Private First Class and Wesley's heart condition exempted him altogether.

Especially significant is the fact that Mrs. May worries over the potential of her sons to secure wives. Obviously, neither son has progressed far enough in his development to acknowledge the feminine side of the self and to relate constructively to the opposite sex. Scofield is an overly differentiated male in his pursuit of success defined by acquiring material goods. He exploits Negroes by selling them insurance they probably do not need. And the hate-filled intellectual schoolteacher, Wesley, obviously directs his rage toward the female elements of his life: we are told that he "didn't like nice girls. . . . he hated living with his mother" (CS, 319), declaring openly to her, "I wouldn't milk a cow to save your soul from hell" (CS, 321). He "snarls" at his mother and belittles her respect for religion—ridiculing her by comparing her to Mrs. Greenleaf ("Why don't you do something practical, Woman? Why don't you pray for me like Mrs. Greenleaf would?" [*CS*, 320]).

In sum, Mr. Greenleaf compares his sons to Mrs. May's in order to taunt his female employer; Mrs. May compares E.T. and O.T. to her sons in order to belittle her own offspring. Following the example of their mother, Scofield and Wesley then compare their mother to Mrs. Greenleaf—thus belittling the one who supports them. Moreover, they bicker and brawl between themselves. All of the characters in this story interrelate by aggressively competing.

The destructiveness of this kind of behavior is suggested by the violent ending of the story when Mrs. May is impaled on the horns of the Greenleaf bull, while Mr. Greenleaf more than likely passively observes the disaster (cf. the death of Guizac in the "The Displaced Person"). The hired hand appears too late, killing the bull only after it has brought Mrs. May to the ground. Mr. Greenleaf seeks revenge because this castrating woman emasculated him when she ordered him to shoot his sons' bull and then gloated over her own phallic power—over controlling "the gun between his knees" (*CS*, 330). Mrs. May's "sacrifice" represents Mr. Greenleaf's triumph over space and time. He aggressively centers himself in the cosmos. His subtle aggression against Mrs. May is prefigured by the "crash as if he had kicked something out of his way" as he enters the harness room to get the gun. He responds to the order to shoot the bull by "violently" wiping his hands and "violently" getting into the car. Mrs. May realizes then that "he'd like to shoot [her] instead of the bull" (*CS*, 330). His complicity in Mrs. May's death is again suggested when we are told that she surmises her hired hand is "loitering in the woods" (*CS*, 332).

Most important, Mr. Greenleaf's complicity in Mrs. May's death is subtly indicated by a repetition of circling images at the end—images clearly associated with Greenleaf earlier in the story. He "circles" the car as they set out after the bull. He "circles" the gate and the hill (*CS*, 331) before he allows his escape. And while Mrs. May waits for Mr. Greenleaf and the bull to reappear, she expects to see Mr. Greenleaf emerge "from the circle of trees" (*CS*, 332). The "green arena" of the pasture where Mrs. May dies is "encircled" by woods (*CS*, 331). Greenleaf approaches her mortally wounded body as if "on the outside of some invisible circle" (*CS*, 334).

The "last discovery" of Mrs. May is made through "the quake in the huge body" of the bull (*CS*, 334), a body defining the physicality

and violence of human secular life and the destructiveness of male/
female antagonisms. Self-sacrifice rather than self-assertion, affiliation
with others rather than competition, the capacity to love others (especially those of the opposite sex), and a capacity for tenderness rather
than aggression are necessary in order to achieve wholeness of self and
harmony within the family.

In all of these stories, the dominance of masculine values, stereotypically defined, results in an attack on the mother, a fragmented family,
and a failure to continue the ongoing chain of human development.
Some of these concerns continue in the next group of stories, but in a
broader context, encompassing social contexts and community.

"The Mystery of Personality" and Society

> An idiom characterizes a society, and when you ignore the idiom, you are very likely ignoring the whole social fabric that could make a meaningful character. You can't cut characters off from their society and say much about them as individuals. You can't say anything meaningful about the mystery of a personality unless you put that personality in a believable and significant social context.
>
> (*MM*, 105)

In the stories discussed so far, family relationships inhibit growth and contribute to the protagonist's insecurity; the individual or parent/child pair is alienated from the community. The stories discussed below depict alienation in a broader sense as it derives from interactions not only between self and family but between self and society.

Establishing the right relationship to community is a major theme of O'Connor's.[40] O'Connor earned her bachelor's degree at Georgia College in sociology. Her course work included six sociology courses, an education course called "The School and Society," a course in educational psychology, and an "Introduction to Modern Philosophy" course. Although her work satirizes the social worker and she hated the prideful do-gooder, some basic concepts of sociology clarify the stories about the individual's relationship to his or her society.[41]

Alienation Versus Group Identity

Erik Erikson points out that ego synthesis requires both ethos (group identity) and ego. The larger social order both contributes to and dissipates our sense of self, depending on whether the group affirms our significance as a leader or whether we become a cipher in the crowd.[42] In "Good Country People," "The Partridge Festival," "A Late Encounter with the Enemy," "Revelation," and "The Displaced Person," O'Connor's characters feel themselves to be insignificant repetitions in the long procession of human life. They are overwhelmed by an identity crisis because they cannot maintain "difference" established by achieving a secure place in the social hierarchy.

Lacking a sure sense of self, these O'Connor characters sometimes seek and sometimes deny their social identities. The symbolic context of these stories develops images of sameness and difference, references to processions, types, and kinds (often expressed by clichés such as "It takes all kinds to make the world"), and obsessions with uniforms or dress generally. On the one hand, O'Connor represents the human tendency to form social aggregates and to identify with classes in power (Mrs. Turpin, Mrs. Hopewell, and Sally Poker Sash and her father). Then it seems clear that social hierarchies develop out of the desire to prove individual significance and to gain power over others through conformity to the group. On the other hand, rebel character types (Hulga Hopewell, Manly Pointer, Calhoun, Mary Elizabeth, and Mary Grace) isolate themselves from others and defy the social order to transcend the group will. Compulsive, bizarre behavior asserts individual difference and self-importance.

Isolating oneself from the social group inhibits personal development as much as depending too much on the group for a sense of self and values. Mechanistic responses to life based on mass values rob us of responsibility and identity, and yet dependence on group life affords a sense of permanence, relieving the pain of an awareness of individual mortality. Immersion in the rituals of group activity represents power over death—the ability to fix reality and to stop time. Especially in the South, conformity to the standards and practices of the group is crucial to a sense of well-being.

Conforming and egoistic character types, however, suffer a frustrated quest for significance (for example, Mrs. Turpin). Only temporarily do they convince themselves they have achieved "significance" by depending on "class" for a sense of status and thereby differentiating themselves from *most* others. Seeking reinforcement of their insecure egos, they associate themselves with those higher on the social ladder and differentiate themselves from those on the lower rung—relying on role playing as well as the power of elitism to feel "significant" in an acquisitive society that undermines the idea of denying oneself for the sake of others. Encouraging stratification of society, they seek the highest possible level in the social hierarchy, a level often determined by false values (money, aggression) and superficialities (clothing, skin color). They are classist and racist.

The two forms of adjustment to modern existence in O'Connor's canon—characters either compulsively conforming or rebelling so emphatically as to be absurd—imply what is missing, that is, responsibility to the group, without dependence or isolation. A unified self achieves "an emotional integration which permits participation by followership as well as acceptance of the responsibility of leadership," as Erikson puts it. The well-integrated self overcomes self-love and a fear of death created by the threat of the collective.[43] When threatened by the great mass of others, individuals escape into materialistic endeavors that the collective encourages through an acquisitive society. O'Connor believes that social maladies are finally caused by human encounters with a materialistic world based on uncertainty rather than faith. Competitiveness rules in those stories representing how the individual relates to the social group or how social groups relate to one another. The competitive spirit, ruthlessly pursued, undermines the Christian ideal of *Caritas*.

O'Connor's obsession with *Human Development* (the book that Mary Grace thrusts at Mrs. Turpin in "Revelation") culminated in the study of Teilhard de Chardin, whom she called "The most important nonfiction writer" for scholars of Catholicism to study (*Letters*, 570). Teilhard contends that "some innate instinct, justified by reflection, inclines us to think that to give ourselves full scope we must break away as far as possible from the crowd of *others*." We overcome a fear of death by our awareness "of the joy of forming part of a whole greater than oneself"—not that we merge pantheistically with "the great current" but that "we are caught up again, invaded, dominated by the divine power." Death, then, should be embraced as "a 'becoming.'"[44]

Teilhard also believes that egoism prevents evolution or "hominisation" of the whole human race. "There is no mind without synthesis. . . . The true ego grows in inverse proportion to 'egoism.'"[45] His conclusions about human egoism deepen an important track in O'Connor's thought: the track formed by Freud's conclusions about egoism—the narcissistic nature of man and his society, which relates to an even more basic track—the Catholic concern for the sin of pride. The stories addressed next all present social stratification resulting from egoistic, materialistic, and mechanistic responses to life. They all depict characters who either isolate themselves from or mindlessly conform to the social group, or sometimes vacillate between these extremes and therefore fail to contribute to the evolution of humanity.

The Young Rebel

In "Good Country People," neither the characters representing group conformity (Mrs. Freeman, Mrs. Hopewell) nor the isolated rebels (Hulga, Manley) avoid conditioned behaviors. The first question to ask about the story is why it begins by focusing on Mrs. Freeman, who seems totally unnecessary to the plot.

Mrs. Freeman's initial appearance contributes to this story's thematic unity, which derives from a complex of symbols, images, and incidents suggesting compulsive repetitions, mindless conformity, and socially conditioned responses. Her limited, mechanistic, and compulsive responses to life are defined in the first paragraph and "turn" the reader down the center of the story:

> Besides the neutral expression that she wore when she was alone, Mrs. Freeman had two others, forward and reverse, that she used for all her human dealings. Her forward expression was steady and driving like the advance of a heavy truck. Her eyes never swerved to left or right but *turned as the story turned* as if they followed a yellow line down the center of it. She seldom used the other expression because it was not often necessary for her to retract a statement, but when she did, her face came to a complete stop, there was an almost imperceptible movement of her black eyes, during which they seemed to be receding, and then the observer would see that Mrs. Freeman, though she might stand there as real as several grain sacks thrown on top of each other, was no longer there in spirit. (*CS*, 271; emphasis mine)

Mrs. Freeman is not free but is grounded in the physical rather than the spiritual world. She compulsively struggles to master life's painful events. Freud viewed mechanistic human behaviors as repressed remnants of infantile behaviors seeking expression and working to master unpleasant realities.[46] Instances of mindless conformity and compulsive behaviors are developed throughout this story—not that O'Connor supported the idea of biological determinism, but she recognized the human struggle required to exercise free will.

Mrs. Hopewell is as limited in expressiveness and subject to mechanical reactions as Mrs. Freeman. Her responses to life are steeped in "favorite sayings" (*CS*, 272–73). Most of these commonplace expressions that she repeats in a variety of circumstances are also repeated by Mrs. Freeman. These two women classify people simplistically—

asserting that people are "different" while ironically behaving according to stereotypes that fail to acknowledge individuality but rather depend on "class." For example, their usual morning dialogue mindlessly (and ironically) claims the capacity to notice difference:

> "Everybody is different," Mrs. Hopewell said.
> "Yes, most people is," Mrs. Freeman said.
> "It takes all kinds to make the world."
> "I always said it did myself." (*CS*, 273)

This is essentially a monologue because Mrs. Freeman mechanically reinforces what Mrs. Hopewell says. This paragraph and those preceding the "dialogue" contain twenty-one instances of "would," indicating habitual behavior. Mrs. Hopewell later repeats the same sentiments expressed in the dialogue above when she encounters Manley Pointer, the Bible salesman (*CS*, 279), and again when she relates her encounter with the young man to Mrs. Freeman (*CS*, 282). All of this undermines her claim to notice distinctions.

The point is that Mrs. Hopewell classifies people as "alike" because she thinks in terms of classes and kinds ("Good Country People," for example)—thereby failing to distinguish important differences. We are told that she has kept the Freemans as her working tenants because "they were not trash. . . . [but rather] good country people," that she considers Mrs. Freeman "the *type* who had to be into everything," and that she judges her previous tenant wives as "the *kind* you would [not] want to be around you for very long" (*CS*, 273–74). Mrs. Hopewell cannot perceive individuality.

The basis of Mrs. Hopewell's determinations becomes suspect when she judges Manley Pointer, the would-be seducer of her daughter, also as a simple country boy. Her responses to her daughter are automatic, conditioned, and conforming. She pities Hulga for having lost her leg (which was shot off in a hunting accident) and for not having "any *normal* good times" (*CS*, 274), defined as dancing and being pretty. Her conformity is further evident when we are told she approves of girls becoming nurses but not philosophers (*CS*, 276). And when she imagines her daughter lecturing "like a scarecrow," it is clear just how much she regrets the fact that "every year she [Joy] grew less like other people" (*CS*, 276). Her pretense to tolerance of "all kinds of people" is suspect.

Hyperaware of *certain* differences, Mrs. Hopewell claims not to be "ashamed" of introducing Mrs. Freeman "to anybody they might meet" (*CS*, 272), but she introduces her as a hired hand. She is sensitive to "kind" determined by class and by social stereotypes. She prefers "simple" boys over her intellectual daughter. Her conformity represents a superficial response to life that O'Connor clearly condemns.

We might expect that Mrs. Hopewell's "opposite," then, the rebel daughter, would receive O'Connor's approving stroke, but Hulga, like Mrs. Freeman and her mother, also responds to others "in a purely mechanical way" (*CS*, 274). When we are introduced to her morning routine, the habitual "would" again recurs, alternating with the conditional "would" so that it is repeated ten times in one paragraph and is implied one other time with the mention of "always" (*CS*, 275). Joy-Hulga, like her mother and Mrs. Freeman, lacks a range of responses to life (*CS*, 273).

Through repetition of the same, sometimes neurotic responses, we confirm our group identity, absolve ourselves of responsibility, and avoid developing, which is always painful. Hulga at times seems a rebel, but actually she has merely chosen to conform to a social group different from her mother's. Since Hulga is less independent than she believes, she fails to reach a mature level of insight. Her regressive tendencies are suggested by her mode of dress—she wears "a six-year-old skirt and a yellow sweat shirt with a faded cowboy on a horse embossed on it" (*CS*, 276)—but more important, by her rebellion against her mother. Hulga feels that being called "Joy" amounts to being classified as "Good Country People" and accepting a deadly "sameness," an eclipsed identity. By changing her name from Joy to Hulga, she denies her mother's wish that she conform and she asserts her independence.

Hulga's preference for the name "Hulga" suggests, however, more than rebellion against her mother. It suggests that she suffers a hyperawareness of the mind/body, freedom/necessity dichotomy. In choosing her name, she asserts her freedom in re-creating the self ("her highest creative act," *CS*, 275). Ironically, she imagines "the name working like the ugly sweating Vulcan"—the Roman god of fire, change, and creativity, but here, like her sweatshirt, limited and concretized by the image of the "sweating" body. Subconsciously, Hulga wishes to avoid the sameness of the body self, that which denies special significance. She would be like Vulcan, called by the goddess and withstanding the flame, therefore immortal. And yet in the last analysis, the name Hulga has chosen for herself evokes the image of hull, husk, the temporal body. The distraught intellectual tries to achieve a unified and whole self representing a fixed reality contrasting with the living ego embedded in consciousness and lacking permanence. There is no escape, however, from life's vicissitudes. Our feelings of "joy" are ever-changing and transient.

In spite of her pretentious parroting of the commonplace expressions of the intellectual nihilists, Hulga, like most of O'Connor's intellectuals, fails to work at any constructive activity in society. Erikson explains that an individual's mastery of tasks provides "a sense of embeddedness in the community, preventing a sense of strangeness and, above all . . . the fear of death."[47] Hulga resists her connection to the whole community; she regretfully acknowledges, "Malebranche was right: we are not our own light" (CS, 276). To acknowledge our relationship to all of humanity is a humbling admission that demands that we accept human weakness and mortality as that which prevents us from claiming to be a separate "light" but also that which should unite us, creating in us a strong sense of community.

Accepting the facts of human mortality and vulnerability is even more difficult in the case of traumas, such as Hulga's loss of her leg. The reenactment of uncontrollable events allows the illusion of control. The psyche preserves traumatic experiences—repeating them in dreams or daily rituals—because the sufferer thereby achieves a sense of mastery over events affirming human vulnerability. Thus, Mrs. Freeman suffers the neurotic compulsion to repeat "the details of secret infections, hidden deformities, assaults upon children" (CS, 275). Mrs. Hopewell responds to Hulga's injury by again and again repeating "the details of the hunting accident, how the leg had been literally blasted off" (CS, 275). Hulga exhibits repetition compulsiveness especially when she fantasizes "that she would run away with [Manley] and that every night he would take the leg off and every morning put it back on again" (CS, 289)—compulsively reenacting what happened when she lost her leg in order to master the loss.

And Manley's theft of Hulga's artificial leg provides the most extreme example of neurotic compulsions repeated in order to overcome trauma. Whatever initially caused Manley's bizarre habit of stealing body parts is hard to tell, but stealing artificial body parts points to an obsession with attaining wholeness—an obsession resulting from an overwhelming sense of psychic fragmentation and a fear of death (castration). Also, these mechanisms such as artificial legs and eyes return us to the portrait of Mrs. Freeman at the start of the story, her mechanistic responses to life operating like the gears of a truck. Images of the fragmented human body and mechanical parts express the psychic fragmentation of the human sufferer lacking self-awareness.

Like "Good Country People," "The Partridge Festival" also targets mechanical responses to life, mindless conformity, and rebellion. The latter story more explicitly develops a conflict between community (the festival celebrants) and individual (the scapegoat and outsider, Singleton). All of the stories about gaining a proper relation to the community end by demanding sympathy for human weakness—however ridiculous and comic. Yet "The Partridge Festival" seems to be one of the least sympathetic of stories; in fact, O'Connor calls it a "farce" (*Letters*, 401) "objectionable from the local standpoint" (*Letters*, 405) because it was written from newspaper clippings about a similar mass murder in Milledgeville during the annual azalea festival. She is sometimes critical of her own community but only as it stands as a symbol for human nature generally, especially those like Hulga and Calhoun who seek an "existential encounter" (*CS*, 436) rather than a personal relationship with someone worth loving.

In "The Partridge Festival," the young (this time male) rebel, Calhoun, returns to his hometown, Partridge, and is greeted by his two great-aunts—both wearing a conforming "sheepish smile" (*CS*, 421). These aunts then initiate the ritual of showing their grandnephew a "miniature" of his great-grandfather, a ritual repeated "every time he came" (*CS*, 422). Calhoun denies his resemblance to his progenitor because he wishes to establish his own unique identity. He in fact sees this relative as bearing "the same general stamp" as the five community dignitaries recently shot by a deranged community outsider named, significantly, Singleton.

Calhoun foolishly identifies with Singleton and idealizes the murderer as a rebel, like himself, "willing to suffer for the right to be himself" (*CS*, 423). Singleton had refused to purchase the required badge during the community's festival and consequently was imprisoned in an outhouse with a goat. Singleton indeed becomes "the scapegoat . . . laden with the sins of the community" and "Sacrificed for the guilt of others" (*CS*, 431). Calhoun denies his own community, while he relishes the idea that "the shape of his [own] face was broad like Singleton's" and notes a "real likeness between them [that] was 'interior'" (*CS*, 423).

By associating himself with the scapegoat, Calhoun feels he is asserting his innocence—a reversal of what is meant by most primitive rituals wherein the community dissociates itself from the scapegoat after having transferred group guilt to it. O'Connor addresses obliquely and ironically the issue of individual responsibility. Calhoun essentially declares Singleton completely innocent when he says his greatest crime was that "He never conformed." The aunts ironically do the same when they rely on what O'Connor considers an invalid excuse exploited by criminals (and wrongly attributed to Freud): "Since he is insane," they rationalize, "he is not responsible." Calhoun then pointedly asks where "does the real guilt lie?" (*CS*, 423)—where does human responsibility reside?

Early in this story, the reader formulates his own suspicions about Calhoun's judgment of Singleton as a hero. He is a "spider-like" man with "reptilian" eyes. When this lecher attacks Mary Elizabeth, exposing himself in the process, it is clear that he is less victimized than Calhoun would have us suppose. Although O'Connor seems to find sympathy for him when she declares, "I am all for Singleton in this, devil though I rightly consider him to be" (*Letters*, 443), the story itself is heavy-handed when depicting Singleton's lack of "grace."

Guilt clearly lies with the prideful individualist; Singleton is a character fragment reflecting Calhoun's pride. Calhoun claims self-knowledge but is basically ignorant of his own inner psychic realities. He is guilty, like Singleton, in that he has not outgrown his narcissistic and aggressive wishes. Freud identifies "the wish to become great" as "one of the immortal infantile wishes."[48] Calhoun's wish to write a novel and expose the town's depravity undermines his credibility. That Aunt Bessie greets him by declaring, "Here's our baby," causes the reader experienced with O'Connor's subtlety to anticipate the portrait of a character longing for significance but hopelessly immature (*CS*, 421).

Although Calhoun identifies with Singleton, O'Connor draws parallels between Singleton and Calhoun that the intellectual rebel would deny. His disdain for his aunts, shown by his trips to town to "escape them," reveals a dishonest, condescending, adversarial we-them mentality: "It would be ridiculous to tell *them*," he thinks to himself (*CS*, 424). He works at developing "his fiercest look" (*CS*, 424) when interacting with them. Further, the intensity of his denial of his great-grandfather—"I'm a different type entirely" (*CS*, 423)—suggests that Singleton acted out Calhoun's part in the Oedipal triangle: the madman killed the dignitaries who were substitutes (look-alikes) for the father.

Calhoun's aggression matches Singleton's. His meanness worsens as the story develops and peaks when he eventually wishes Mary Elizabeth physical harm. When driving her to see Singleton, he hopes "the girl [would] go through the windshield" (*CS*, 439). What he fails to understand is that this girl's "fierce expression" (*CS*, 422) reflects his. Rather, he prefers to see himself as a heroic type—gifted with great insight, a depth of vision, and an artistic sensibility—claiming that "The mystery of personality . . . is what interests the artist [meaning himself]" (*CS*, 436). This "hero" claims mastery over that subject, but then he envisions Singleton, like himself: "an individualist . . . a man who would not allow himself to be pressed into the mold of his inferiors . . . a man of depth living among caricatures" (*CS*, 431). The prideful intellectual cannot achieve a depth of insight regarding himself.

Calhoun sees his conformity to the community, his social self, as an intrusion on "his real self—the rebel/artist/mystic" (*CS*, 424). He suffers a sense of "guilt . . . doubleness" that can only be eliminated, he is convinced, if he can write something to "vindicate the madman" (*CS*, 424), who, unlike himself, represents the "purity" of being able to express "the right to be different. . . . The right to be yourself" (*CS*, 429). Conforming to the community represents a kind of pollution of self to Calhoun.

The "doubleness" or dividedness Calhoun suffers is clearly evident when the young man contemplates his own "unremarkable-looking and innocent" image in a barbershop mirror and searches "desperately for its hidden likeness to the man [Singleton]" (*CS*, 429–30), whom he considers "spiritual kin" (*CS*, 436). While Calhoun analyzes his own and Singleton's "innocence," the narcissistic stance (looking in the mirror) reveals his guilt, his self-involvement. Ironically, his own sense of "guilt" intensifies when he accepts the occupational role of salesman (his alter ego) for the summer months in order to support himself in the role of rebel the rest of the year. What disturbs him is that he realizes he enjoys selling because then he is "carried outside himself" (*CS*, 425), a movement he nonetheless considers destructive.

Thus, Singleton ambivalently represents the other individualist self Calhoun would seek and the other guilty self he would deny. Mary Elizabeth represents the other self he eventually acknowledges. Calhoun's relationship with this young intellectual clarifies even further the extent of his confusion not only with moral judgments and judgments about reality but also confusion as to the boundaries of his own self. When he and the girl watch a beauty pageant from her father's law office, we are told that Calhoun "stared at her so long that he was afraid her image would be etched forever on his retina" (*CS*, 435). He later struggles "to obliterate her from his consciousness so that he could reestablish Singleton there" (*CS*, 438).

Calhoun denies that Mary Elizabeth and he are obviously two of a kind: he asserts that their "forms are different," meaning that she writes nonfiction and he writes fiction. Yet O'Connor suggests throughout that they are the same. Finally, when they feel this sameness, what they feel (unity in self-righteousness), the reader perceives ironically (unity in guilt). Calhoun anticipates meeting Singleton in a "predestined convergence" (*CS*, 442), which becomes a perverse seduction when Singleton exposes himself to Mary Elizabeth. This grotesque and comic incident ironically reinforces the idea that human physicality confirms our sameness. Singleton finally asserts, "You and me are two of a kind," and Calhoun later sees "a miniature visage . . . in [Mary Elizabeth's] spectacles" of himself: "Round, innocent, undistinguished as an iron link" and a member of the human community. Calhoun's denial of community is destined to failure from the start.

Calhoun sees various members of his community as "enemies" and dehumanizes them into abstractions as much as the townspeople dehumanize Singleton as "criminal." This attitude toward others represents the human tendency toward exclusiveness—which promotes racism, classism, elitism, and other types of hierarchical thinking proclaiming certain individuals superior to certain others.

Group Power

A similar narcissistic drive for power and significance apart from the crowd (or audience) is what motivates General Sash in "A Late Encounter with the Enemy." Ironically, he tries to differentiate himself by donning the "uniform" of a leader. Likewise, the General's granddaughter, Sally Poker Sash, claims special significance reinforced by the social hierarchy when she aims to graduate from college.

That the General's uniform refers us to the Civil War seems especially significant given the behavior of the grandfather and the granddaughter here. The Civil War itself—an attempt of a region to differentiate itself from its mother country—becomes a symbol for the philosophical and psychological issue of how the individual preserves his or her identity given a particular place in the family and in society. In this story, we are again presented with a parent/child relationship, such as earlier cases in which the parent's egoism eclipses the identity of the child. The relationship of this pair, General Sash and Sally Poker Sash, to the larger community seems, however, as important, if not more important, than the relationship between them.

Both Sally and the General associate themselves with group power and dissociate themselves from whatever threatens their individuality—especially being an undistinguished member of the community. Their "we/them" mentality (the basis for war) leads them to perceive most everyone else in the world as a kind of "enemy." A sixty-two-year-old student trying to differentiate herself by earning a college degree, Sally wants her grandfather to live long enough to attend her graduation so that she can prove "what all was behind her [as she puts it], and was not behind *them*" (*CS*, 135; emphasis mine). As the author then tells us, "This *them* was not anybody in particular. It was just all the upstarts who had turned the world on its head and unsettled the ways of decent living" (*CS*, 135).

Sally seeks order in what seems chaos, decency in what seems by her standards (defined by the social status quo) indecent. She most certainly conforms to her society's values rather than developing her own, just as she depends entirely on her grandfather's feigned "accomplishments" for a sense of self-worth. She values education because society rewards it; she values the old traditional "Dignity" (*CS*, 135), which her grandfather ironically represents, because society admires it. She wants to distinguish herself, but she resorts to accepting the role of "daughter" to a distinguished man—a role that actually eclipses her self-importance rather than bolstering it.

Most of the critical interpretations of this story (and there are far too few) have focused on the General. And yet it is Sally whose dilemma is central to the plot. She is the one seeking power and significance—seeking to become the "heroine" but in a confused manner. The old man feels he has already attained "significance."

Sally seems a rebel in that she has decided at a late age to seek a college degree, but soon it is evident that she accepts a conforming, subsidiary role. This would-be scholar and teacher only pretends to pursue the option of developing herself. Convinced her graduation will not be worthwhile if the General dies before the occasion, she undermines her self-worth and exists in a deadly solipsistic circle including only her grandfather and herself. Both the General and Sally depend on external trappings to project their identities—he on his uniform, which turns out to be a mere costume for a movie premiere, and she on a black dinner dress and a gilded corsage. Sally's college degree is mere ornament, since she refuses to use what she has learned about teaching: "she always taught in the exact way she had been taught not to teach" (*CS*, 135).

The fragmentation of self that Sally suffers is suggested frequently, especially during the movie premiere when her grandfather is asked to display himself before the audience as a symbol of the South. He is given a Confederate General's uniform that does not even match his actual rank in the war (an event that he does not even remember), so that his pride in the uniform exceeds his pride in the actual war. The gaps and disjointedness of the General's memories match the fragmentation of self that Sally suffers. When her grandfather is spotlighted before the crowd, we see only "a weird moon-shaped slice of Sally Poker" (*CS*, 138). And then the revelation that she forgot to wear her silver slippers and that instead "two brown Girl Scout oxfords protruded from the bottom of her dress" (*CS*, 138) suggests immaturity.

An unpleasant reality underlies the flamboyant and superficial Hollywood-inspired "show" held in Atlanta. O'Connor suggests that the "show" defines how Sally and the General live every day, denying their inadequacies by presenting a "show" of power based on empty claims.

Our society, of course, validates the idea of the father as the most powerful figure in the family group and the military leader as a potent leader of society. General Sash sees himself as "five feet four inches of pure game cock" (*CS*, 135). By relying on him for her own sense of worth, Sally means to participate in his strength. The fallacy of her struggle is shown when he depends on *her* "to keep him from falling" (*CS*, 137). The General's and Sally's self-delusions are only too apparent. The old man, naked in his wheelchair, confusedly makes his way to his granddaughter's bedside in the middle of the night. That General Sash exposes himself to his granddaughter expresses his wish to return to the paradisal state of childhood when we feel no shame. His narcissistic desire to be displayed before various audiences is another version of the exhibitionist's impulse.

O'Connor describes how the General's "feet . . . hung down now shriveled at the very end of him" and mentions thereafter his refusal to wear teeth (*CS*, 135). The suggestions of detumescence and castration here refer to the impotence of old age and also to moral impotence. This old man's infantile behavior reveals the child in the old man, a failure to develop. He regresses to an infantile state because he uses others to bolster self: "To his mind, history was connected with processions and life with parades and he liked parades" (*CS*, 136). The General is in fact physically and morally weak—determined to participate in life's parade and to ignore death's procession.

Ordinarily, we conceive of a uniform as something that robs us of individual identity, aligning us instead with the group identity. But the General feels his uniform will differentiate him from the "long procession of teachers and students in their robes." Indeed, the very notion of a human "procession" calls attention to the idea of human development—a process that both the General and Sally have avoided. The "enemy" is finally the reality of death, "The black procession . . . dogging [the General] all his days" (*CS*, 143)—a reality, however, which if faced encourages human development.

The General's and Sally's insensitivity to the reality of death seems the final point of his story and is concretized in the image of John Wesley—totally unaware of his great-grandfather's death as he wheels around the corpse. That the graduation procession seems less important here than the "long line at the Coca-Cola machine" provides a comment on the value of the schoolteacher's diploma. Sally appropriately disappears into the crowd of "her kin" (*CS*, 144) at the end.

Other Mature Conformists

The first stories in this group focus on pseudointellectual types who differentiate themselves from the community by pointing to the very thing that should allow them to accept their responsibilities to others, that is, their intelligence. The stories remaining focus not on the rebel but on the mature conformist benefiting from the social hierarchy. The desire to differentiate oneself from those not belonging to one's own "kind" or class is perhaps no more clearly evident in O'Connor's stories than in "Revelation." Just as Sally Poker Sash relies on the General and the social values his uniform represents and just as the General relies on the group identity of the Confederate Army for a sense of significance, so Ruby Turpin in "Revelation" derives a sense of self not only from her occupational group but also from her social class, her religious affiliation, and her race.

Ruby Turpin's primary mode of attack as she fortifies her sense of self while waiting in a crowded doctor's office is to categorize and to criticize the other patients there. She pretends to be egalitarian and open, declaring "It's all kinds of *them* [Negroes] just like it's all kinds of *us*" (*CS*, 495; emphasis added), but she rigidly classifies people according to their dress, possessions, and speech. The various levels of Southern society are stereotypically represented in this story: poor black by the delivery boy, poor white by the "trashy" woman, working middle class by the Turpins themselves, and upper class by the "stylish" mother of the Wellesleyan student.

When the story opens, Mrs. Turpin, a woman of great size, "sized up the seating situation" (*CS*, 488)—thereby immediately exhibiting a hierarchical habit of mind. That she primarily measures the worth of people in the waiting room according to their clothing ought to remind us of the General and Sally Poker Sash. The emphasis is on Mrs. Turpin's superficial vision; she sees only surfaces. Her vision lacks depth because she is too quick to judge (she "saw at once," *CS*, 488; "She had seen from the first," *CS*, 490). She notices in detail the clothing of each person she scrutinizes, and their shoes. She concludes for example that what the "white-trashy woman" was wearing, "bedroom slippers, black straw with gold braid threaded through them," was "exactly what you would have expected her to have on" (*CS*, 491). Ruby in fact relies on what she expects to see given the stereotypes of her materialistic culture.

As mentioned earlier, the tendency to rely on cliché, like the tendency to establish rigid class lines, is symptomatic of a conforming mind. Even the titles of O'Connor's stories ("A Good Man Is Hard to Find," for example) point to the special importance of cliché, and she sometimes provides small touches of them, as in this story, or sometimes uses them heavy-handedly, as in "Good Country People." Mrs. Turpin and the "pleasant lady" parrot our culture's often superficially realized ideals of tolerance and love for others—expressed in the bromide Mrs. Turpin reiterates most often: "It takes all kinds to make the world go round." Moreover, Ruby rationalizes using the cliché, "fat people have good dispositions." She is not receptive to the inner reality of others but rather sees only the outward trappings—social masks.

Mrs. Turpin establishes herself in a select group differentiated from most others to avoid being herself designated as "common" (*CS*, 491), but when she contemplates how society ought to be stratified, she finds she cannot maintain a consistent system:

> On the bottom of the heap were most colored people, not the kind
> she would have been if she had been one, but most of them, then
> next to them—not above, just away from—were the white-trash;

then above them were the home-owners, and above them the home-and-land owners, to which she and Claud belonged. Above she and Claud were people with a lot of money and much bigger houses and much more land. But here the complexity of it would begin to bear in on her, for some of the people with a lot of money were common and ought to be below she and Claud and some of the people who had good blood had lost their money and had to rent and then there were colored people who owned their homes and land as well. . . . by the time she had fallen asleep all the classes of people were moiling and roiling around in her head, and she would dream they were all crammed in together in a box car, being ridden off to be put in a gas oven. (*CS*, 491–92)

Like Old Dudley's need to separate the races ("black and white and yellow") so that humanity is not "all mixed up like vegetables in soup" (*CS*, 7), Mrs. Turpin needs to maintain rigid racial lines. She objects "because they [Negroes] got to be right up there with the white folks" (*CS*, 493). Her fear of "people . . . moiling and roiling around in her head" also relates to what threatens Mrs. Shortley when she contemplates "The Displaced Person" and his "kind" of people, depicted in newsreels "piled high . . . all in a heap, their arms and legs tangled together" (*CS*, 196). The preordained roles of the social hierarchy enable Mrs. Turpin to escape an unpleasant sense of fragmentation and insignificance.

Ruby Turpin claims to be a "respectable, hard-working, church-going woman" (*CS*, 502) who would "help anybody out that needed it . . . whether they were white or black, trash or decent" (*CS*, 497), but her tendency to categorize people as "white or black" undermines her assertions of being charitable and egalitarian. This all-knowing woman of "experience," grateful to be herself, "a good woman," easily accepts white rationalizations about blacks and the lower classes, such as the notion that it is proper to deprive them of the world's goods "Because if you gave them everything, in two weeks it would all be broken or filthy" (*CS*, 497). A rich store of stereotypical attitudes is provided through numerous examples of dramatized conformity. The white-trashy woman, although more honestly expressing her racism than the others, also accepts unthinkingly her culture's givens—for example the idea that Negroes all want to marry whites to "improve their color" (*CS*, 496). Although adversaries throughout, Mrs. Turpin and the trashy woman seem more alike as the story progresses. We see their resemblance when Mary Grace throws her book at Mrs. Turpin. The trashy woman then exclaims, "I thank Gawd . . . I ain't a lunatic" (*CS*, 502), thus repeating Mrs. Turpin's self-congratualtory stance of gratitude for being herself.

Mary Grace calls Mrs. Turpin a wart hog from hell, and an ugly reality finally breaks through the light-hearted surface of this story—a surface created by dialogue that stresses the conflict between the inner and outer realities of human personality. The story line vacillates between exterior dialogue (what Mrs. Turpin says to express her "good woman" projections) and interior monologue, revealing what Mrs. Turpin thinks—nasty belittling thoughts about others (*CS*, 493–94). Politeness is countered by meanness. Mrs. Turpin's vision is finally blocked by her inability to be self-aware. Mary Grace looks "directly through Mrs. Turpin" (*CS*, 492), but ironically Mrs. Turpin thinks that the girl is looking at something "inside" that Mrs. Turpin needs to see—her own egoistic pride reinforced by mindless conformity to mass values.

When the "stylish" lady uses her sense of class allegiance with Mrs. Turpin to form ranks and to attack her own daughter for not being grateful that her parents "would give her anything" (*CS*, 499), and when Mary Grace responds by throwing her book at Mrs. Turpin, leaving the self-satisfied woman with a feeling of being "hollow," O'Connor communicates exactly the empty inner reality of Mrs. Turpin suggested throughout the story. Mrs. Turpin is finally "a great empty drum of flesh" (*CS*, 500) because she has not developed herself by relating constructively to others; she dimly perceives that the girl's attack is justified—"that the girl did know her . . . in some intense and personal way, beyond time and place and condition" (*CS*, 500)—beyond class.

This glimmer of recognition indicates that in spite of her faults, Ruby Turpin gains in self-knowledge and faces the facts of her own physicality. She achieves "a gesture hieratic and profound" (*CS*, 508) when she goes home to contemplate her neat, clean, and decent pig parlor with the knowledge that keeping it clean will not whitewash the self or purify the flesh. Her apocalyptic vision involves the recognition that measures of virtue based on social status are worthless—and that the last shall be first and the first last, the basic message of the book of "Revelation," which closes the Holy Scriptures. At the end of O'Connor's story, Ruby imagines "a vast horde of souls . . . rumbling toward heaven" (*CS*, 508), places herself at the end of that "procession," and accepts the fact that we all are "just common" (*CS*, 491)—

thus relinquishing the notion of being "singled out" or of achieving anything "single-handed" (*CS*, 502, 505). This recognition allows her to join "the immense sweep of creation," as O'Connor puts it, and to participate in "the evolutionary process" (*Letters*, 477).

"The Displaced Person" most emphatically depicts the dangers of failing to love one's fellows, of feeding one's ego by wielding power over others, of forming ranks in order to overwhelm what threatens one's identity, and of mindlessly accepting mass values—even using them to rationalize immoral action. Mrs. McIntyre is much like Mrs. Turpin, whose pretense of egalitarianism ought to repel us: she refers to her black help and asserts that "you got to love em if you want em to work for you" (*CS*, 494). Mrs. McIntyre is, however, not as fortunate as the "visionary" who attains her "Revelation" before she has reached a level of alienation too drastic to be overcome.

In "The Displaced Person," O'Connor again represents the Southern social hierarchy: poor blacks (Sulk and Astor), poor white-trash (the hired hands, Mr. and Mrs. Shortley), and the rising industrial aristocracy (Mrs. McIntyre, a widow who has taken over the management of her husband's dairy farm). The added representation of the suffering foreigner (Mr. Guizac) and the priest, however, greatly enlarges the context and provides the broadest philosophical base of the stories concerned with social groups in the O'Connor canon.

This story is distinctive in that O'Connor fashions the alliances across class lines rather than within them and forms them according to the arbitrary whims of the person in power, especially Mrs. McIntyre. The story's pattern of loyalties constantly shifts between warring factions. Fickle, irresponsible, selfishly determined rationalizations form the basis for human allegiances. Individual members of various groups cut ties without regret. At the start, Mrs. Shortley and Mrs. McIntyre seem a somewhat harmonious pair, especially as seen from Mrs. Shortley's perspective, but finally it is Mrs. McIntyre's firing of Mr. Shortley that causes the distress and eventually the death of Mrs. Shortley. Displaced bonds deteriorate into contests, even deadly antagonisms. Friends become enemies. Affections transmogrify to betrayal. The story ends with Mrs. McIntyre, Mr. Shortley, and a black servant in collusion as the tractor rolls over and kills Guizac, the displaced foreigner. This final closing of the ranks occurs not between members of the same family or social group but between members of disparate groups not ordinarily aligned but united by a common cause: self-interest.

The point of this story is that human beings concerned with "place" or social status in the modern industrial world can only "displace" each other as they form ranks against anyone who seems at the time to threaten their position. Forming ranks, choosing sides, asserting differences, denying sameness, and aggressively undermining rather than accepting others are basic human drives that must be overcome in order to establish a unified human family, rather than one divided against itself. Mrs. Shortley is morally incomplete: "short" on humility and the qualities needed to establish a firm link with others. Mrs. McIntyre is complete ("entire") only in her delusion of total self-sufficiency. The structure of the story forms its contours around this central pair, so that part 1 focuses on Mrs. Shortley (how she differentiates herself from those beneath her and associates herself with those above her on the social scale), part 2 on Mrs. McIntyre (how she struggles for power over Mrs. Shortley and others), and part 3 on the priest, who clarifies the deficiencies of the pair.

In part 1, Mrs. Shortley's progress suggests what is needed for human development: she is first seen as isolated from others but finally participates in human suffering. She becomes like the Jews she condemns. The beginning of this tale establishes a we/them opposition, an insider versus outsider conflict, a disinterested observer versus involved participant dichotomy—which is most vividly manifest when Guizac is crushed in the presence of "disinterested" observers, who in fact aggressively wish him dead. There are those who trespass and those who belong, those who violate the rights of others and those who are dominated. Even the sun (a symbol of God in O'Connor's works) is presented as "an intruder," and the peacock, whose "eyes in the tail stand for the eyes of the Church" (*Letters*, 509), seems an eavesdropper, not unlike Astor and Sulk, the Negro workers who hide behind a mulberry tree in order to watch the arrival of the displaced persons from Poland who have recently been hired by Mrs. McIntyre. These "intruders" and the priest form a group of outsiders pitted against those who consider themselves "insiders."

Mrs. Shortley pridefully asserts her position as an "insider," with Christ on one side and Mrs. McIntyre on the other, to bolster her weak sense of self. Mrs. Shortley only briefly notices the similarities, the convergence, between the three different groups that now make up Mrs. McIntyre's hired help: when the Guizacs first arrive on the farm, this wife of the hired hand notes that the foreigners are "only hired help, *like* the Shortleys themselves and the Negroes" (*CS*, 194; emphasis mine), but she spends the rest of the story noting differences between them, drawing outsider/insider lines based on race and class. She wishes to be differentiated from anyone she feels is her inferior (that is, both blacks and foreigners). She aligns herself with those of this-worldly power in order to attain a position above and apart from *most* others. Mrs. Shortley establishes her self-worth by comparing herself favorably to Mrs. McIntyre and by giving orders to the blacks.

Aware of what separates the classes, Mrs. Shortley is hypersensitive to *certain* differences between group members, but when other distinctions ought to be made, she fails to make them: she confuses the victims of crime (the Jews) with the perpetrators of crime (the Germans). The rest of the time she is carefully fitting everyone into her particular scale of values, which develops from simplistic judgments that establish her elevated status (white, Protestant, aspiring to the middle class). This arrogant farm woman depends on white/black polarities such as "advanced" (the Americans) and "backward" (the Poles). In her eyes, the Guizacs' Catholic beliefs have "none of the foolishness . . . reformed out of [them]" (*CS*, 198).

Mrs. Shortley's Puritanical Southern Protestanism encourages misanthropy, racism, and classism. This "lady's" revulsion for anything different from herself is shown by her obsession with physical appearance and her association of the Guizacs with dirt (insects), revealing an aversion for physicality based on primitive, infantile experiences (an idea more fully developed below). Mrs. Shortley's is not a sliding scale of values, except when she notes that Mr. Guizac's daughter is *prettier* than her own daughter, a problem that she eliminates by placing her in an entirely different species due to her "bug's name," Sledgewig. A similar aversion is shown when she thinks of the whole family, "the Gobblehooks," in terms of "rats with typhoid" (*CS*, 196). Her self-worth depends on being able to associate herself clearly with dominant white Protestantism, representing purity, order, and cleanliness rather than with the black race, representing evil, disorder, and dirt—or the foreign Jew, representing dirt and death. Since the Guizacs are associated in her mind with death, differences must be scrupulously maintained. Garbling their name is a way of asserting difference. This nickname she gives them suggests Mrs. Shortley's own existential alienation, her own fear of being engulfed, eaten, "gobbled" up. That she associates them with death is evident even when she considers their language: "She saw the Polish words, dirty and all-knowing and unreformed, flinging mud on the clean English words until everything was equally dirty. She saw them all piled up in a room, all the dead dirty words, theirs and hers too, piled up like the naked bodies in the newsreel" (*CS*, 209). Here "dirty" means "mortal."

Considering only appearances, the physical beauty of her daughter, and emphasizing how her son "could sell anything" (*CS*, 197), Mrs. Shortley's values are in fact this-worldly values. Her competitiveness when defending her children while comparing them to the Guizac children matches her defense of her husband. Jealous of Guizac's efficiency and industriousness, Mrs. Shortley asserts (ironically using religion to bolster her case): "It is no man . . . that works as hard as Chancey, or is as easy with a cow, or is more of a Christian" (*CS*, 205). The alliteration of "cow" and "Christian" ought not to be missed as it seems to equate disparate elements, thus undermining Mrs. Shortley's argument in a subtle way, not to mention what happens to spiritual hierarchies with animals at the bottom and pious souls near the top.

O'Connor most importantly satirizes Mrs. Shortley's religious pretensions: her use of religion as a status symbol and of alleged "grace" as a token of worth in the material world. When she compares her family with Guizac's, she feeds her own ego on the idea that her son went to Bible school and is therefore "superior" to the Guizac boy (*CS*, 197). These "religious" aspects of her family are given equal emphasis with the materialistic ones. And yet, she denies religion itself: "She felt that religion was essentially for those people who didn't have the brains to avoid evil without it. For people like herself, for people of gumption, it was a social occasion providing the opportunity to sing." And she "considered the devil the head of it and God the hanger-on" (*CS*, 203–4). The hypocrisy of her earlier claim that her religion was more progressive than that of Guizac seems clear. Nevertheless, she ironically uses religion to differentiate herself from the "inferior" Guizacs who threaten to destroy the category of "white, clean, neat," and "progressive" Christian (Protestant, not Catholic).

All categories collapse when Mrs. Shortley suffers a stroke and participates in a scene similar to what she sees in the newsreel depicting the Holocaust ("a small room piled high with bodies of dead naked people all in a heap, their arms and legs tangled together . . . a hand raised clutching nothing," *CS*, 196). The farm woman, like the dead Jews, is exiled from her home, a fact pointing to a sameness that transcends racial, social, and national boundaries. The last view of Mrs. Shortley—with one leg "twisted under her and one knee almost into her neck," and "clutching at everything she could get her hands on"

(*CS*, 213)—points to sameness, not difference. Mrs. Shortley is like the Jews, "clutching nothing," and O'Connor stresses the fact that we all suffer the same fate and must learn to overcome narcissistic tendencies that cause us to want separation from and superiority over others—preventing us from facing our own mortality.

Whereas Mrs. Shortley is obsessed with asserting differences, even complaining when Guizac fails to notice white/black racial lines and shakes the Negroes' hands "like he didn't know the difference" (*CS*, 207), Mrs. McIntyre is obsessed with sameness—repeatedly declaring that the Jewish Guizac family, the white Shortley family, and the blacks are all "the same" (*CS*, 220). Everyone else, however, converges in her mind so that she may diverge. She further distances herself from what *they* represent when she asserts: "I am not responsible for the world's misery" (*CS*, 223).

Part 2 of this story focuses on Mrs. McIntyre's development as it parallels Mrs. Shortley's, for both women are finally shocked into an awareness of sameness. But Mrs. McIntyre of course differs from Mrs. Shortley: this farm manager heads the social hierarchy and misuses her power. Finally, she discards the Shortleys because for all practical purposes she no longer needs them. She relates to others only as they meet her needs and support her concepts of herself as controller of the top rung. She speaks to Mrs. Shortley but only in a "monologue" (*CS*, 203). Although dependent on others to carry out her will, she denies this dependency, which is transferred to the Negro servant, Astor, when Mrs. Shortley leaves. Mrs. McIntyre converses with Astor by using the personal, first-person plural form ("We've seen them come and seen them go," *CS*, 214), but obviously, she again is running a monologue. The Negro only serves to reflect her own thoughts. Astor repeats both what Mrs. McIntyre says (ironically paraphrasing her words with "Black and white . . . is the same" [*CS*, 215]) and what the Judge used to say. This suggests Astor's dual role: he serves as her black double now, the Judge's shadow formerly.

The threat of miscegenation is the ultimate threat to Mrs. McIntyre's desire to feel control over her own fate. In a striking image that occurs following the incident when Mrs. McIntyre openly condemns Guizac's plan to save his cousin from the concentration camp ovens by marrying her to the Negro, Sulk, Mrs. McIntyre "climbed to the top of the slope. . . . and she narrowed her gaze until it closed entirely around the diminishing figure [of Guizac] on the tractor as if she were watching him through a gunsight" (*CS*, 224).

Mrs. McIntyre's aggression toward Guizac is clear, his "murder" prefigured. Her aversion for Guizac—"no larger than a grasshopper in her widened view" (*CS*, 224)—and for what she calls "a half-witted thieving black stinking nigger" (*CS*, 222)—is an aversion for the body self that threatens decay. Mrs. McIntyre feels as if "some interior violence had already been done to her," and consequently, she allows Guizac to be run over by the tractor. Finally, it is Mrs. McIntyre who is displaced: "she felt she was in some foreign country where the people bent over the body were natives, and she watched like a stranger" (*CS*, 235).

Mrs. McIntyre's tendency to treat everyone else except herself as "the same" reaches its peak when she equates "the devil and the priest" and the displaced person and Christ (*CS*, 230). The first equation is absurd, the second one ironically true in that Guizac and Christ both partake of the divine and are united in suffering. The priest represents true independence, charity, and faith—what is needed to recognize the mystery of the Incarnation represented, for example, not only in Guizac's gesture to save his cousin but also in the "tail full of suns" (*CS*, 198). The priest represents the imaginative unifying perspective in this story. Mrs. McIntyre is his opposite—standing for isolation. She ends her life as a debilitated, old woman totally dependent on two black figures that serve as symbols for unity through suffering: that is, the priest and the Negro woman (*CS*, 235).

Racial Conflict

O'Connor once noted that the following is considered by many as "good Georgia advice: Don't marry no foreigner. Even if his face is white, his heart is black" (*Letters*, 209). In the stories above, we have seen human conflict as characters battle across generational and class lines, then join the ranks of the suffering. Both conflicts within the family and class conflicts underlie racial conflict, a major theme in the O'Connor canon. These conflicts are best understood by considering what the psychoanalytic theorists and social psychologists of the forties and fifties were saying about the grounds for racial prejudice. Lawrence S. Kubie, Joel Kovel, and Mary Ellen Goodman are representative in this regard; they explain that attitudes toward the body (associated with darkness, dirt, and death) profoundly affect human responses to dark skin.[49] Attitudes toward death and the body profoundly affect attitudes of the dominant, puritanical, white culture in America.

Many parallels exist between what Goodman says about responses of whites toward dark skin and the traits of O'Connor's racist characters. Goodman tells us that white children commonly call Negroes "Dirty Nigger." In an earlier version of "Judgement Day," O'Connor defines Tanner's daughter's aversion for Coleman. The daughter complains about "that filthy stinking old nigger . . . making the place smell like a bear pit at the zoo" (*FO* 194a, 3–4). Tanner's need to assert power over others in order to bolster his own sense of self (a phenomenon Goodman also observed in the children she studied who used race to that end) provides a generous target for O'Connor's satiric sensibility. When the perspective is more clearly that of the author and not of the character being satirized, Negroes are described as "coffee-colored" (*CS*, 254, repeated 255), "tan-skinned" (*CS*, 542), or "tan" (*CS*, 255). Goodman recommends describing Negroes as "coffee-colored" or "cinnamon-colored" when helping children overcome aversive tendencies.

O'Connor's stories and manuscripts frequently represent aversive tendencies; racial prejudice is associated with aversions toward dirt, the excremental body, and death. In "Judgement Day," Tanner associates a black woman with "dung" (*CS*, 549). O'Connor's unfinished novel depicts the protagonist, Walter, riding the train home, aware that his body has

> a peculiar smell, a kind of alive and luxuriant rancidness to which he had become so accustomed that it appeared the only steady dependable thing he knew. It seemed to have a dull haze that belonged to humanity; then penetrating that, rising above it, something acrid and sharp and purely personal. In the last week he had thought about death so much that death in his mind had taken on almost a personality. He fell asleep once during the night for an instant and dreamed that death was a huge colored woman who smelled exactly as he smelled and who sucked all the breath out of him with kisses. (*FO* 213a, 22)

O'Connor's stories are very subtle as they render racial conflicts in America, but they are not without sympathy for the suffering of blacks. Some critics still complain that O'Connor's treatment of the Negro depends too much on negative stereotypes. Others charge her with racism. Josephine Hendin argues that in O'Connor's work, "Racial conflict is a *spectacle*."[50] And yet it is Flannery O'Connor who stridently

O'Connor says she's not realist [handwritten annotation]

declares: "There is nothing that screams out the tragedy of the South like what my uncle calls 'nigger statuary'" (*Letters*, 101), which is "a terrible symbol of what the South has done to itself" (*Letters*, 140). It is also O'Connor who explains that black stereotypes in the stories represent the "conciliatory mask which [the Negro] manipulates for his own protection" and that "The uneducated Southern Negro is not the clown he's made out to be" (*MM*, 234). So why is it difficult to find clear evidence in the letters and essays that racism is a major theme?

There is good reason for this misunderstanding. Constantly wary lest her works be read as social realism and she be classified among the prideful, intellectual integrationists of the sixties often satirized in her work, O'Connor downplays the importance of racial issues when she discusses her work. She misleads her readers to think she is unconcerned about race, for example, when she says, "The topical is poison" (*Letters*, 537). Her attitudes toward race are complex and have been obscured by her reluctance to play a pious, self-righteous role, by her reluctance to be openly critical of her community, and also by presumptions regarding her Southern background. It is true that she did want to establish her art as a poetic and philosophical kind not limited to depicting "social forces" in the mode of social realism but rather expressing "deeper kinds of realism" (*MM*, 39). But the author's comments should not be used as a license to ignore the implications of her artistic vision—a vision sympathetic to the suffering of blacks. The question of O'Connor's attitude toward racial conflicts may be clarified by considering the psychology of racism as we read her stories.

Instances of mistreatment of blacks by whites abound in the stories and in the manuscripts. In an early, unpublished story, "The Coat," O'Connor assumes the persona of a black laundress whose husband is shot to death by whites just as his Coleman lamp burns out in the dark woods. The first story of her master of fine arts thesis at the University of Iowa, the last story of her last collection, and her unfinished novel all depict dark/light pairs: respectively, Rabie/Old Dudley, Tanner/Coleman, and Roosevelt/Tilman. These stories depict suffering or handicapped blacks serving white males. In these master/servant doublets, the Negro character projects a stereotypical mask that becomes a dark mirror reflecting the narcissism of the white character using his black servant to expand the boundaries of his own self.

In a 1960 interview at the College of Saint Teresa in Minnesota, O'Connor said she did not "feel capable of entering the mind of a Negro." She was dissatisfied with her early efforts to write from a black perspective (not only in "The Coat" but also in "Wildcat"). And so for most of her lifetime, she wrote stories depicting narcissistic whites depending on blacks to meet their most basic needs. In her unfinished novel, the debilitated Tilman relies on his servant Roosevelt to take him to the toilet, and in "The Displaced Person," Mrs. McIntyre ends up an invalid "with only a colored woman to wait on her" (*CS*, 235). In each case, the black person bolsters the white person's sense of superiority until the latter is humbled because of his or her own selfish behavior. The point of this is that O'Connor's compassion for the black race is indirectly revealed throughout the stories by her depictions of white narcissists.

O'Connor does present racial pairs superficially conforming to definitions promoted by the repressive dominant culture (for example, black/white pairs symbolizing evil/good, dirty/pure, body/soul, or mortal/immortal polarities). She sides, however, with the darker member of the pair. Her satires are directed toward the prideful, dominant Caucasians, even though we also feel sympathy for them. In an early draft of "Judgement Day," Dr. Foley, a half-breed, buys Tanner's land out from under him. He is described as having a malignant aspect, a "meanness," which "came from his white blood" (*FO* 194d, 7). Those who misunderstand O'Connor's satirical thrust do so because of her enormous gift to evoke a reader's response of sympathy as well as criticism—to involve the reader in the traumas racist characters suffer as well as to distance the reader from prideful "meanness." As Kahane notes about O'Connor's work: "violent confrontations arouse dread and anxiety even under the surveillance of wit," because her "imagery . . . evokes archaic fears . . . infantile fears—of devouring, of penetration, of castration"[51]—of what Freud sees as the substance of the uncanny. This element of sympathy that the reader feels has deep roots and has resulted in the successful enactment of O'Connor's religious impulse, requiring a humble awareness of our connectedness to the human community unified by suffering.

The Negro race is above all an icon for suffering, and we ought to consider here the author's insistence that sensitivity to suffering forms the very ground of her thought. O'Connor points to her treatise on the suffering of a child, a terminal cancer patient, and declares this piece necessary "in order to make legitimate criticism" of her work (*Letters*, 442) (see part 2 for an excerpt of this important authorial statement).

The "Mary Ann piece" is O'Connor's introduction to a story written by nuns running a home for hopeless cancer patients. These nuns were inspired by the case of a three-year-old girl afflicted by disfiguring cancer and given but a short time to live. O'Connor was first asked to write the girl's story; finally she did serve as editor and also as preface-writer for the book. In her introduction, O'Connor reveals her insights about human suffering—insights that apply to the issue of aversive tendencies and racism. She first clarifies the human tendency to ignore anything that evokes pain, fear, or guilt in the viewer—focusing her attention on the story of Nathaniel Hawthorne's revulsion for a sickly child, as reported by his daughter, the founder of the particular cancer home in question. Hawthorne's daughter explains how the young Hawthorne overcame his revulsion for a rheumy child who raised his arms, inviting himself to be picked up. His memoirs report that he embraced the child and then chastized himself and humanity in general for the "ice in the blood" that underlies our inability to embrace what seem grotesque human shapes when we first confront them but which actually reveal our own humanity.

What is true of our response to the sick is true of our response to the disadvantaged. The ability to face suffering squarely, whatever the source, requires a special kind of tenderness that O'Connor sees as essentially Christian and that when lacking "ends in forced labor camps and in the fumes of the gas chamber"—that is, in racism and aggressive/narcissistic behavior. In this *Memoir to Mary Ann*, O'Connor's allusion to the Jewish people during the war clearly links physical suffering, aversive tendencies, and racism.[52]

O'Connor's last story about race, "Judgement Day," most explicitly condemns the dominant white's relation to the black as one-sided and narcissistic. The white face reflects and perpetuates the black mask without understanding the Negro's need for distance from white stereotypes of blacks. Time and experience sharpened O'Connor's satiric impulses in this story, which clearly directs our attention to interactions between the races and defines the racist character with no uncertainty: Tanner's heart is "hard and tough as an oak knot" (*CS*, 545), a criticism with a Hawthornian edge. In an early draft (*FO* 194d), Tanner considers killing Negroes who "Make a monkey out of him." In the published story, Tanner considers murdering the black doctor who buys the land out from under his shack (*CS*, 536), and he threatens his black workers with stabbing (*CS*, 537). A very early draft even more clearly reveals Tanner's aggressive instincts. As he contemplates his abilities to work Negroes, he explains that he refrains from murder because "he was not going to hell for killing a nigger. There was too little pleasure in it" (*FO* 194d, 12), a comment reminiscent of The Misfit in "A Good Man Is Hard to Find." Tanner prides himself on his ability to overpower the blacks with his wit, but he often exhibits murderous impulses.

Ironically, this powerful "master" first appears in the story as an impotent old man. The story starts with its "hero" in the stance of an infant being dressed by his daughter. The outer reality of his infantile stance matches that of his inner, regressive, moral state: he sees his daughter as what he must "escape," someone he wants to get "out of the way" (*CS*, 531). Tanner in fact sees his daughter as a threat, and he sets up barriers against her intrusions like a small child defending his territory. This authority figure becomes so encapsulated in his own narcissistic concerns that he cannot relate constructively to others. Tanner fails to develop channels of communication with his daughter. His daughter and servant are mere reflections of his own needs.

Barriers between family members—evident when Tanner's daughter talks to herself rather than to her father, for example—lead to the issue of barriers between races. Tanner in fact cannot relate to blacks except as inferiors. His daughter treats them as things, measuring one's status, when she brags about how many blacks used to work for her father. Tanner gloats over his daughter's reduced status because a Negro moves into the apartment next door, showing that his attitudes formed the source of hers. Tanner's condescending approaches include calling the black neighbor "John" ("Head"?) (*CS*, 543), thus refusing him his true identity—and also "preacher" (*CS*, 544), which, according to the sexist view, is one of the more feminine and passive occupations open to Negroes. These subtle attacks by Tanner create in this black "actor" "some unfathomable dead-cold rage [which] seemed to . . . shrink him." He further feels "A tremor [which] racked him from his head to his crotch" (*CS*, 544–45)—a tremor suggesting impotence as this white man emasculates the black man by refusing to allow him his role as "actor."

There is much in this story to suggest that O'Connor's sympathies are with the Negro actor and not with Tanner. In the first place, Tanner's treatment of his black servant parallels his treatment of the neighbor in that it is reductive and involves a show of masculine power. Tanner drains Coleman's power. When Coleman first meets Tanner, he is said to watch the white boss "as if he saw an invisible power" (*CS*, 538); he focuses on the white man's power, even though he himself, being twice Tanner's physical size, very visibly represents physical strength. Coleman's name contains the idea of "coal," a powerful energy source and the source of punning in an earlier draft when Tanner says, "You don't look like no coal man" (*FO* 194). In the unpublished story mentioned above, "The Coat," a black man is in fact murdered after his Coleman lamp runs out of fuel.

That Tanner finally drains Coleman of power is communicated by depicting his shrinkage over time:

> The old Negro was curled up on a pallet asleep at the foot of Tanner's bed, a stinking skin full of bones, arranged in what seems vaguely human form. When Coleman was young, he had looked like a bear; now that he was old he looked like a monkey. With Tanner it was the opposite; when he was young he had looked like a monkey but when he got old, he looked like a bear. (*CS*, 534)

This striking comparison using the bear-monkey metaphors does not appear in early drafts and was consciously added at a late stage of the writing process. It suggests that Tanner drained Coleman of his sense of identity, his power to be his own self. An earlier version also offers a suggestion of shrinkage and even more clearly supports the idea of Tanner's being walled up within his own self. He does not understand reciprocal relationships: "Coleman had been on his hands for forty years. They were both old now, him sewed up in a wall of flesh and the other twisted double with no flesh at all" (*FO* 193, 5). Coleman is Tanner's "doubled-up shadow" (*CS*, 535), an image suggesting not only that at bottom they are alike because they belong to the same human species but also that this black servant suffers enormous pain.

Tanner represents, on the other hand, the inability to understand true suffering. He is characterized by "failing vision" (*CS*, 531)—and this blindness Tanner would impose on others: that is, the blindness of being unable to see that we all suffer a "common lot" (*CS*, 539). In order to assert his power over Coleman and to make him see the world his way—to see differences rather than similarities between them—he carves a pair of glasses for his black worker. The glasses force Coleman to "see" and "accept" the master-servant relationship.

When Coleman puts on the glasses, however, what is emphasized is *Tanner's* inability to see. Tanner's whole sense of existing depends on his assuming the social role of superior white rather than on developing his own integrity. The insubstantial nature of Tanner's dependence on role-playing and the racist's false sense of self-worth is suggested often. Tanner experiences only "an instant's sensation of seeing before him a negative image of himself, as if clownishness and captivity had been their common lot. The vision failed him before he could decipher it" (*CS*, 538–39). Tanner sees for only an instant that Coleman is suffering like himself: his vision is fleeting, lost.

It is difficult to see Coleman as "sharing" anything of Tanner's; he is merely surviving in a world where the power lines are not on his side of the track. I do not wish to underestimate the importance of ambivalence in Tanner's relationship to Coleman. There is certainly love involved, but it is primarily self-love. There is no *real* giving on Tanner's part; the giving is Coleman's.

Tanner expects "Judgement Day" to confirm his own salvation, but O'Connor intimates his damnation throughout this tale. When Tanner attempts to "escape" his daughter, his body is described as being "like a great heavy bell whose clapper swung from side to side but made no noise" (*CS*, 548). There is no substance to his inner self because it depends on assuming the social role of superior white rather than on developing his own integrity.

Far more sympathetic than Tanner but also limited in terms of his ability to relate constructively to others, Grandfather Head in "The Artificial Nigger" assumes the role of moral guide as he encourages his grandson Nelson to conform to his own view of the community (the city) from which he chooses to isolate himself. Central to his view are his insecurities about himself and a related negative attitude toward Negroes. O'Connor's techniques in dealing with race are most subtle in this story, which defines Head's racist aversions toward the black community through a rich metaphoric process of repetitions that are clearly related to the then current theories about racism developed by Kubie, Kovel, Goodman, and others, as mentioned above. We limit our interpretations of this story when we consider only Head's state of grace, O'Connor's Catholic views, and authorial statements about racial issues in the canon—statements accepted without considering their context.[53]

At the very start, "The Artificial Nigger" establishes mind/body, "Head"/sewer dichotomies. The initial rendering of Head's room establishes an ironic distance between reader and protagonist because of the disparity between Head's shack (replete with "slop jar," "privy," and "horse stall") and the old man's exalted view of himself as he

75

prepares for "the moral mission" of initiating his grandson into manhood by taking him to the city, which is "not a great place" (*CS*, 251) because Negroes live there. A major gap in Nelson's knowledge is his inexperience with Negroes. Head plans to acquaint the boy with Negroes in order to encourage him "to stay at home for the rest of his life." This simple, narcissistic wish of the father to possess the son and to keep him at home in an innocent, dependent state hardly seems "moral." Head wants to belittle his grandson—not allow him independence or educate him. If we admit that he wants to educate him, we must realize with Kenneth Scouten that he wants "to educate his grandson about Negroes who, apparently, represent evil for the old man."[54]

Evil here is defined in terms of the body. The sheer number of excremental images in this story is remarkable: references to the slop jar, privy, and horse stall mentioned above encourage a pun on "Head." The attention given to the toilet on the train and the sewer in the city cannot be explained as mere setting. In the initial scene, a "displacement upward into language" and away from unpleasant realities of the lower body is achieved.[55] That is, O'Connor presents Head as he transforms a humble scene into a romanticized setting more suited to his idealized version of himself. O'Connor expresses Head's elaboration of self by offering her readers an imaginative piece of fictional prose drawing on Dante and the fanciful imagery of Hawthorne's "The Custom House." The similarities between the imagery describing Hawthorne's "Old Manse" and Head's shack were cited in my 1984 dissertation; W. R. Allen made the same observation in his 1984 article, although again he emphasizes Head's "conversion," whereas I emphasize the way that Head's very human insecurities about himself result in an overactive imagination envisioning an elegance of self and place sadly absent.[56] These parallelisms (Hawthorne/Head; "Old Manse"/Head's shack) call attention to the mind/body split—to imaginative constructs and physical limitations, thus undercutting Head's heroic posture.

O'Connor's art gradually develops the implications of Head's behavior so that we gain a greater understanding not only of the narcissistic parent but of the racist mind. From the very first argument about Nelson's ignorance of Negroes to the final encounter with "The Artificial Nigger," the reader's attention is drawn to Head's urge to control/overpower Nelson and his aversion for dark-skinned persons. The racist's urge to establish control over blacks in order to prove white superiority is not unlike Head and Nelson's urges to outdo one another. Head repeatedly belittles Nelson by trying to demonstrate that older means smarter. He claims to be the more knowledgeable about the city and Negroes—a claim developed throughout the story to emphasize the competitive nature of Head, who even worries about being the first one up on the morning of their trip.

Superiority is most emphatically measured by who has the most knowledge of Negroes. Head claims superior knowledge because the city is "full of niggers," and he has been to the city more times than Nelson (*CS*, 252). But only one more time if we count Nelson's birth there, O'Connor reminds us. A poignant truth underlies Head's claim to knowledge, the fact that he lives in an isolated shack probably in a sparsely populated, all-white, rural area. O'Connor knows that the most insidious kind of racism is sometimes found in the North, where deep-seated aversions develop without direct contact with blacks to contradict them. Although Head does not live in the North, the fact that Nelson has not yet been introduced to or even seen a Negro suggests a similar kind of isolation from and aversion to Negroes.

In spite of Nelson's ignorance of Negroes, he too claims knowledge. Head and Nelson argue about whether to count Nelson's experience as an infant in the city. Their efforts to outdo one another often become ridiculous. This particular argument, however, also brings up a provocative question. Nelson's insistence that his infantile experience "counts" in fact supports the Freudian contention that we are governed by unconscious infantile experience. In an early draft, after Nelson suffers ridicule for not recognizing a Negro as a "black," he feels "a fierce fresh hate" while he looks at his own reflection in the train window and sees "something sinister and inadequate out of his past, when ten years ago he had been born in the city" (*FO* 158d, 11). The "sinister and inadequate" years of infancy seem related to the present emotion—his hatred for his grandfather's belittling behavior that has been displaced by the hatred for the Negro. The very human struggle for control over others results in aggressive behavior—like the kind Head exhibits when he competes with his grandson.

The regressiveness of sibling rivalry ironically defines the grandfather/grandson relationship; Head and Nelson "looked enough alike to be brothers" and brothers "not too far apart in age." This impression is reinforced by images of the grandfather's "youthful expression" and the grandson's "ancient" expression (*CS*, 251). We see here an inversion of the normal developmental process—indicating "a resistance to psychological evolution [and revealing] the old man in the young child, the young child in the old man," as Gaston Bachelard puts it.[57] Head is especially regressive when he instinctively threatens his grandson with those experiences infants fear most (engulfment in the sewer, hunger, and abandonment)—stimulating Nelson's insecurities but acting himself like an insecure child. He exploits his authority and experience in order to manipulate his own grandson, whom he treats as a rival.

One way to overpower a rival is to treat him as if he were a thing, a compulsion Kovel calls "thingification" and relates to racism. American slave owners counted Negroes among their possessions and dehumanized them—reducing them to things. Kovel argues that "dehumanization, the desire for property, and the need to dominate have all somehow contributed to the institutional forces that bind us in the chains of racism."[58] The title of O'Connor's story, "The Artificial Nigger," itself focuses on the phenomenon of a person turned into a thing—a Negro formed into a statue and fixed in a subservient role.

Head's tendency to "thingify" the Negro is pervasive throughout this story. He tells his grandson that he won't like the city because "It'll be full of niggers" (CS, 252). When a "coffee-colored man" strides down the aisle on the train, Head asks, "What [not who] was that?" (CS, 255), and exclaims to a fellow passenger, "That's his first nigger" (CS, 255), as if the encounter was like getting a first bicycle. Later, when he directs Nelson toward the kitchen, Head's comment about the black waiter equates Negroes and cockroaches—a display of verbal abuse more overtly aggressive than previous innuendoes referring to Negroes as "things." The Negro shoe polisher is the "thing" that marks their way once they get to the city. They realize when passing him a second time that they are lost. At the end of the day when they try to escape the black section of town, the decreasing number of blacks is another "thing" that suggests they are going the "right" way.

Nothing in this story indicates that the "right" way on a sociological level is an avoidance of blacks. Lost in the black part of town, Head goads Nelson into asking directions from a black woman—sarcastically allowing his grandson to be the expert because, as he puts it to him, "This is where you were born" (CS, 260). This black woman for an instant seems to answer Nelson's craving for maternal love, a craving intensified by his one-parent, paternal upbringing. Nelson's quest for self-definition is in fact a quest for origins. Knowledge of the city (image for woman) amounts to knowledge of the mother he never knew.

He seeks the mother in order to discover, as he puts it, "where I come from" (*CS*, 259). He is transfixed by the black woman, a symbol of maternity. In an earlier draft, this woman is represented as pregnant: "Her stomach was broad and full with a small round shadow in the center of it" (*FO* 158d, 2). O'Connor specifies that she "meant for her in an almost physical way to suggest the mystery of existence to him . . . a black mountain of maternity" (*Letters*, 78).

Nelson's confused response to the black mother figure is due to an earlier incident when Head again instills revulsion for blacks in the boy by showing him the excremental view of the city—"the sewer system . . . [which] contained all the [city's] drainage and was full of rats" (*CS*, 259). O'Connor provides clear clues that these two incidents (encounter with sewer and encounter with black woman) are related. That is, the excremental vision of the city, which has been repeatedly associated with Negroes, causes Nelson to feel fear and revulsion for the black woman. When he stands before her, Nelson feels "as if he were reeling through a pitchblack tunnel" (*CS*, 262)—a phrase repeated word for word both during the sewer scene (*CS*, 259) and during the encounter with the black woman. Moreover, in an early manuscript, Nelson feels "horrified that the wish to be smothered [mothered] in her black kiss had come from inside him" (*FO* 158d, 23) because earlier Head had represented the sewer as a "black evil-smelling hole" (*FO* 158d, 18) associated with the city and Negroes. The associations Head encourages during the sewer scene between the bowels of the city, dirt, darkness, and by implication, Negroes who live in the city, elicit aversive fears in Nelson. Head ensures his grandson's perpetual dependence in this way.

Head's indoctrination of Nelson at first does not have the desired effect. The boy quips, "You can stay away from the holes" (*CS*, 259), after he views the sewer. But as the story progresses, Nelson becomes more and more dependent, Head more and more sadistic, even abandoning the boy when he falls asleep on the sidewalk. Head's racism, then, develops an equation: city equals Negroes; city equals sewer and threat of engulfment; and Negroes equal darkness, dirt, sexual temptation, and death.

Kubie explains that for most of us "all body secretions are dirty." In a hierarchy of dirt, defined as any of the bodily products emerging from the apertures, excrement clearly evokes the greatest aversion. And "much of the white man's prejudice against the pigmented races comes from his feelings about excrement. . . . The white child . . . has little feeling against the Negro, until he is stimulated to it by the adults"— exactly the process going on in this story.[59]

Earlier drafts were more obvious in establishing the association of Negroes with dirt, an association clarifying Head's aversion and not O'Connor's prejudice. In one case, "Colored children played in the gutters" (*FO* 20), and in another instance, black servants are described as being as "much a part of the place as the dirt underfoot" (*FO* 205, 8). The polarities between good/pure/white/immortal (guardian angel in the opening scene) and bad/dirty/black/mortal (products of the slop jar) are crucial to O'Connor's treatment of racism and her understanding of the human tendency to dissociate the self from the body, which represents disease, dirt, and death.

One early draft of this story tells us that "Mr. Head was sixty years old" and that "this was the first time he had ever suffered" (*FO* 158b, 28). Head weeps when Nelson rejects his grandfather for abandoning him, but when the two travelers encounter the "artificial nigger" and acknowledge the suffering he represents, they are mysteriously reconciled to each other. O'Connor in fact declares that the central black form in this story represents "the redemptive quality of the Negro's suffering for us all" (*Letters*, 78), a timeless Roman Catholic theme. Nelson and Head's reconciliation does seem to be a redemptive moment: they recognize in the statue's "wild look of misery" (*CS*, 268) the misery and sense of alienation they are currently suffering. They become more or less reconciled to each other, and this is why O'Connor declared that this "is a story in which there is an *apparent* action of grace" (*Letters*, 160; emphasis mine). That the grandfather and grandson are reunited is of course significant. Head does mature and realizes his own dependence on his grandson.

And yet I would argue that Head's progress is diminished by the fact that Head and the white community he represents still fail to respond to the suffering of the black community. Head and Nelson retreat to their segregated and isolated shack, while Nelson declares, "I'm glad I've went once, but I'll never go back again" (*CS*, 270). This, the last line of the story, indicates that the original purpose established at the very beginning has been fulfilled. Nelson conforms to his grandfather's will by changing from an independent self who declares he has been to the city "twict" to a dependent self conforming to Head's view that the boy had only been to the city once and that the city and blacks ought to be avoided. Nelson's stature withers as he conforms to Head, who fails to overcome his racism and his narcissistic need to dominate his grandson. Whenever O'Connor presents a story about a parent/child pair that begins with a rebellious child seeking a sense of self and ends with the child mirroring the parent, the parent's integrity is questionable.

Although the reader is invited to feel a certain compassion for Head at the end, his portrait throughout the story sheds a great deal of light on the psychology of racism. Head and Nelson *do* reconcile themselves to each other when they feel the statue "dissolving their differences like an action of mercy" (*CS*, 269). But what *differences* are there to "dissolve" between these two look-alikes? O'Connor stresses their sameness: "The two of them stood there with their necks forward at almost the *same* angle and their shoulders curved in almost the *same* way and their hands trembling *identically* in their pockets" (*CS*, 268; emphasis mine). We are then told that the artificial Negro is the *same* size as Nelson and that Nelson and Head see the *same* feeling of misery in his eyes as they feel.

The degree of misery the statue represents puts Head's and Nelson's misery in perspective. Even though the grandfather and grandson experience a perplexing moment because they recognize that their own and the Negro's misery is the "same," and even though suffering reconciles them to each other, we must realize that what they suffer is not the "same" as what blacks over the years have suffered. There are enormous "differences" between the amount of suffering the artificial Negro represents and the amount of suffering the grandfather and grandson have experienced. Moreover, Head and Nelson's reunion represents a widening of the rift within the human community, a widening in the division between the two races, because Nelson adopts his grandfather's ideas. Head attempts to make a "lofty statement" (*CS*, 269) but concludes with a childish, racist statement: "They ain't got enough real ones here. They got to have an artificial one." The old man then asserts that "no sin was too monstrous to claim as his own" (*CS*, 270), and Nelson looks at his grandfather "with . . . suspicion." Head never acknowledges or overcomes his aversion to blacks or his narcissistic pride, and his inadequacies are reemphasized when he returns with Nelson to the dominant white ranks of his isolated community.

O'Connor wrote that in the last paragraphs of this story she has "practically gone from the Garden of Eden to the Gates of Paradise" (*Letters*, 78). "Paradise" as Head views it might be construed as this-worldly control over his grandson.[60] And the almost flippant tone here qualifies that word, "practically." She is here discussing her attempts to respond to Caroline Gordon's suggestion that she needs "a larger view" in her endings. The larger view must be a consideration of the whole community. The psychoanalytic context suggests regressive behavior and the excremental references not only undercut Head's claims to virtue but also point to the larger issue of racial conflicts.

In "Everything That Rises Must Converge," O'Connor again represents a generational pair that in subtle ways defines racism: we find in this story one of the most grim antagonisms between a mother and a son. Taken from Teilhard de Chardin, the title is, as O'Connor tells us, "a physical proposition that I found in Père Teilhard and am applying to a certain situation in the Southern states and indeed in all the world" (*Letters*, 438). It is a story that she also says "touches on a certain topical issue in these parts and takes place on a bus" (*Letters*, 436). Teilhard in fact sees the basis for racism in the individual's desire to differentiate him or herself from others—a failure to "converge" that is "all the more insidious . . . [because] flattering to collective egotism, keener, nobler, and more easily aroused than individual egotism."[61]

Julian's actions in this story confirm his isolation from others rather than his convergence. He separates himself from his mother, only condescending to take her to her weight class once a week. He establishes barriers against "the general idiocy of his fellows" by existing in "a kind of mental bubble," where he feels "safe from any kind of penetration from without" (*CS*, 411). His idea of the perfect neighborhood is one of widely separated houses—a sharp contrast to his mother's neighborhood where all the homes seem "of a uniform ugliness" (*CS*, 406). And during a conflict with his mother on the bus, he distances himself by looking at her and "making his eyes the eyes of a stranger" (*CS*, 412). He criticizes his mother for her classist memories of lost property and status but secretly longs for the Godhigh mansion.

An egotistical, hypocritical intellectual incapable of self-knowledge, Julian's sense of superiority ironically rests on the idea that he is *not* classist or racist. And yet he has never been successful in making a black friend, dreams of being engaged to a Negroid-*looking* woman in order to disturb his mother, and imagines making friends with upper-class blacks, perhaps a "distinguished Negro professor" (*CS*, 414). Finally, he is actually annoyed when on the bus a Negro woman sits next to him—until he sees this as a way to punish his mother. O'Connor raises the question of whether the larger human family will ever "converge" when individuals deny their own immediate family.

Julian's contempt for his mother is worse than his mother's contempt for the blacks, although she too is in "reduced" circumstances morally as well as materially. She wishes to "reduce" her weight and gain in social status when she ought to be gaining in sympathy for her community. Both Julian and his mother pretend to self-knowledge (she claims, "if you know who you are, you can go anywhere," *CS*, 407), but neither one clearly understands their own motivations.

Julian's mother is blinded by her dependence on mass values as is the case with so many O'Connor mother types. She loses herself in the petty details of the material world, frets over whether she should have spent $7.50 for a hat, and depends on cliché to express her view of the world ("You only live once"; "Rome wasn't built in a day"; "It takes time . . . the world is in such a mess," *CS*, 411). And she depends on societal stereotypes defining her "kind of people" (*CS*, 407). Hierarchy, not convergence, represents security for her. She avoids sameness and buys the expensive hat in order to avoid seeing herself "coming and going" (*CS*, 407)—to avoid acknowledging her connection to others.

While Julian and his mother assert "difference," O'Connor establishes patterns of sameness. The black woman and Julian's mother wear the same hat. The dark/light, mother/son pairs established when the two mothers seem to switch sons on the bus suggest sameness. Julian and his mother are alike in their failure to develop: the mother seems like "a little girl" (*CS*, 406)—recall the "youthful" expression of Head—and Julian ends in the stance of a little boy crying out for his "Mamma" (*CS*, 420). Both the mother and the son dream of the past. He accuses her of living in "her own fantasy world" of "imaginary dignity" (*CS*, 409), but he also lives according to a romanticized version of himself cultivated in his own "mental bubble."

These two characters differ primarily in that Julian is more self-centered and selfish than his mother. She at least is unselfish in that she supports her son while ignoring his failures, whereas her son feels "an evil urge to break [his mother's] spirit" (*CS*, 409). He succeeds. Julian's aggressively critical stance toward his mother develops until the mother and son can no longer recognize each other. She faces his contempt for her and sees "nothing familiar about him" (*CS*, 419). Her identity depends on his, and when she can't "determine his identity," she can't determine her own. She suffers a stroke, and he is described as "looking into a face he had never seen before." She then searches his face, looking for recognition but finding "nothing" (*CS*, 420).

The ending of this story emphasizes the human tendency toward interdependence and the idea that an inability to recognize sameness, and thus to "converge" or "love," results in destructiveness. Hatred expressed between family members and between different social groups is only overcome when individuals suffer moments of insight coincidental with moments of "guilt and sorrow"—the final words of this story taken directly from Teilhard de Chardin and reminiscent of the "misery" that reunites Head and Nelson.

Good/Evil Conflicts

At times, O'Connor represents in her characters, and produces in her readers, a revulsion for the physical world and the physical body so vividly rendered that we cannot help but polarize the forces of good and evil in our own minds. Thus, O'Connor has been accused of being Manichaean and Jansenist.[62] Certain O'Connor stories dramatize the war between the forces of good and evil—depicting ethical dualities that define not only the pain of being divided internally between mind and body, but also painful contradictions in society and the world. O'Connor's art is not, however, Manichaean but affirms the Incarnation:

> When I know what the laws of the flesh and the physical really are, then I will know what God is. We know them as we see them, not as God sees them. For me it is the virgin birth, the Incarnation, the resurrection which are the true laws of the flesh and the physical. Death, decay, destruction are the suspension of these laws. I am always astonished at the emphasis the Church puts on the body. It is not the soul she says that will rise but the body, glorified. . . . flesh and spirit united in peace. (*Letters*, 100)

In the stories about good/evil conflicts, O'Connor defines the problem of limited human perspectives—the inability to see "as God sees" and thus the tendency to see the physical world as evil. Superior in this regard, the artist reconciles the "apparent" and the "real," the profane and the sacred dimensions of reality, and achieves a certain insight or "epiphany," as Joyce puts it—an epiphany that transcends the usual human limitations, however fleeting. Joyce's epiphanies are this-worldly, but O'Connor affirms "epiphany" in terms of the sacred glimpse physical reality affords those who seek spiritual dimensions: "St. Augustine wrote that . . . this physical, sensible world is good because it proceeds from a divine source. . . . only when the natural world is seen as good does evil become intelligible as a destructive force and a necessary result of our freedom" (*MM*, 157).[63] O'Connor's emphasis on the flaws of human judgment and her conservative view of "evil" places responsibility for disasters in the world squarely on human shoulders. In fact, the most heinous crimes in human history— for example, gassing Jews, the stark reality behind the image of dead and disjointed bodies in "The Displaced Person" and elsewhere in O'Connor's stories—sometimes resulted from someone's wish to support an "apparent good" (improving the gene pool), which was instead "evil" or at least a "privation of good" in the form of bad judgment.

The stories in this group, then, are concerned with mankind's destructive will and limited perceptions regarding physical life. "A Good Man Is Hard to Find," "The Life You Save May Be Your Own," and "A Circle in the Fire" define the forces of human will most clearly; "The River," "A Temple of the Holy Ghost," and "Parker's Back" define the limitations of human perspectives in relation to physical life.

O'Connor's dark view of human will developed from her Catholicism, a dark view intensified by the Calvinism of American romance and Southern Protestantism—all supporting notions that man is innately depraved—incapable of virtuous action in a world that by its very nature promotes evil. When considering O'Connor's "sinners" and those who fail to perceive the divine potential in the physical world, we ought to remember, however, that she defines sin as a "suffering-with" (*MM*, 166). Her letters chastise pious, elitist attitudes toward sin—those who acknowledge it only in others. She makes the point that we should not disown what comes in human form nor accept with sentimentality what offends our humanity. Depicting the worst in human nature is for O'Connor an act of faith, a repetition of God's intention to shock us into "grace." What some readers see as cynical and distorted views of human life, O'Connor sees as honest representations—however exaggerated and symbolic—of human suffering and sin repressed by the community in order to assuage the guilt of individual members. Her art indirectly asserts that we ought "to look at the worst" and accept it (*MM*, 148) and that "it is when the individual's faith is weak, not when it is strong, that he will be afraid of an honest fictional representation of life" (*MM*, 151).

The Evil of Active Human Will

"A Good Man Is Hard to Find" precisely presents the worst of O'Connor's tragic events—the extermination of an entire family. At the start, the humorous depiction of a family vacation in the family car engages the reader's attention. Captivated by the all-too-familiar personality of the domineering grandmother, the reader delights in observing this willful matriarch's efforts to engineer her family's vacation according to her own whims and fancies (she takes her cat as a stowaway and tries to pressure everybody to go to Tennessee instead of Florida). Reader involvement in the folly of this family hinges on our familiarity with the event and our identification with the immediately recognizable human types presented: for example, the husband who dominates his wimpy wife because he is henpecked by his mother; the bratty children. The initial depiction of this family must surely outdo the "funny papers" and the "comic magazines" (*CS*, 117, 119) being read by June Star and John Wesley—as well as the funny story the grandmother tells about a former suitor, thus tickling "John Wesley's funny bone" (*CS*, 120). Nowhere in O'Connor's art is the comic impulse clearer; nowhere is the tragic impulse clearer.

The conniving grandmother threatens her family with the news that if they proceed with their plans they will be heading in the path of an escapee from federal prison, The Misfit. Her obstinacy about going to Tennessee is so great that she convinces herself and the family that the Tennessee plantation she recalls from her girlhood is nearby—when actually the family is driving through the Georgia countryside. She convinces her son, Bailey, to follow her directions by riling up the children over nonexistent secret panels they hope to discover in the old house. Startled by her recollection that the house she seeks is in Tennessee and not Georgia, she tips her basket, holding the cat she has smuggled aboard against her son's wishes. The cat then jumps on the harried father's shoulders and causes an accident, thereby placing the whole family in a vulnerable position when the carload of criminals happens upon the scene of the accident. Without much ado, the three agents of evil proceed to exterminate their victims.

The grandmother's development culminates when she feels sympathy for the murderer just before her death. This sympathy is a positive value, even though her gesture of love is brutally rejected when the killer shoots the old woman pointblank. We condemn The Misfit's perverse will, but see his relation to the self-assertive grandmother. The grandmother and The Misfit belong on the same continuum measuring degrees of willfulness, although the cantankerous old woman is of course far more sympathetic than the escaped convict. The Misfit represents the grandmother's willfulness magnified to the most extreme degree possible. This story is a study of human will and the need to control/overpower others in the physical world. Subtle patterns of imagery centered on the body reinforce the facts of human biology/ physicality and the materialistic tendencies underlying the grandmother's and The Misfit's deficits.

Freud teaches us that dreams respond to biological needs and are motivated by wish fulfillment. Dreams strive to satisfy basic instincts— biological needs for nourishment and sexuality, demands for love, and wishes for a sense of security in the world. Dreams also enable us to achieve mastery over life's traumas and frustrations. Repetition in dreams of repressed experiences allows this sense of mastery. The fact that the grandmother "recalls" the house of her childhood (repeated four times on two pages, *CS*, 123–24) suggests the kind of compulsive recurrences that characterize dreams. The house is in fact a common symbol in dreams for the organism as a whole. This imaginative grandmother's manipulation of the family defines that special sense of power dreams sometimes evoke. The movement of this story follows the progression of dreams that begin with a sense of infinite power and end in nightmare—a sense of total helplessness.

Our first impressions, then, center on the grandmother's power to manipulate her family, and underlying the obvious focus on the old matriarch, there is a subtle focus on the body's physical needs, especially for food. In other O'Connor stories, characters suffer hunger, signifying spiritual longing (for example, Parker in "Parker's Back"), but in this story, characters are constantly satisfying their hunger. The mother feeds the baby at the start of the journey. Just past the outskirts of the city, the children eat lunch, and the grandmother eats a peanut-butter sandwich. Then she tells a story about a former beau, Mr. Teagarden ("tea"/"eat"), who once brought her a watermelon with his initials, E.A.T., carved on it. The melon, she explains, was eaten by a Negro boy when he passed the porch where her suitor had left it and interpreted the initials as license to indulge his appetite. The watermelon of course is associated in slang with pregnancy. Moreover, the eating of this forbidden fruit alludes to Eden. The focus on eating, pregnancy, and the loss of innocence suggests a certain queasiness about the physical world and prepares us for the murders. A failure to develop beyond physical needs and wishes results in human beings "devouring" one another.

Images of eating then intensify when the family stops to eat at a roadside café—a barbeque "pit" ironically called "The Tower" and owned by Red Sammy Butts, a stereotypical materialist and entrepreneur. This axis mundi permits a breakthrough to the underworld rather than to heaven. Guarding the entrance to Red Sammy's eating establishment is a chattering monkey, a Cerberus figure that doubles for the physically repulsive Butts and suggests the tendency to imitate (monkey see, monkey do). The monkey is "catching fleas on himself and biting each one carefully between his teeth" (*CS*, 122) as the family arrives. Images and incidents involving eating call attention to a great bodily need and also to the family's materialism.

The play with infernal imagery when the family enters the café is obvious and points to the limitations of a strictly materialistic perspective. The family enters the eating establishment and "a long dark room" where they encounter Red Sammy's wife, "a tall burnt-brown woman," and Red Sammy's "sweating red face." The grandmother "hisses" (*CS*, 121) as she scolds June Star for being rude. Then they all lament the absence of good men in the world, a cliché-filled exchange. The sweat, the excremental darkness, and the snake imagery allude to the body self. The interplay between images of eating and images suggesting gross materialism (Red Sammy's commercialism) function to prepare us for the grandmother's folly and The Misfit's nihilism. The grandmother, Red Sammy, and The Misfit rely only on what they can see and measure in mundane experience. The family itself values only what it can "possess," expressing the values of our commercialized culture.

Like so many O'Connor mother figures, the grandmother has unthinkingly acquired materialistic values of the American commercialized culture. She is dressed "fit to kill" in a dress trimmed with white lace so that "anyone seeing her dead on the highway would know at once that she was a lady" (*CS*, 118). O'Connor here obviously undercuts the old woman's materialistic values and concern for physical "appearances." Immersed in the stream rather than contemplating the end of life, the grandmother judges a "good" man according to superficial first impressions and materialistic values. Her former suitor, Mr. Teagarden, is good because "good-looking" and wealthy from his Coca-Cola stock. She concludes "at once" that Butts is a good man (*CS*, 122) and presumes that dressing up wins not only suitors but also God's favor.

Images of feeding and dressing up the body transmogrify to images of cannibalism. The family encounters The Misfit, whose smile "showed a row of strong white teeth" (*CS*, 127). The epigraph for the collection of short stories taking the title of this story seems particularly relevant here: "The dragon is by the side of the road, watching those who pass. Beware lest he devour you. We go to the Father of Souls, but it is necessary to pass by the dragon."[64] The dragon is not a beast or devil external to the self but is found wherever human will exerts itself at the expense of others. Materialistic goals and sadistic impulses reassuring the self that it can control mortality are evil forces prevalent in the modern world.

Just after Bailey and his son are murdered, the wind moves "through the tree tops like a long satisfied insuck of breath" (*CS*, 129)—dramatically evoking the horror of human physicality. O'Connor knows that we experience the body self as an evil force, a notion as ancient as Plato and as modern as Freud. June Star feels an aversion because The Misfit's sidekick reminds her of "a pig" (*CS*, 131), a common image for repulsive, human physicality that recurs throughout the canon. The Misfit first appears naked to the waist and ironically apologizes for his exposed body self, a travesty of social taste that receives more of his attention than the murders.

The manner in which The Misfit coolly "recalls" his past but fails to remember why he was imprisoned (for patricide, according to the prison psychiatrist) reveals that he is conveniently unaware of his own aggressive impulses against his father. He represses any sense of guilt resulting from unresolved Oedipal conflicts. The grandmother, then, sees The Misfit as someone "familiar to her as if she had known him all her life" (*CS*, 126). O'Connor knows that what is "familiar" in Freudian terms is what we all have in "common"—uncontrolled aggressive wishes deriving from infantile experiences. These aggressive impulses are not "nice," but the old woman concludes that The Misfit is "a good man" who does not have "common blood" and who comes from "nice people" (*CS*, 127)—the third such judgment (Teagarden and Butts were earlier candidates).

The grandmother's flattery (undoubtedly meant to save her own skin) is ineffective. This criminal explains that he has "seen a man burnt alive" and "a woman flogged"—events probably observed with as disinterested and sadistic a manner as he currently exhibits. He achieves a sense of control over his own aggressive impulses through violence. He equates himself with Christ ("It was the same case with Him as with me," *CS*, 131), thus confusing the sufferer who sacrificed himself for the sake of others with the inflictor of suffering on others for the sake of his own pleasure: "No pleasure but meanness," The Misfit says. Although once a gospel singer, this prophet of death now functions as an "undertaker." Unable to believe in Christ's Resurrection because he was not there at the time and cannot intuit beyond the material world, The Misfit examines life but concludes with nihilism. As The Misfit's chat with the grandmother progresses from his personal past to the history of Christianity, the parallelism between a denial of patricidal impulses and a denial of religious truth results in a poignant irony. Indeed, The Misfit finally stands for the entire human race repressing murderous impulses and unable to believe in God.

Only when facing death does the grandmother finally manage to recognize exactly what she and this criminal have in "common." This recognition goes beyond the fact that the criminal is wearing her son's shirt designed with "blue parrots," another image suggesting mindless imitation. Both The Misfit and the grandmother derive from the same human family tainted by sin and suffering in the material world. Thus, they are kin: he is one of her "own children" (*CS*, 132). The likeness she sees amounts to an epiphany; she faces the fact that the worst of us is a relative, an essential move of Christianity as Roman Catholics see it. Ironically, this lady finally dies in an unladylike pose, "with her legs crossed under her like a child's" (*CS*, 132), and this image of the child represents "innocence" paradoxically earned through suffering and sin.

Finally, The Misfit's conclusion that the grandmother "would of been a good woman . . . if it had been somebody there to shoot her every minute of her life" reflects O'Connor's Catholicism. God's violence unseats the spiritually complacent and forces the recognition of what establishes commonality—the physical body and the fatalism represented by death and decay. This story affirms a transcendence through love, which is sadly lacking in contemporary human relations.

The Evil of Destructive Passivity

In "The Life You Save May Be Your Own" (a companion piece to The Misfit's story), we meet Mr. Shiftlet and Mrs. Crater—again an encounter between a diabolical young man and a motherly older woman. A satanic figure looms over the innocents, but unlike "A Good Man Is Hard to Find" the comic impulse lasts from start to end. In this story, O'Connor draws on popular American humor, which celebrates the rascal and commonly presents an interaction between the con man and the gullible victim.[65] To complicate matters here, the gullible victim ineptly aims to con the rascal into marrying her retarded daughter. Although we are told that "she had no teeth" (*CS*, 146), Mrs. Crater belongs to O'Connor's coven of devouring mothers, this time "ravenous for a son-in-law" (*CS*, 150). Her nature is phallic, aggressive, wooden, and unfeeling—mechanically comic. Described as being "about the size of a cedar fence post," she wears "a man's gray hat" (*CS*, 146). She lives alone with her handicapped daughter in a desolate spot, but still the mother fearlessly greets the vagabond, Shiftlet—because she "could tell, even at a distance" that he is "no one to be afraid of" (*CS*, 145).

Mr. Shiftlet converses with Mrs. Crater, and he bears "no particular expression on his face." She likewise responds automatically to his philosophical questioning and repeats her favorite phrase, "That's right," so often and in so many different circumstances that O'Connor again intimates a limited human response like other characters who speak in clichés. The singleness of Mrs. Crater's responses and motivations ironically contrasts with the suggestions of duplicity—suggestions reinforced by the fact that the mother and daughter bear the same name (Lucynell Crater), which itself repeats the notion of emptiness (nell, crater). The daughter is a mere shadow of the mother's will.

The one-armed Shiftlet with his "jutting steel-trap jaw" suggests the devouring quality of The Misfit and spiritual deformity. Paradoxically, Shiftlet appears before Mrs. Crater's porch and stands so that "his figure formed a crooked cross" (*CS*, 146). This handyman then resurrects the old woman's automobile and feels "as if he had just raised the dead" (*CS*, 151). The only life this anti-Christ intends to save, however, will be his own in a materialistic world where innocent young women are sacrificed for possessions—things like automobiles. Shiftlet marries the idiot daughter only because he wants the old woman's car and then promptly deserts her when she falls asleep at the counter of a roadside diner.

Mr. Shiftlet's duplicity is as obvious as Mrs. Crater's and is suggested by his name (T. T. Shiftlet) and his hometown of Tarwater, which suggests split ("tear" meaning "rip"). Shiftlet ironically says he might have come from "Singleberry" (*CS*, 147), while asserting his honesty. Mrs. Crater pointedly asks if he is "single," and indeed, he is actually one-dimensional or single-minded in his exploitation of others and his inability to see beyond the material world: he declares that "the spirit . . . is like an automobile" (*CS*, 152).

The comic incongruity between the ideal of true philosophical discourse and Shiftlet's philosophical smokescreen, meant to hide his immoral intentions, is bombastic. A mock philosopher, Shiftlet asks, "What is a man" (*CS*, 148), an echo of *Hamlet*. He postures as a social critic, a scientist studying "the mystery of flame," and a "good" man, who complains that most people lack morals and don't "care if they did a thing one way or another . . . [but] he hadn't been raised thataway." This fragmented man tells a story about a surgeon who "cut the human heart . . . out of a man's chest and held it in his hand" (*CS*, 147), while he himself cuts the heart out of everyone he meets—unaware of his own crimes and constantly projecting blame onto others. Shiftlet himself lights the match of human suffering and passively watches it burn. His critical stance only serves to highlight his failure to be self-critical.

Although O'Connor says that "moments [of Grace] are prepared for (by me anyway) by the intensity of the evil circumstances" (*Letters*, 367–68), we sense no grace in this story—unless it be in the satire itself, which attacks the traditional role of Southern woman and the ideal of "simple-mindedness in females." Martha Chew notes that O'Connor toys with the premise of the retarded woman as good wife material.[66] Shiftlet, however, is not in the market for a "good" wife. Like The Misfit, Shiftlet progresses from gospel singer to undertaker. Unlike the more aggressive criminal, Shiftlet does not actively destroy his victims. He passively deserts Lucynell, failing to care for her after marrying her to get her mother's car. His passivity reminds us of what we saw in Mrs. McIntyre when she allowed the destruction of Guizac. As O'Connor puts it, Mr. Shiftlet is "of the Devil because nothing in him resists the Devil" (*Letters*, 367). His passivity and materialism deprive him of spiritual values.

Being depressed and feeling guilt serve as evidence of conscience, a sacred force in O'Connor's view. Human beings are free to choose whether or not they obey commands of conscience. Significantly, Shiftlet feels "depressed" just before he deserts Lucynell and "oppressed" (*CS*, 155) when he picks up a young boy, a runaway. The extent of Shiftlet's depravity, hidden from himself by his self-righteous masque, is clear when the young boy attacks the older man for a sentimental, tear-filled speech about motherhood, supposedly an attempt to discourage the boy from leaving home. In this speech, he expresses the point of the story: "a man with a car [has] a responsibility to others" (*CS*, 155). The child sees through Shiftlet's hypocrisy and shocks him with the truth: "My old woman is a flea bag and yours is a stinking pole cat" (*CS*, 156).

But Shiftlet is intent on denying his own culpability to the very end; he projects his evil impulses outward until he feels the world's "slime" (what his name suggests is "shit") engulf him (*CS*, 156). That his initials are T. S. suggests another possible interpretation of his hometown, Tarwater. That is, tarwater is a primitive laxative thought in the eighteenth century to be a kind of cure-all. The gap between the physical reality and the professed spirituality is also evident in Shiftlet's "smile [that] stretched like a weary snake waking up by a fire" (*CS*, 152). An early version of this story depicts Mr. Shiftlet's return to a wife whom he then beats to death with a club, a criminal act more suited to The Misfit. It is clear that O'Connor condemns both brands of evil—that which is active and that which is passive. What she demands is that, unlike Mr. Shiftlet, we consider our responsibility to others and master our actions so that they accord with our philosophy.

This story of abandonment alludes to the earliest form of abandonment we all experience—that of the mother's retreat (weaning) from the child. The incidents ending this story conflate the mother's abandonment of the child (in Shiftlet's case), the child's abandonment of the mother (in the hitchhiker's case), and the final abandonment of Lucynell. And the reader feels a sense of abandonment when the rascal escapes. The humor ends. The story satirizes our desire as readers to have the sheriff, preacher, father, or mother arrive in the last scene to administer justice. Instead, Shiftlet rides off to Mobile in his stolen automobile and escapes with the "guffawing peal of thunder"—"his stump sticking out the window"(*CS*, 156) in a dehumanized gesture.

Metaphysical Evil

The stories analyzed above make the point that first and foremost evil is an absence of good due to human will—whether as assertion of active, perverse will (in the case of The Misfit) or a perverse passivity (in the case of Shiftlet's inability to love beyond the self). "A Circle in the Fire" is O'Connor's study of paranoia—the human response to what the Catholics consider to be one-fifth of the world's evil, that is, the forces of evil mysteriously beyond the realm of human will.

The struggle between evil and good is surrealistically suggested in the first sentence establishing the setting: "the last line of trees . . . was almost black and behind it the sky was a livid glaring white" (*CS*, 175). Mrs. Cope is most sensitive to this struggle and suffers existential dread—an obsession with metaphysical evil, including dread over the enormity of the universe but more particularly natural calamities such as fires in woods and other destructive forces not controlled by human will. Mrs. Cope focuses especially on her fear of natural calamities threatening her property—she works "at the weeds and nut grass as if they were an evil sent directly by the devil to destroy the place" (*CS*, 175). Her "opposite," Mrs. Pritchard, focuses on metaphysical evil threatening the physical body. Both women seek to gain control over their fears and represent two different responses to the presence of metaphysical evil in the world—one active, the other more passive.

Mrs. Pritchard passively leans against the "chimney"—her "shelf of a stomach" establishing her gross physicality. She focuses on her "four abscess teeth" (*CS*, 177)—on physical pain rather than psychological pain, such as Mrs. Cope's paranoia. But Mrs. Pritchard only seems to respond to life passively, failing to resist evil, for example, when she recommends to Mrs. Cope that when trouble comes all at once, "it wouldn't be nothing you could do but fling up your hands" (*CS*, 178), or when she gloats over the boys getting the best of her employer ("Like I toljer . . . there ain't a thing you can do about it" [*CS*,188]).

And yet the fact that Mrs. Pritchard dwells on the physical suffering of the world is itself more active than might at first be imagined. She compulsively indulges in morbid gossip about other people's disasters—habitually repeating "calamitous stories" and even relishing funerals (she "would go thirty miles for the satisfaction of seeing anybody laid away" [*CS*, 175]). In this way, she achieves mastery over physical suffering and death.

Unlike Mrs. Pritchard's seeming acceptance of life's inevitable tragedies, Mrs. Cope actively displaces her fears of disaster by tearing at the nut grass and constantly trying to consider "something cheerful" (*CS*, 175). She sees evil in the nut grass but not in the self, and in spite of their physical differences (the contrast between Mrs. Pritchard's corporeality and Mrs. Cope's trim body), we notice that they are also alike. These two "opposites" wear "identical hats," both are subject to neurotic fear, and both fail to resist evil in fruitful ways. They fail to be self-aware, judging the source of the world's evil to be predominately beyond the self rather than, as in the Roman Catholic view, predominately caused by failures in human will (active and passive). Mrs. Cope identifies destructive forces in everything outside the self, even the Negroes, whom she accuses of being "as destructive and impersonal as the nut grass" (*CS*, 177).

Mrs. Cope's phobias "about fire in the woods" or being "destroyed by a hurricane" (*CS*, 177), however, finally represent the pain humans suffer because they anticipate death. The destruction she fears is ultimately not destruction of her woods but self-destruction. She declares her gratitude that her problems come one at a time or "They'd destroy me" (*CS*, 177), as she puts it. Her defensive posture prevents her from feeling compassion when three homeless boys appear at the door. Not able to see beyond her material "place," she only briefly feels compassion for these boys when she realizes that they are hungry, but her sense of "pain" over their predicament is short-lived. The next day she feels "faintly provoked" (*CS*, 185). This mother figure who comments on Powell's "familiar" face (*CS*, 179) is in need of some self-awareness. Her encounter with Powell lacks the grandmother's epiphany in "A Good Man Is Hard to Find." That is, Mrs. Cope does not recognize that the boys belong to the same human "family." When told by Mrs. Pritchard that the boys were disobediently riding the horses, Mrs. Cope bears an "expression . . . the same as when she tore at the nut grass" (*CS*, 186). thus distancing herself from the boys and denying her own destructive lack of compassion.

The facts of human vulnerability, self-centered aggression, and the transience of the physical world are repressed by O'Connor's characters as they grapple with threats to their self-satisfied sense of security and identify forces outside the self, especially forces inherent in the nature of things, as being responsible for their woes. The physical world, not the self, is evil in the view of The Misfit, Mr. Shiftlet, and Mrs. Cope.

Limited Perspectives:
The "Evils" of the Physical World

In the last of the stories depicting good/evil conflicts, revulsion for or fear of the physical world haunts characters seeking a spiritual reality. From O'Connor's Catholic viewpoint, the human body is God's handiwork. But the characters in "A Temple of the Holy Ghost" and "Parker's Back" suffer the physical world as an evil force. O'Connor views God's creatures as incomplete and grotesque in their incompleteness but, more important, in the process of becoming whole. Images of the fragmented and deformed body—the freak and the crippled human being—finally suggest the potential for wholeness and spirituality. Moreover, what we might view as evil and grotesque O'Connor often accepts sympathetically as inherently good—only "appearing" evil because of our limited vision, an orthodox Roman Catholic view expressed in "The River."

In "The River," O'Connor's mastery falters. This story depicts a neglected child convinced by a born-again preacher conducting his baptismal and healing service at river's edge that the river offers a new "life." The boy returns to the river and drowns. The destruction of a child cannot be seen as "good" for most of us, and this story does not do enough to overcome that reader reaction. "Parker's Back" affirms physical life; "The River" condemns it. The material world may appear "good" only if we ignore the fact that it is filled with drunken parents, vicious children, and child molesters. Death, and the consequent loss of the world, might be considered then a positive "good"—a release. Bevel "comes to a good end," O'Connor asserts. "He's saved from those nutty parents, a fate worse than death. He's been baptized and so he goes to his Maker."[67] This suggests that the material world is a vehicle for attaining the spiritual one, and although considered "good" from that standpoint, still the spiritual self ought to count the world as dung, as Augustine tells us.[68]

O'Connor herself obviously felt revulsion for physical life at times ("the people I write about certainly don't disgust me entirely though I see them from a standard of judgment from which they fall short" [*Letters*, 221]). Her faith demanded acceptance; her work reflects the struggle between affirmation and negation: "If you believe in the divinity of Christ, you have to cherish the world at the same time that you struggle to endure it" (*Letters*, 90). This may explain the ineffectiveness of "The River," an early attempt to grapple with the problem of the suffering of innocent children.

O'Connor knows how hard it is for most of us to accept the idea that evil and suffering are mere appearance. Images of limited perspectives dominate "The River" and develop a pattern underlining the difficulty of attaining the vision needed to accept suffering. Manipulation of point of view in this story demands that the reader notice incidents emphasizing limited perspectives and consider the philosophical implications of dramatic disparities between two possible interpretations of what the characters say and do—one an interpretation limited to the secular world, the other suggesting Catholic doctrine. The Ashfield's banter about their son Harry—"He ain't fixed right. . . . Well then for Christ's sake fix him" (*CS*, 157)—refers to his clothes being in disarray from their own perspective and his spiritual development being at risk from the author's perspective. O'Connor's method is perhaps too subtle here. She implies that the distance between what the characters see and what the reader deduces infers on a lower plane the disparity between the human and the divine view of the world.

In the second incident of this story, perspective is emphasized further. The babysitter, Mrs. Connin, because of her limited knowledge of modern art, cannot appreciate or understand a painting of "black lines crossing into broken planes of violent color" (*CS*, 157). The color matches this family's violent mode of existence, and the "broken planes" imply what Maritain says about our limited vision being due to "the fundamental, irreducible, dissymmetry between the line of good and the line of evil."[69] This supposedly "good" woman plans to take the boy to a healing, where "The Reverend Bevel Summers" might cure the boy's "hunger" and the mother's hangover. That the babysitter appears as a "speckled skeleton" (*CS*, 160) foreshadows Harry's unfortunate end by ironically suggesting that this woman represents death leading the boy, not salvation—again a judgment depending on perspective, on whether one believes that death leads to life and resurrection.

The perspectives of Mrs. Connin, the parents, the parents' friends (who value *The Life of Jesus Christ* only in monetary terms, *CS*, 170), and Harry are all shown to be extremely limited at some point in this story. Harry's distortions seem the most severe. First, a gap in religious training is revealed when the boy puzzles over a picture of a man wearing a white sheet (*CS*, 163). Later, the boy's limited vision is depicted when the three Connin children—seated on the top of the hog pen with a clear view of the dangerous hog contained therein—suggest to Harry, seated below on the ground, that he remove the bottom board, thus allowing a better look but also releasing the enraged animal. Finally, Harry's misreading of the world causes him to find death in what the preacher calls "the River of Life" (*CS*, 165).

If O'Connor intended to imply that the boy's view of the river was after all correct and that this preacher and the river truly offer salvation, one wonders why this servant of God works in an infernal setting. His "sideburns that curved into the hollows of his cheeks" and "his face . . . all bone" (reminiscent of Mrs. Connin) glare in the "red light reflected from the river" (*CS*, 164). Other details adding to this impression are the two silent birds that "revolved downward" and then "sat hunch-shouldered as if they were supporting the sky" (*CS*, 165–66).

The buzzard is the most common bird circling Georgian skies. And the imagery of a diseased city nearby undercuts this preacher's effectiveness: "Behind, in the distance, the city rose like a cluster of warts" (*CS*, 165). Finally, Summers fails to cure Mr. Paradise's cancer, Mrs. Connin's ulcer, or the "old woman with flapping arms whose head wobbled" and who "turned a time or two in a *blind* circle until someone reached out and pulled her back into the group" (emphasis mine; *CS*, 166). The helping hand comes from the crowd, not from the Reverend. What emerges here is a sense of enormous human need poorly met by the Southern evangelical mode of worship. It is difficult not to see this story as a satire of born-again theology.

The final distortion in perspective occurs when the drowning boy sees his would-be rescuer, Mr. Paradise, as "a giant pig bounding after him, shaking a red and white club and shouting." From his point of view, what the boy ordinarily might see as appetizing, the candy cane meant as a lure, becomes threatening, a club. Although it is true that we feel no regret for Mr. Paradise's loss—for "the old man [who] rose like some ancient water monster . . . empty-handed" (*CS*, 174), and although we would rather see him caught "empty-handed" than "red-handed," still the reader mourns for what the boy loses. The boy's "low cry of pain and indignation" preceding his release from "his fury and fear" (*CS*, 173, 174) expresses only too well our desire to live—and in this world. Mr. Paradise's name is meant ironically to express a limited view of what the material world seems to us. O'Connor subtly intimates that this repulsive man represents a profane material world we should deny.

Even so, the fisted hand of Mr. Paradise is not repulsive enough for us to reject the old man's attempts to save the boy as entirely self-serving. The sacred presence of the long gentle hand saving the boy from "life" is not emphasized enough throughout the story. The only developed representatives of faith, Mrs. Connin and Bevel Summers, are presented just as grotesquely as the primary representative of evil, the old man. And the repetition of incidents involving limited perspectives is so subtle that most readers don't seem to notice it. Consequently, the larger perspective that would help us to see that the death and suffering of innocent children is "good" fails to emerge. What does emerge is a sense of human error, the inability to locate the sacred properly.

It is difficult to maintain faith in divine dimensions of worldly operations that permit the suffering of children and even more difficult to believe in the sacred dimensions of human biology, in O'Connor's view. But "Parker's Back" does convey faith in the Incarnation, a significant accomplishment by an ailing author suffering the most painful moments of her disease. While O'Connor's earlier attempts to address human biology from an adolescent perspective were not as successful, they should be analyzed first in order to clarify the accomplishment of her last and perhaps best story of those concerned with the problems of defining "evil" in the physical world.

At no time is one's bewilderment over the body self more intense than during adolescence, a kind of disease everyone suffers. "A Temple of the Holy Ghost" deals with the identity crisis that often occurs at this critical time when an awareness of the body self leads to the questions of "Who?" and "What am I?". This story tries to answer these questions with Catholic doctrine (you are "A Temple of the Holy Ghost") and presents a sensitive, twelve-year-old, preadolescent girl who confronts a sacred/profane duality ineffectively reconciled.

O'Connor thought it "odd" that this story did not receive more critical attention and was never "anthologized" (*Letters*, 487). O'Connor's gift does reside in tapping the reader's sympathy for the most unseemly characters (the chauvinistic egoist O.E. in "Parker's Back," for example). When she wrote "A Temple of the Holy Ghost," however, this gift was not yet mature enough to grasp the need to involve the reader more deeply in this child's suffering, especially given society's conditioning to respond unsympathetically toward the struggles of young girls.

This particular girl struggles to accept the body self and to discover a sacred dimension in the profane reality around her. The profane constantly violates a sacred reality, especially by threats to the "purity" of the body. O'Connor admits that, as she puts it, "my upbringing has smacked a little of Jansenism even if my convictions do not." She then comments: "'A Temple of the Holy Ghost' all revolves around what is purity" (*Letters*, 117).

And yet the story concentrates on impurity and disunity. Told through the limited perspective of "the child" as she experiences a visit from her unwelcome cousins, the story focuses on the body self represented in part by the "positively Ugly" girls (as seen from the child's perspective). The cousins remove their sacred convent clothing and adorn themselves with profane "red skirts and loud blouses," which seem to mock "their Sunday shoes" as they strut in front of the mirror. From their own perspectives they are beautiful; from the child's, ugly. She feels a jealous antagonism toward her cousins. These attitudes toward the body self and familial conflicts obviously exclude a sacred dimension.

The cousins jest over the mother's suggestion that they should stave off sexual advances by reminding boyfriends that their bodies are temples of the Holy Ghost. Of course, staving off sexual advances is far from what the girls intend, and "None of their ways were lost on the child" (*CS*, 236). The physical reality the child would deny is soon to be repeated in her own blossoming sexuality—seen as repulsive. The child equates birth with "spit" (*CS*, 246) and suggests that the taxicab driver, Alonzo Myers, and old Mr. Cheatam (both obese and repulsive) would make appropriate suitors for the girls. The child's own obesity ("her fat cheeks," *CS*, 237) ironically matches that of Alonzo's, whose bodily odors do not improve even on Sunday (*CS*, 247). Her loathing for others must be understood as self-loathing based on a disgust for the body.

But O'Connor intimates that this disgust is due to the child's limited perspective. In the evening, the child notices that the garden lanterns "made the girls sitting at the table look prettier than they were" (*CS*, 242). In turn, the reader should also reevaluate this youthful critic who judges herself as "ugly"—a judgment repeated by the cook and by her mother. The reader should see the child as a sensitive and intelligent adolescent struggling with profound questions. How do we accept the threatening cycles of regeneration (represented by the rabbit giving birth through its mouth, *CS*, 246)? Such juxtapositions of spit (death) and birth declare our impermanence.

When the child's cousins leave with their dates to go to the fair, she studies from a distance the "long finger of light . . . revolving up and around and away, searching the air as if it were hunting for the lost son." She yearns to see more than the profane reality, "the beacon light from the fair" (*CS*, 242). But the circus itself represents the disparity between the profane and sacred realities, between what we must suffer and what we desire. Another such disparity is seen when the boys' "hillbilly song" is juxtaposed with the sacred Latin hymn. Timeless sacred truths reassert themselves in a modern profane milieu. The hymn reads, *Et antiquum documentum/Novo cedat ritui* (*CS*, 241), meaning that the old ceremony gives way to a new ritual (the circus). Modern and early Christian times mingle in the image of the human faces painted on the faded canvas tents, which the child sees as "martyrs waiting to have their tongues cut out by the Roman soldier" (*CS*, 243).

Tension builds between sacred and profane perspectives, between spiritual aspirations of the girl and the secular world. She desires to be a saint but acknowledges her sloth; wishes to be a martyr but wonders if "she could stand to be torn to pieces by lions or not." She envisions the Romans attempting to burn her, but "to their astonishment she would not burn down." She repeats this daydream in order to master the facts of her own mortality: "She rehearsed this several times, returning each time at the entrance of Paradise to the lions" (*CS*, 243).

The girls return from the fair and relate their story about a sideshow featuring a hermaphrodite who exposes himself. Again we find a conflict between sacred and profane dimensions. The primitive hermaphroditic god is common in myth and is here violently yoked with the modern freak show. On the one hand, O'Connor suggests the sacred nature of the body when the child imagines the men watching the hermaphrodite "more solemn than they were in church" (*CS*, 246). On the other hand, the profane setting overwhelms the sacred: the materialistic ends of freak shows appeal to the sexual curiosity of the masses. The physical reality of the hermaphrodite is an ugly reality that appears to deny the sacred nature of the world—of a god that would afflict his creatures with the pain of a freakish body. The hermaphrodite himself expresses revulsion for the body self and accuses God of being a merciless, punishing force: "If anybody desecrates the temple of God, God will bring him to ruin and if you laugh, He may strike you thisaway" (*CS*, 246). And yet the hermaphrodite also represents an uncanny sense of power gained through a unification of the sexes. Thus, we feel both revulsion and attraction for this "freak" of nature seeming to overcome gender barriers and represented in myth as a god.

The return to the convent is meant to reconcile the conflict between the sacred and the profane realities developed throughout the story— a reconciliation achieved through the Eucharist and "the big nun" who warms the child's "frigid frown" with an embrace, a gesture of love, however awkward (the nun is shown "mashing the side of [the child's] face into the crucifix," *CS*, 248). This expression of God's love in the physical world occurs just after the child participates in the Eucharist, which transforms her from continuing "in the same ugly vein" to praying "Hep me not to be so mean" (*CS*, 247). During this service, the child overlays her view of the host with a vision of the hermaphrodite.

The reader feels an enormous disparity between the spirituality represented in the symbol of the Host and the primitive expression of divinity that the hermaphrodite evokes, not to mention the primitive reality of circus life.

The child apparently feels the disparity, too, and still puzzles over the mystery of physical life on the way home from the convent. She meditates on "three folds of fat" in Alonzo's neck and his piglike ears (*CS*, 248). She is then, however, capable of a transcendent vision that seems to distill a sacred symbol into everlasting substance. That is, she sees the sun (a symbol of God according to O'Connor) as a "huge red ball like an elevated Host drenched in blood." As this sun sets, it trails the straight line of "a red clay road" (*CS*, 248) in the sky. The juxtaposition of "clay" and "sun," like that of "hermaphrodite" and "Host," suggests the miracle of the Resurrection as the Catholics perceive it— the miracle of the body purified.

And yet, O'Connor represents profane physicality with so much vividness and power that we are not convinced by an ending that seems a patch rather than an outgrowth of an organic whole. The child's "divine" impulses and the nun's embrace of love are not developed enough. The spiritual potential of flesh in this story is overshadowed by imagery, incident, and character suggesting a profane reality more real than any sacred one.

In "Parker's Back," O'Connor does manage to express what she attempted in "A Temple of the Holy Ghost." The sense of struggle between the body, felt from our limited perspective as evil, and the spirit seems clear. Parker feels "as if the panther and the lion and the serpents and the eagles and the hawks [his tattoos] had penetrated his skin and lived inside him in a raging warfare" (*CS*, 514). But however much Parker's spirit struggles against the body (represented by animal imagery) and however much Parker suffers a terrible sense of a body/spirit duality, the reader finally sees divine potential in the image of the tattooed Christ and in Parker's gesture of love for Sarah Ruth, whose stern Puritanical Protestantism ironically symbolizes "spirit." Parker is O'Connor's final and most brilliant portrait of a divided self. Proclaimed by her as an attempt at a story "too funny to be as serious as it ought" (*Letters*, 427), this portrait reaffirms the author's deep involvement with exploring "the mystery of personality" and human life—a mystery because inherently contradictory—comic *and* tragic, sacred *and* profane.

Obadiah Elihue Parker is attracted at the age of fourteen to a tattooed man who represents unity and wholeness, "a single intricate design of brilliant color" (*CS*, 512). As he studies this man, Parker feels incomplete, divided, and spiritually empty, like most adolescents encountering the demands of the body and the realities of the adult world with a new intensity. It is at this time that Parker questions "the fact that he existed" and feels "a peculiar unease" (*CS*, 513). His encounter with the tattooed man seems to be a symbolic encounter with the biological self, which for Parker represents a first awareness of the mind/body dichotomy.

Dividedness, fragmentation, and a sense of alienation from body are exactly what Parker aims to overcome: "Whenever a decent-sized mirror was available, he would get in front of it and study his overall look. The effect was not of one intricate arabesque of colors but of something haphazard and botched. A huge dissatisfaction would come over him" (*CS*, 514). He struggles for unity of self, a secure identity that cannot be achieved without acceptance of the body and mortality, not to mention positioning himself as a constructive member of the whole human community, the first step accomplished by marriage.

Having identified that which makes him feel fragmented, that is, the body, Parker aggressively wages an attack on the self by trying to transform himself into a unified image with tattoos, a strategy that fails. Parker momentarily stops getting tattoos when only his back remains undecorated; he cannot stand the further fragmentation suggested by needing two mirrors to see his tattoos (*CS*, 518). He seeks control of his destiny symbolized by control of his body, mastery of existence sought through his sense of masculinity, and a secure identity symbolized by Sarah Ruth's acknowledgment/acceptance.

Parker's first efforts to establish a sense of a whole and sound identity depend on physical appearance. Parker feels he is physically "attractive" because his tattoos attract women. He displays his body by removing his shirt whenever possible, especially when his female boss is watching (*CS*, 511). Parker is disturbed by the fact that she "looked at him the same way she looked at her old tractor" (*CS*, 511), even though she is an unattractive, old woman. On the other hand, because she is an old woman, he may subliminally long for the attention of his mother's eye. With tongue in cheek, O'Connor presents this drive of the exhibitionist and then declares that Parker has "an extra sense." Unfortunately, Parker's extrasensory perception hopelessly expresses bodily drives—not spiritual insight. It indicates to him "when there was a woman nearby watching him" (*CS*, 511).

Parker lacks any awareness of the spiritual dimensions in human life and is therefore obsessed with his own physical appearance. Tormented by the disparity between what he feels he is (attractive) and what he appears to be in the eyes of his new wife (repulsive), he refuses to acknowledge Sarah Ruth's disgust for his tattoos—a disgust for the body. Parker's experience with Sarah Ruth intensifies the identity crisis Parker suffered earlier at age fourteen when he became obsessed with tattooing. His behavior is adolescent. Erikson identifies the behavior of adolescents precisely as a morbid preoccupation with identity determined by "the eyes of others."[70] This preoccupation shows a terrible uncertainty, a wavering sense of self, and a dependence on others for reassurance as to one's own identity.

Parker's attraction to Sarah Ruth resides in the fact that, unlike himself, she seems to know who and what she is (a Chosen One—all Spirit). Parker does not know who or what he is, but he hopes his wife will help him to gain a sense of his own identity. Ironically, what she does is to confuse her husband further because of her denial of the body.

Just as Sarah Ruth's quest for fulfillment through the spirit alone seems suspect, so fulfillment of Parker's desire for completeness cannot be achieved through the body alone: no wholeness can be attained by focusing on the physical body, which itself represents death and fragmentation. Parker's exhibitionist impulses cannot be explained by the Freudian framework alone. Parker behaves as if he were physically hungry: "a boy whose mouth habitually hung open . . . as ordinary as a loaf of bread" (*CS*, 513). What is emphasized throughout, however, is not his empty stomach or physical frustrations but his empty eyes, the seat of the soul. He is in fact repulsed by physical hunger when he sees Sarah Ruth's family: we are told then that "Hungry people make Parker nervous" (*CS*, 515). He is not one to deny the body, but he is spiritually hungry. He is confused about how to satisfy his need. Sarah Ruth, although she claims to be spiritually satisfied, likewise is divided and confused. Subtle allusions to Eve undercut Sarah Ruth's "relish" for the apple Parker gives her (*CS*, 516).

It is the spiritual self that seeks satisfaction in O'Connor's work. It is the spiritual quest that drives Parker to seek wholeness. Karl Abraham shows that in a great number of languages the word for "doubt" (for example, *zweifeln*) is connected with the word for two (*zwei*), and in one of the late biblical documents, Psalm 119, "doubter" means "one who is divided." Doubt and dividedness signify weak faith. According to the orthodox Roman Catholic view of the Incarnation, as long as one believes, one achieves unity of body/spirit.[71]

O'Connor's disapproval of Sarah Ruth's Manichaean character is directly evident. Sarah Ruth's worst fault is "ice in the veins"—the Hawthornian sin of a cold heart suggested by the "icepick" eyes of her first description. A castrating phallic woman wielding a broom, she drains Parker of vitality when she misreads his tattoo of an eagle. From her perspective, it is merely a chicken.

Sarah Ruth avoids self-examination by repressing her own weaknesses and by "sniffing up sin" (*CS*, 510) in others. She defines "sin" in terms of indulgences of the body: smoking, drinking, sex—ladies painting their faces to attract men and Parker tattooing himself to attract women. Repulsed by the body, she examines Parker's supposedly wounded hand as if it were "a poisonous snake" (*CS*, 512). She pays him as much heed as "a stray pig" (*CS*, 515). Parker is defined by his boss as a mechanism and by his wife as an animal—both comparisons pointing to twentieth-century fears. Sarah Ruth counts his tattoos as "vanity of vanities" (*CS*, 515), and yet her own piousness is vanity also. Her revulsion for physical life is conveyed repeatedly (she prefers her husband "dressed and with his sleeves rolled down") and in contexts that suggest O'Connor's disapproval.

Parker's dissatisfaction with life is not overcome by marrying this Manichaean woman. In a last, desperate attempt to achieve love and recognition from his wife, he tries to envision a tattoo for his back that she "would not be able to resist" (*CS*, 519). Worrying over what might succeed with her, he accidentally runs a tractor into a tree and watches it explode. This brush with death causes him to feel "that there had been a great change in his life, a leap forward into a worse unknown" (*CS*, 521). Parker's crisis is a positive experience that enables him to act "authentically" in the world, as Heidegger puts it.[72] Previously, Parker's sense of identity could only be satisfied by receiving love and recognition from his fellow human beings, not by giving love.

Alarmed when the tattoo artist doesn't recognize him, Parker demands recognition: "You KNOW me!"—he shouts. When he returns to his wife and wants her to look at his back, newly decorated with a Byzantine Christ, he also demands Sarah Ruth recognize and accept him finally. Parker's gesture of love is what allows him to feel "that his dissatisfaction was gone" (*CS*, 527). We ought to be moved by his desire to please Sarah Ruth, especially given her unyielding disposition and his previously narcissistic motivations. Parker has changed from behaving according to the exhibitionist's self-involvement to wanting for the first time in his life to "please" someone else (*CS*, 527). When Sarah Ruth Cates beats the man who wants so much to win her love and inflicts wounds on the face of the tattooed Christ, there can be no doubt where the reader's sympathy lies. Parker becomes a kind of Christ figure, and the story ends with biblical resonances: "There he was—who called himself Obadiah Elihue—leaning against the tree, crying like a baby" (*CS*, 530).

In the letters discussing this story, O'Connor tells us that "Sarah Ruth was the heretic—the notion that you can worship in pure spirit" (*Letters*, 594). By concretizing the sacred/profane split in the characters of Sarah Ruth, who focuses her attention on "purity," and Parker, who focuses his attention on the body—rather than using subtle imagery as in "A Temple of the Holy Ghost"—O'Connor achieves control of her reader's response, thus avoiding the misunderstanding that her art expresses her own revulsion for physical life.

All of humanity at some time feels a revulsion for the body because it declares our impermanence—the excremental/reproductive truths about ourselves. O'Connor's art acknowledges this fact, but also acknowledges it as something to overcome. The motif of revulsion for human physicality is also found in many other modern works, not least Kafka's story, "The Metamorphosis." In this story, the father at one point responds to his son's metamorphosis into an insect (a "dung beetle") with the mandate that "family duty required suppression of disgust."[73] Like Kafka, O'Connor asserts the importance of recognizing and accepting what is human, no matter how grotesque. Self-awareness leads to such recognition and acceptance, a necessary step toward integration of the whole human family.

Although Parker and Sarah Ruth's relationship fails to express love, O'Connor, by winning the reader's compassion for Parker, advocates an acceptance of the physical world as an arena for divine love expressed through a very human medium. What we might have seen as repulsive because most readers associate tattoos with crime, O'Connor elevates, even celebrates. Hendin complains that O'Connor's characters lose "all sense of human kinship," and yet we certainly should feel a sense of kinship with Parker. In fact, Bleikasten concludes that Parker is "an artist figure" and "a comically distorted projection of the writer."[74] Finally, O'Connor maintains that the body is both a primary arena for struggle and a means of expressing love. Ironically, Parker's first name suggests the author's own struggle with the body at the time she wrote this story: O-BOD-DIE-AH.

Conclusion

As the pain of living with her own disease increased, Flannery O'Connor might have ended her career with a bitter story. But "Parker's Back," written on her deathbed, is one of the most comic, the most sympathetic toward the central protagonist, and the most affirmative generally of all the stories she wrote. It is also one of her very best; this story rather than the usually anthologized "A Good Man Is Hard to Find" should be the starting point when beginning study of O'Connor's work.

Parker's final gesture of love is the antithesis of The Misfit's destruction of the grandmother, Mr. Shiftlet's abandonment of Lucynell, Mark Fortune's brutality toward his granddaug..ter, Sheppard's neglect of Norton, the Ashfields' neglect of their son Harry, Mrs. McIntyre's complicity in the death of Guizac, Mr. Greenleaf's conspiracy against Mrs. May, and Calhoun's identification with Singleton, the rebel who murders the dignitaries of his community. There is a point behind these acts of aggression that have become the focus of O'Connor criticism. The point to be made by inverse logic has much to do with the gestures of love in the stories—gestures just as dramatic as the violence but often missed.

Some critics perhaps rightly view O'Connor's destructive characters as if on "a trip in a glass-bottomed boat" (*Letters*, 376), but it is simply wrong to view the more sympathetic characters such as Parker, the child in "A Temple of the Holy Ghost," Mrs. Turpin, and Asbury Fox as evil oddities. O'Connor defended herself ineffectively against charges that she was obsessed with depicting Southern grotesques: she sided with the rebels ("I'm all for Singleton in this" [*Letters*, 443]) only because they must have seemed a notch above pious readers consigning all of her characters to the category of "freaks"—nothing to do with me.

Nor should we join the pious reader who proclaims that all of O'Connor's characters are sympathetic, even the devourers who murder, abandon, neglect, and maim others in order to feel themselves less psychologically "maimed," less physically crippled, or less incomplete. One of the worst problems in O'Connor studies is the urge to extend sympathy everywhere, even to vicious characters who try to overcome their insecurities in the physical world by violent or materialistic assertions of will. This tendency to extend sympathy too far developed in response to early critics who saw sympathy nowhere. With a better understanding of O'Connor's methods of indirection, her alignment with New Criticism and the poets, and her involvement with modernist thought, the lines of sympathy ought to be more certainly established. That Wayne Booth's meticulous reading of "Everything That Rises Must Converge" identifies this story as an example of "stable irony" exactly demonstrates my point here.[75]

Flannery O'Connor's irony, her comic impulse, and her involvement with modern philosophy is never clearer than in *Wise Blood,* her first novel. This novel was met for the most part with criticism narrowing the lines of response to its theological implications. And yet in the novel we find a complex and subtle satire of the nihilist, the existentialist, the modern materialist who aims to use religion for profit, as well as the born-again Southern Protestant alienated from his community because of his idiosyncratic or destructive methods of affirming his faith.

We find in this novel some of the most comic moments in O'Connor's art and some of the most grotesque—especially when considering the allusions to infanticide, self-blinding with lye as an affirmation of faith, and murder. One of the more comic incidents demonstrates the central issue in the novel—that of adjusting to modern life. Sabbath Lily, the preacher's daughter, writes the newspaper for advice about whether she should "neck or not" because she is "a bastard and a bastard shall not enter the kingdom of heaven" anyway. She is not satisfied with the response to her letter: "your real problem is one of adjustment to the modern world. Perhaps you ought to reexamine your religious values to see if they meet your needs in life. A religious experience can be a beautiful addition to living if you put it in the proper perspective and don't let it warf you." Sabbath Lily replies: "What I really want to know is should I go the whole hog or not? That's my real problem. I'm adjusted okay to the modern world."

None of O'Connor's characters are adjusted to the modern world, but every possible method of achieving some kind of adjustment is explored—from promoting the Church without Christ to murdering those who represent a more vulnerable aspect of the self in order to affirm power over death. Hazel Motes, The Misfit of *Wise Blood,* tries both of these methods to "adjust," among others. We tend to focus on his grotesque attempts to adjust rather than on the gestures of love found in the novel, gestures that might have succeeded. Enoch and Mrs. Flood try to befriend this perverse "hero," but he rebuffs everyone. While Hazel's rebellion against the Southern Protestantism that alienates him from his community is satirized in this novel, his nihilism does not help his "adjustment."

This novel was, in fact, one of the first works that critics and readers tried to understand, but it might have been better understood after first reading the stories. The stories more readily develop our appreciation for O'Connor's comic impulse and clearly express her focus on the importance of community and on the simple gestures of love that might finally help us to adjust to the modern world. Hazel's alienation from his community and inability to love results in psychic fragmentation. Mrs. Flood sees in his eyes at the end a mere "pinpoint of light"—his humanity nearly snuffed out.

In *The Violent Bear It Away,* the second novel, Mason likewise snuffs out his grand-nephew's hopes to develop beyond adolescence into an independent self responsible to the community. The pattern in the stories of a child's identity eclipsed by a parent's will is here represented in its most vivid form by the fate of Francis Tarwater. The novel ends as Francis mirrors the behavior of his uncle, who believes himself a prophet. Francis becomes like the "jagged shadow" that leads him toward the perverse "goal" of perpetuating his granduncle's will.[76] This same pattern is seen in the stories when Nelson adopts Head's racist view of the city, when the child in "A Circle in the Fire" acquires her mother's dread—"the new misery she felt [which] on her mother looked old" (*CS*, 193), and when Mary Fortune Pitts demonstrates a degree of aggression to match her grandfather's ruthless will.

When finally establishing O'Connor's place in American letters, we should acknowledge that her best works—"Parker's Back," "Revelation," "Everything That Rises Must Converge," "Greenleaf," "Good Country People," "The Displaced Person," "A Late Encounter with the Enemy," "The Artificial Nigger," "Judgement Day," "The Life You Save May Be Your Own," "A Good Man Is Hard to Find," and *The Violent Bear It Away*—represent so remarkable an achievement in terms of the comedy and the tragedy expressed that this very young and brilliant author should be acknowledged as one of America's masters of short fiction.

The challenge Flannery O'Connor offers her readers is to cross gender, racial, and class barriers, not for the sake of her destructive characters but for the sake of those "grotesques" who still manage a gesture of love in spite of their other failings, which epitomize human failings everywhere. Parker's gesture of love toward Sarah Ruth, Ruby Turpin's toward Claude, Julian's toward his mother, Head's toward Nelson, Mrs. Fox's toward her son Asbury, Thomas's mother's toward Sarah Ham, the grandmother's toward The Misfit, and even Guizac's toward his cousin are crucial events in a storyline that focuses on human nature struggling under pressure. We must not simply remember the worst of O'Connor's characters but must overcome our initial shock so as not to miss the wonderful human comedy magnificently played out by characters exhibiting a vitality true to the best as well as the worst in human nature.

Flannery O'Connor's mastery is suggested by the intense critical response to her work—a response that has prevented us from truly understanding the complexity of her art and from seeing ways to reconcile contradictory judgments about her characters. Her ability to involve us emotionally in the life of the work should not blind us to the need for rationally contemplating her stories in light of the fullest range of implications given the complexity of her mind and methods. Her interests in the social, psychological, philosophical, and theological issues of modern times must be considered. Then we can, depending on our own inclinations, fully give in to despair or, better, to the comic elements that ultimately draw us closer to O'Connor's characters as we recognize our own need for freedom to assert ourselves and freedom from the fear of physical or mental infirmity. O'Connor's rare gift of expressing the comic impulse in all-too-human portraits of serious intent is what has caused her art to earn so much interest today in Japan, the next arena of critical research. Her mix of the comic and the tragic elements of human life is also what will preserve her art in the centuries to come—especially as her insights into modern life and "the mystery of personality" are better understood.

Notes

1. For an article about the contradictions between *Mystery and Manners* and *The Habit of Being,* see Clara Claiborne Park, "Crippled Laughter: Toward Understanding Flannery O'Connor," *American Scholar* 51, no. 2 (1982):249–57.

2. Robert Coles devotes an entire chapter to this issue in his *Flannery O'Connor's South* (Baton Rouge: Louisiana State University Press, 1980).

3. "A" is a writer friend and correspondent who chooses to remain anonymous.

4. Melvin J. Friedman and Lewis A. Lawson, eds., *The Added Dimension: The Art and Mind of Flannery O'Connor* (New York: Fordham University Press, 1976), 231; "An Interview with Flannery O'Connor and Robert Penn Warren," *Vagabond* 4 (1960):14.

5. Sister M. Bernetta Quinn, "View from a Rock: The Fiction of Flannery O'Connor and J. F. Powers," *Critique: Studies in Modern Fiction* 2, no. 2 (1958):21.

6. Frederick Asals discovered this O'Connor statement in an unpublished document. See *Flannery O'Connor, the Imagination of Extremity* (Athens: University of Georgia Press, 1982), 130. Park in "Crippled Laughter" complains that O'Connor followed "the neo-critical orthodoxy of the self-sufficiency of the work to a fault" (249–57). O'Connor says she "distrusts" books on "the short story form" but calls "invaluable" (*Letters*, 83) Cleanth Brooks and Robert Penn Warren's *Understanding Fiction* (New York: F. S. Crofts, 1945); the first and second editions included an appendix on craft, an important consideration when reading O'Connor.

7. Murray Krieger, *The New Apologists for Poetry* (Minneapolis: University of Minnesota Press, 1956), 26.

8. Allen Tate, "Tension in Poetry," in *The Modern Critical Spectrum*, ed. Gerald Jay Goldberg and Nancy Marmer Goldberg (Englewood Cliffs, N.J.: Prentice-Hall, 1962), 83–92.

9. James Joyce, *A Portrait of the Artist as a Young Man: Text, Criticism, Notes*, ed. Chester G. Anderson (New York: Penguin, 1977).

10. I am indebted to Professor Chester G. Anderson for this observation and the example of "Eveline," Joyce's character who "sat at the window watching the evening invade the avenue"—an invasion that defines Eveline more than the setting.

11. Josephine Hendin, *The World of Flannery O'Connor* (Bloomington: Indiana University Press, 1970); Claire Katz [Kahane], "Flannery O'Connor's Rage of Vision," *American Literature* 46 (1974):54–67; Carol Shloss, *Flannery O'Connor's Dark Comedies: The Limits of Inference* (Baton Rouge: Louisiana State University Press, 1980); Martha Stephens, *The Question of Flannery O'Connor* (Baton Rouge: Louisiana State University Press, 1973); Ruth Vande Kieft, "Judgment in the Fiction of Flannery O'Connor," *Sewannee Review* 76 (1968):337–56.

12. Subsequent references to O'Connor's stories will appear parenthetically and are from *The Complete Stories* (New York: Farrar, Straus & Giroux, 1971); hereafter abbreviated *CS* followed by page number.

13. Edward Kessler traces recurring instances of grins and smiles in O'Connor's works and places her in the company of apocalyptic poets like Blake and Eliot. See "The Violence of Metaphor," in *Flannery O'Connor and the Language of Apocalypse* (Princeton, N.J.: Princeton University Press, 1986);

Cleanth Brooks and Robert Penn Warren, *Understanding Poetry* (New York: Holt, Rinehart, & Winston, 1960), 76, 292.

14. Cleanth Brooks, "The Formalist Critic" and "The Uses of Formal Analysis," in *Modern Critical Spectrum*, ed. Goldberg and Goldberg, 106.

15. Friedman and Lawson, *Added Dimension*, 229, 248.

16. Søren Kierkegaard, *Fear and Trembling and the Sickness unto Death*, trans. Walter Lowrie (Princeton, N.J.: Princeton University Press, 1954).

17. Nathan A. Scott, Jr., "Flannery O'Connor's Testimony: The Pressure of Glory," in Friedman and Lawson, *Added Dimension*, 138ff.

18. Sigmund Freud, "Archaic and Infantile Features in Dreams," in *Standard Edition of the Complete Psychological Works of Sigmund Freud*, trans. James Strachey, Anna Freud, and Alan Tyson, 24 vols. (London: Hogarth, 1957).

19. All references to O'Connor's drafts were taken from the manuscript files housed in the Ina Dillard Russell Library of Georgia College and will be cited parenthetically by file folder number preceded by the abbreviation *FO*.

20. See also Saul Bellow's *Dangling Man* (New York, 1944); such images are found throughout O'Connor's first novel; Friedrich Nietzsche, *Thus Spake Zarathustra* (New York: Dutton, 1960).

21. Claire Kahane, "The Artificial Niggers," *Massachusetts Review* 19 (1978):183–98.

22. This story is entitled "The Turkey" in *The Complete Stories*.

23. Friedman and Lawson, *Added Dimension*, 228.

24. See my article, "Apocalypse of Self, Resurrection of the Double: An Analysis of Flannery O'Connor's *The Violent Bear It Away*," *Literature and Psychology* 30, no. 3/4 (1980):100–111, for an analysis of O'Connor's second novel, the most obvious example of death-haunted adult males seeking to become parents in order to remake a child and thus extend their will in time. Moreover, O'Connor's first novel, *Wise Blood*, represents a death-haunted, aggressive, adult male quester, although, like the earlier types, not a parent.

25. O'Connor does say "What I call a moral basis is a good deal more than a masculine drive" (*Letters*, 126) and "all that feminine principle stuff . . . is . . . a regression . . . from what St. Paul means by charity" (*Letters*, 394), but she read Jung and Neumann in 1955 (*Letters*, 103) and declares "I admire [Jung] and . . . have been interested in the subject for some time" (*Letters*, 382). See C. G. Jung, *Modern Man in Search of a Soul* (London: K. Paul, Trench, Trubner, 1933); Erich Neumann, *The Origins and History of Consciousness* (Princeton, N.J.: Princeton University Press, 1971).

26. Otto Rank, *Beyond Psychology* (New York: Dover, 1958), 237.

27. Teilhard de Chardin, *The Phenomenon of Man* (New York: Harper & Row, 1959); *The Divine Milieu* (New York: Harper & Row, 1960); *On Suffering* (New York: Harper & Row, 1974).

28. Rank, *Beyond*, 223.

29. Joseph Campbell, *The Hero with a Thousand Faces* (New York: Meridian, 1956), 122.

30. Neumann, *Consciousness*, 218; Plato, *Dialogues of Plato*, trans. Jowett (New York: Washington Square Press, 1961), 177–78.

31. Claire [Katz] Kahane, "Flannery O'Connor's Rage of Vision," *American Literature* 46 (1974):54–67.

32. Frederick Asals, "The Double in Flannery O'Connor's Stories," *Flannery O'Connor Bulletin* 9 (1980):49–86.

33. Neumann, *Consciousness*, 16, 35.

34. Asals, "The Double," 70.

35. Ibid.

36. Ernest Becker, *The Denial of Death* (New York: Macmillan, 1973); *The Collected Poems of W. B. Yeats* (New York: Macmillan, 1950), 184; Sigmund Freud, *Civilization and Its Discontents* (1930), Vol. 21 of *Standard Edition* (London: Hogarth, 1957), 57–145.

37. Frederick Asals, "The Mythic Dimensions of Flannery O'Connor's 'Greenleaf,'" *Studies in Short Fiction* 5 (1968):317–30.

38. This acceptance of female impotence is also seen in "Why Do the Heathen Rage?" when the farm manager mother declares to her son: "Walter . . . you're a man. I'm only a woman" (*CS*, 485).

39. Mircea Eliade, *The Sacred and the Profane: The Nature of Religion* (New York: Harcourt, Brace, 1959).

40. See Friedman and Lawson, *Added Dimension*, 241; also *MM*: "The novelist is concerned with the mystery of personality, and you cannot say much that is significant about this mystery unless the characters you create exist with the marks of a believable society about them. The larger social context is simply left out of much current fiction, but it cannot be left out by the Southern writer" (198).

41. O'Connor's dislike for the social scientist was reinforced during her stint in 1948–49 at Yaddo, a writer's haven in Saratoga Springs, New York. There she confronted another writer with charges of having communist affiliations because she worried that a philanthropic endeavor designed to help artists was being misused. A counterattack from the Left became vicious, and O'Connor left Yaddo feeling disillusioned: she later writes about "the subject of [her] Yaddo deal and the general rottenness of Social Science" (*Letters*, 19). She also says that "the help [at Yaddo] was morally superior to the guests" (*Letters*, 364).

42. Erik H. Erikson, *Childhood and Society*, 2d ed. (New York: Norton, 1963); Erikson was a psychiatrist at Harvard.

43. Erikson, *Identity : Youth and Crisis* (New York: Norton, 1968), 269.

44. Chardin, *On Suffering*, 8–9, 11.

45. Chardin, *Phenomenon of Man*, 180, 263.

46. Sigmund Freud, *Beyond the Pleasure Principle* (New York: Liveright Publishing, 1950).

47. Erikson, *Identity*, 32.

48. Sigmund Freud, *Civilization and Its Discontents*.

49. Lawrence S. Kubie, "The Fantasy of Dirt," *Psychoanalytic Quarterly* 6 (1937):388–425; Joel Kovel, *White Racism: A Psychohistory* (New York: Random House, 1970), 177–230, 41; Mary Ellen Goodman, *Race Awareness in Young Children* (Cambridge, Mass.: Addison-Wesley, 1952).

50. Josephine Hendin, *The World of Flannery O'Connor* (Bloomington: Indiana University Press, 1970), 155.

51. Kahane, "Artificial Niggers," 184.

52. The Dominican Nuns of Our Lady of Perpetual Hope Home, *A Memoir of Mary Ann* (New York: Farrar, Straus & Cudahy, 1961), 19.

53. My reading of this story does not concern itself with Head's redemption. The early critical consensus was that theological issues were most important when reading this story: e.g., Asals, *O'Connor*; Turner F. Byrd, "Ironic Dimension in Flannery O'Connor's 'The Artificial Nigger,'" *Mississippi Quarterly* 21 (1968):243–51; A. R. Coulthard, "From Sermon to Parable: Four Conversion Stories by Flannery O'Connor," *American Literature* 55, no. 1 (1983): 55–71; Bob Dowell, "The Moment of Grace in the Fiction of Flannery O'Connor," *College English* 27 (1965):238; David Eggenschwiler, *The Christian Humanism of Flannery O'Connor* (Detroit: Wayne State University Press, 1972); Sister Kathleen Feeley, *Flannery O'Connor: Voice of the Peacock* (New Brunswick, N.J.: Rutger's University Press, 1972); Carter W. Martin, *The True Country: Themes in the Fiction of Flannery O'Connor* (Nashville: Vanderbilt University Press, 1971); James J. Napier, "'The Artificial Nigger' and the Authorial Intention," *Flannery O'Connor Bulletin* 10 (1981):87–92; Paul W. Nisley, "The Prison of Self: Isolation in Flannery O'Connor's Fiction," *Studies in Short Fiction* 17 (1980):49–54; Sister M. Bernetta Quinn, "Flannery O'Connor, a Realist of Distances," in Friedman and Lawson, *Added Dimension*; Kenneth Scouten, "'The Artificial Nigger': Mr. Head's Ironic Salvation," *Flannery O'Connor Bulletin* 9 (1980):87–97; Carol Shloss, *Flannery O'Connor's Dark Comedies: The Limits of Inference* (Baton Rouge: Louisiana State University Press, 1973).

54. Scouten, "Ironic Salvation," 90.

55. Norman N. Holland, *The Dynamics of Literary Response* (New York: Norton, 1975), 134.

56. Suzanne Morrow Paulson, "Flannery O'Connor's Divided Vision," Ph.D. dissertation, University of Minnesota, 1984; W. R. Allen, "Mr. Head and Hawthorne: Allusion and Conversion in Flannery O'Connor's 'The Artificial Nigger,'" *Studies in Short Fiction* 21 (1984):17–23.

57. Gaston Bachelard, *The Psychoanalysis of Fire* (Boston: Beacon Press, 1964), 4.

58. Kovel, *White Racism*, 41.

59. Kubie, "Dirt," 404.

60. Consider, for example, what "Paradise" might mean for Mr. Paradise, the child molester in "The River."

61. Teilhard de Chardin, *Phenomenon of Man*, 238.

62. Thomas M. Carlson charges that Stanley Edgar Hyman erroneously labels O'Connor a dualist and that as a writer she opposes all Manichaean attempts to separate flesh and spirit (see "Flannery O'Connor: The Manichaean Dilemma," *Sewanee Review* 77 [1969]:254–76). Frederick J. Hoffman (*The Art of Southern Fiction: A Study of Some Modern Novelists* [Carbondale: Southern Illinois University Press, 1967]) says that O'Connor herself criticizes "the Manichaean spirit of the times," as she puts it (94). Gene Kellogg (*The Vital Tradition: The Catholic Novel in a Period of Convergences* [Chicago: Loyola University Press, 1970]) says that O'Connor's imagination is formed by Jansenism (26). Allen Tate ("Flannery O'Connor: A Tribute," *Esprit* 8 [1964]:48–49) refers to O'Connor's "temperamental Jansenism." Marion Montgomery writes about "Flannery O'Connor and the Jansenist Problem in Fiction," *Southern Review* 14, no. 3 (1978):438.

63. According to the Catholic view, evil is the absence or negation of good and the direct result of perverse human will. Jacques Maritain likewise asserts that "evil is only a vacuum or a lack of being, a nothingness and a privation," in *God and the Permission of Evil*, trans. by Joseph W. Evans (Milwaukee: Bruce Publishing, 1966).

64. Attracted by what she called a "wonderful quotation," (*Letters*, 126), O'Connor borrows from Saint Cyril of Jerusalem.

65. See Walter Blair and Hamlin Hill, *America's Humor* (Oxford: Oxford University Press, 1978), for an analysis of "Vernacular characters," the coda "It is good to be shifty in a new country" (163), and a description of Longstreet's Simon Suggs (194), a possible influence.

66. Martha Chew, "Flannery O'Connor's Double-Edged Satire: The Idiot Daughter versus the Lady PhD," *Southern Quarterly* 19, no. 2 (1981):17–25.

67. "An Interview with Flannery O'Connor," *Censer* (College of St. Teresa), Summer 1965, 53.

68. See Saint Thomas Aquinas's discussion of Augustine and the presence of evil in the world as due to the greater good, that is, man's freedom (Anton C. Pegis, *Introduction to Saint Thomas Aquinas* [New York: Modern Library, 1948]), 216ff.

69. Maritain, *Permission of Evil*, 9.

70. Erik H. Erikson, *Identity: Youth and Crisis* (New York: Norton, 1968), 109.

71. I am indebted to Professor Chester G. Anderson, University of Minnesota, for many such observations about doubt and repression of guilt as a source of dividedness.

72. This story and others in the canon may be understood as gaining

authenticity by overcoming what Heidegger calls the "tranquillization about death" that occurs when we consider death as applicable only to others (see *Existentialism*, ed. Robert C. Solomon [New York: Modern Library, 1974], 112–14).

73. R. V. Cassill, ed. *The Norton Anthology of Short Fiction* (New York: Norton, 1986), 792.

74. Hendin, *World*, 29; André Bleikasten, "Writing of the Flesh: Tattoos and Taboos in 'Parker's Back,'" *Southern Literary Journal* 14, no. 2 (1982):17.

75. Wayne Booth, "Ready-made Values: 'Everything That Rises Must Converge,'" in *The Rhetoric of Irony*. (Chicago: University of Chicago Press, 1974).

76. *Three by O'Connor* (New York: Farrar, Straus & Giroux, 1983), 267.

Part 2

THE WRITER:
SELECTED COMMENTS BY O'CONNOR, HER FRIENDS, HER MENTORS, HER EDITORS, AND HER CRITICS

Introduction

You cannot read a story by what you get out of a letter.

(Letters, 170)

To provide a sense of O'Connor as an individual working in a particular time and place, this section presents short excerpts from her letters, lectures, manuscripts, and interviews. The comments of critics, interviewers, journalists, reviewers, and community members alternate with the author's own words. In the first section, I contrast O'Connor's own comments about her art, her reader, and her community with certain newspaper, magazine, and journal articles that misquote or misinterpret O'Connor to some degree. This section ends with carefully selected comments by those well-qualified to speak of her art and her person. Margaret Meaders was the editor for the Georgia College newspaper when O'Connor was submitting cartoons for publication; Caroline Gordon is a writer friend with whom O'Connor shared early drafts of her stories; and Professor Ted R. Spivey is a family friend who teaches at Georgia State University in Atlanta. Published here for the first time are the interview of Margaret Meaders and the comments of Paul Engle, O'Connor's mentor at the University of Iowa Writer's Workshop; Robert Giroux, her publisher and friend; and Cecil Dawkins, a close writer friend and teacher.

The second section focuses on the critics who judge O'Connor's narrative voice as cruel. I hope that interweaving short excerpts from O'Connor's more or less off-the-cuff remarks and criticisms of the stories will clarify why O'Connor was, as Melvin J. Friedman puts it, "ill-tempered" in response to what was said about her art. This sampling of critical commentary begins with the most recent comments by Friedman in 1985 and then provides examples of similar criticisms in the seventies, the sixties, and the fifties. These criticisms are directed more toward O'Connor as a person than to her stories.

To correct misreadings of her work, O'Connor responded to specific criticisms of herself and her stories by projecting a gracious Southern mask, sometimes confusing rather than clarifying the issue. Although some sound insights are to be found by studying O'Connor's life, her letters, and her essays, readers should focus primarily on the poetic texture of the stories, the complex metaphoric patterns found there, her methods of indirection, the nature of the comic impulse, the genre O'Connor claims as her own (grotesque tragicomedy), and the modernist tradition in which she wrote.

In fact, it is important to notice that O'Connor adjusts what she says, depending on her correspondent or reader. For example, when writing to Hawkes she reinforces his judgment that as a narrator her satiric edge puts her on the side of the devil. But when writing to others, it is clear that she disapproved of what he said. She does give in, however. She sometimes adopts Hawkes's view and that of those who considered her "odd" or, as she puts it in the quote below, "eccentric." This latter judgment originated in her community and was a hard one for her to overcome. Even a dorm mom at Georgia College declared to me in 1982 that "Flannery was an odd duck—a man before her time!"

Most of the manuscript files are not dated, but wherever possible, I have included dates.[1] Chronology may or may not be significant. As previously mentioned, the sequence of critical commentary, begins with the most recent criticisms and works backward. Chronology is also important in the sequence of O'Connor's responses to John Hawkes's judgment that her narrative voice is "on the devil's side." And yet as I was deciding about the arrangement of this part of the book, I considered content first of all. The final long excerpt is from the introduction to *A Memoir of Mary Ann,* the only authorial statement O'Connor specified as being necessary to understanding her art.

Note

1. The quotations on pages 123, 125–28, 139–40 and 146 below from the unpublished manuscripts are copyright © 1988 by the Estate of Flannery O'Connor and used with their permission and that of the author's literary executor, Robert Giroux.

The Author's Art, Her Reader, and Her Community

Flannery O'Connor, letter to Father J. H. McCown, 9 May 1956: "art is wholly concerned with the good of that which is made; it has no utilitarian end. If you do manage to use it successfully for social, religious, or other purposes, it is because you make it art first."[1]

Flannery O'Connor, essay: "The Southern writer is forced from all sides to make his gaze extend beyond the surface, beyond mere problems, until it touches that realm which is the concern of prophets and poets. . . . The direction of many of us will be more toward poetry than toward the traditional novel."[2]

Flannery O'Connor, manuscript: "Henry James said that the morality of a piece of fiction depends on the felt life that was in it. This means the depth at which life is felt and the deepest acts of feeling and vision certainly include moral judgment. Two writers may look at the same event and not see the same thing at all, because one looks with indifference and one looks with horror. It's the business of the novelist to reproduce what he sees, but it is his business to see as deeply into everything as possible, and it is here, that if he is a Catholic, his faith should enter in. . . . When we look at the serious fiction written by the Catholics in these times, we find a striking preoccupation with what is seedy and evil and violent. The pious argument against such novels goes something like this: if you believe in the redemption, your ultimate vision is one of hope so in what you see you must be true to this ultimate vision; you must pass over the evil you see and look for the good because the good is there; the good is the ultimate reality.

"The beginning of an answer to this is that the good is the ultimate reality, but the ultimate reality has been weakened in human beings as a result of the fall, and it is this weakened life that we see. And it is wrong, moreover, to assume that the writer chooses what he will see and what he will not. What one sees is given by circumstances and by the nature of one's particular type of perception. A writer writes about what he is able to make believable."[3]

The Writer

Time, review of *Everything That Rises Must Converge,* 1965: "Mary Flannery O'Connor had the luck of the Irish, or seemed to. At 25 she was pretty, witty, and had published fiction in some of the best little magazines. At 26, she came down with an incurable form of *lupus erythematosus.* . . . But Author O'Connor had the stubbornness of the Irish, too. . . . Before her death last August, she had published two novels . . . of rare intensity, and one volume of ten short stories (*A Good Man Is Hard to Find*) that included four macabre masterpieces. . . .

"A lifelong Catholic, Author O'Connor wrote exclusively of ultimate things: sin and salvation, death and rebirth, the old Adam and the new life. But she was a poet of region as well as religion, and in this new collection of nine stories, which belong among the finest examples of American Gothic, she celebrates in Southern guises the old violent dialogue of the demonic and the divine. . . .

"Author O'Connor was a verbal magician whose phrases flamed like matches in the dark revealing a face in a flash (a child's features contorted with grief into 'a puzzle of small red lumps'), a life in a single insight ('a sniveler after the ineffable'). But the motivation of character and the imitation of life did not finally interest Author O'Connor. 'The meaning of a story,' she once wrote, 'begins at a depth where these things have been exhausted.'"[4]

Flannery O'Connor, essay: "The fiction writer presents mystery through manners, grace through nature, but when he finishes there always has to be left over that sense of Mystery which cannot be accounted for by any human formula."[5]

Flannery O'Connor, interview, *Esprit,* 1959:
Question: "What is a short story?
Answer: "This is a hellish question inspired by the devil who tempts textbook publishers. . . . The best I can do is tell you what a story is not: (1) . . . a joke, (2) . . . an anecdote, (3) a lyric rhapsody in prose, (4) . . . a case history, (5) . . . a reported incident. It is none of these things because it has an extra dimension . . . [which] comes about when the writer puts us in the middle of some human action and shows it as it is illuminated and outlined by mystery. In every story there is some minor revelation which, no matter how funny the story may be, gives us a hint of the unknown, of death."[6]

Flannery O'Connor, essay: "Fiction is about everything human and we are made out of dust, and if you scorn getting yourself dusty, then you shouldn't try to write fiction."[7]

The Author's Art, Her Reader, and Her Community

Flannery O'Connor, manuscript: "I think the average reader believes that the fiction of the South can be divided into two kinds, which he would call the Romantic and the Realistic. The Romantic would be the magnolia novels of Southern history and the Realistic would be the kind that describes how a whole family goes to town to buy a collective toothbrush. The former are good publicity and the latter are not.

"There was such a spate of these so-called Realistic novels in the thirties that once Story Magazine had a parody of them that began: 'Where's Paw?—Oh Paw, he's down resting on the manure pile.'

"People seem to feel that the Realism of a novel is in direct proportion to the sordidness of the material, but actually, although this sort of thing is commonly called Realism, it is only Romanticism running in the opposite direction. At one end there is a sentimentality of the veranda and at the other a sentimentality of the outhouse."[8]

Margaret Turner, *Atlanta Journal and Constitution*, 1960: "According to critics, Flannery writes better than nearly anybody else now living. Her writing has been compared to the works of Tennessee Williams, William Faulkner, and the Russian novelist and short-story writer Dostoeyevsky [*sic*]. All are distinguished by their character studies which are in the realm of abnormal psychology."[9]

Flannery O'Connor, letter to a professor of English, 28 March 1961: "I am not interested in abnormal psychology."[10]

Celestine Sibley, "Baboons Differ with Giraffes," *Atlanta Constitution*, 1957: "That prize-winning short story writer, Miss Flannery O'Connor, came up from her home in Milledgeville the other night to speak of writers and writing at Emory University. . . . despite her scorching scorn for amateurs and people who write mostly to 'fill their pockets,' she was the hit of the season. . . .

"Not that the quiet, shy-seeming Miss O'Connor was so blunt as all that. She did compare the Emory course to a sort of portable zoo, wherein the animals appear one at a time 'and what the giraffe says this week will be contradicted by the baboon next week. . . .' But her fierce and single-minded devotion to good writing, her intelligence and unrelenting honesty gave everything she said value and made it not only palatable but altogether captivating to those of us who are either earnest amateurs or seekers after a fast buck. . . .

"She quoted a man who said writing a novel was like 'giving birth to a sideways piano.'"[11]

Flannery O'Connor, manuscript: "Some writer has said that when he finished his book he felt as if he had given birth to a Steinway piano.

There is a sense of relief but there's usually another Steinway piano on the way and the relief does not last long."[12]

Flannery O'Connor, interview, *Motley*, 1958:

Question: "How much entertainment should a critical reader get from a novel? . . .

Answer: "This depends on what you mean by entertainment. If you mean pleasure for the mind, the answer is 100%. . . . If you mean amusement, none is necessary."[13]

Vivian Mercier, *Hudson Review*, 1960: "Whether one reads *The Violent Bear It Away* ironically or as the story of a genuine vocation, the realistic convention in which it is written jars too sharply against the basic improbability of the plot. Only if set in a dream world . . . could this fable remain convincing after one has put down the book. I read it with breathless attention, as one reads the short stories in Miss O'Connor's *A Good Man Is Hard to Find*, but ultimately I felt cheated. No form of entertainment is less satisfying than a performance by a conjuror."[14]

Flannery O'Connor, manuscript: "After my book came out I had a letter from a relative saying, 'You are correct. I do not like your novel. The world is depressed enough as it is and your mission is to cheer us up.' My cousin was confusing the mission of the novelist with that of the organ-grinder. . . . These people see the novel as an escape from reality, whereas the novelist sees it as a penetration of reality."[15]

Flannery O'Connor, manuscript: "I think that the fiction writer comes in for more ignorant criticism today, by just anybody, than does any other kind of artist. There's always a loud voice coming from somewhere that tells him he is not doing his duty. . . . Anyone who can read a seed catalogue thinks he can read a novel or a short story. Painters and musicians are protected somewhat because they don't deal in what everyone already knows about, but the fiction writer writes about life and so anyone *living* considers himself an authority on it."[16]

Flannery O'Connor, manuscript: "I used to think it should be possible to write for some supposed elite, for the people who attend the universities and sometimes know how to read, but I have since found that though you may publish your stories in the *Yale Review*, if they are any good at all you are eventually going to get a letter from some old person in California or some inmate of the federal penitentiary or the state insane asylum or the local poor house telling you where you have failed to meet his needs."[17]

Flannery O'Connor, letter to "A," 14 November 1959: "I am not afraid that the book [*The Violent Bear It Away*] will be controversial, I'm afraid it will not be controversial. I'm afraid it will just be damned and dropped, genteelly sneered at, a few superior kicks from one or two and that will be that."[18]

Flannery O'Connor, manuscript: "I have read any number of reviews which call my own stories savage and brutal and which hint at impiety, whereas the fact is that they could all be read with profit in any self-respecting Sunday school."[19]

Flannery O'Connor, letter to "A," 25 December 1963: "C. Carver [her editor] thought ['Revelation'] one of my most powerful stories and probably my *blackest*. Found Ruby evil. Found end vision to confirm same. . . . suggested I leave it out.

"I am not going to leave it out. I am going to deepen it so that there'll be no mistaking Ruby is not just an evil Glad Annie.

"I've really been battling this problem all my writing days."[20]

Flannery O'Connor, interview by Harvey Breit, 1959:

Breit: "Is there something to being a Southerner in terms of literature?

O'Connor: "I think it's easier for a Southerner to begin writing than for anyone from almost any other section of the country, because we have so many conventions and so much tension in the South. We have a content to begin on.

Breit: "Somebody once tried to relate the South as it exists now and in the past twenty years to the Russia of the late 19th century, where a great novel came out with Tolstoy and Dostoevsky, and Gogol, and Turgenev, and Chekhov. That there was the same type of situation— a great tension and a great impact of the new social life on the old conventions. Do you think there's something in that?

O'Connor: "I think there is. . . . to overcome regionalism, you must have a great deal of self-knowledge. I think to know yourself is to know your region, and that it's also to know the world, and, in a sense, paradoxically, it's also to be exiled from the world."[21]

Flannery O'Connor, *Esprit*, 1963: "Unless the novelist has gone utterly out of his mind, his aim is still communication and communication suggests talking inside a community. One of the reasons Southern fiction thrives is that our best writers are able to do this. They are not alienated."[22]

Flannery O'Connor, essay: "As a fiction writer who is a Southerner, I use the idiom and the manners of the country I know, but I don't consider that I write *about* the South."[23]

Flannery O'Connor, manuscript: "This discovery of being bound to a particular society and a particular history, to particular sounds and a particular idiom, is for the writer the beginning of a recognition of himself as finite subject, limited, the beginning of a recognition that first puts his work in a real human perspective for him. It is a perspective which shows him his creaturehood."[24]

Flannery O'Connor, manuscript: "An idiom characterizes a society; we carry our history around in our idiom as well as everything else essential to us as a people bound together by common experiences."[25]

Flannery O'Connor, letter to John Hawkes, 1961: "The herd has been known to be right, in which case the one who leaves it is doing evil. When the herd is wrong, the one who leaves it is not doing evil but the right thing."[26]

Flannery O'Connor, manuscript: "The chief event of the spring when I was growing up was the annual garden club pilgrimage of homes. Then various houses in Milledgeville, including our own, were opened to the public, which trouped through in respectful solemnity to view the past. This was a past which happened to be in excellent working order and in which I lived. My attitude toward these occasions was pride, the outward face of which was boredom and mockery. I signed my name and the name of my chicken, Colonel Egvert, in the guest book and listed our address as Hungry and doubtless died laughing at myself. These pilgrimages still go on . . . and now I notice that the children dress up in antebellum costume and some of the ladies do, too. Probably if I were still eleven this would only add to my merriment—for a child eats up fakery—but now beneath an appreciation of its comic character, it increases my unease."[27]

Flannery O'Connor, manuscript: "Parochial school authorities looked askance at my efforts to attract attention in third grade composition by substituting 'St. Cecelia' for 'Rover' in sentences running, 'Throw the ball to Rover.' . . . Eventually being graduated to a progressive high school, I was pounced upon as Specimen D of the self-expressive adolescent. . . . Literary expression was here encouraged in all matters except reflections on progressive education and critical teaching. It was a source of some small discomfort to these teachers that I could add only with the use of my fingers, confused history with a foreign language, and put 90% of my originality into my spelling. They overlooked such matters, however, on the assumption that if I ever became a writer, I could cease using my brains altogether."[28]

Time, review of *"The Complete Stories,* 1971: "This collection brings together for the first time in one book all of Miss O'Connor's stories. Every one is good enough so that if it were the only example of her work to survive, it would be evident that the writer possessed high talent and a remarkably unclouded, unabstract, demanding intelligence. The best are among the best American short stories ever written.[29]

Thomas Merton, *Raids on the Unspeakable,* 1964: "When I read [O'Connor] I don't think of Hemingway, or Katherine Anne Porter, or Sartre, but rather of someone like Sophocles. What more can be said of a writer? I write her name with honor, for all the truth and all the craft with which she shows man's fall and his dishonor."[30]

Robert Giroux, letter to Suzanne Morrow Paulson, 1987: "When I first met Flannery O'Connor, before I had become her publisher, I sensed behind her soft-spoken speech, clear-eyed gaze, and shy manner her tremendous strength as a writer. As her stories and novels came in, I noted the spectacular development of her sense of comedy, and I marvelled at the fecundity of her imagination, her great intelligence, and unsparing honesty. With the posthumous publication of her essays and letters, I recognized the whole truth: she is a genius and a classic, whose work belongs in the pantheon of American writers."

Paul Engle, director of the University of Iowa Writer's Workshop, interview by Suzanne Morrow Paulson, 1982: "Flannery was the most sensible and self-aware student ever at Iowa. She had no illusions whatsoever about the complexity of life, and that's why she put so much complexity into her fiction. No writer was ever more aware of what she wrote. She was a complicated person—a subtle person. Simple and unsubtle readers are not her proper readers."

Margaret Meaders, adviser for the Georgia College newspaper and friend of the family, 1962: "Through my office window I watched the senior cross the street, enter the main campus, and move along the broad walk under the old, plumed elms. We Southerners would say that she 'moseyed.' I never remember seeing her hurry. Many years had to pass before it occurred to me that if you know where you're going soon enough and get started in that direction, you don't have to hurry. And I'm sure now that Flannery O'Connor has known most of her life where she was going.

". . . Flannery would soon turn out to be one of the powerful writers of her generation. . . .

". . . O'Connor offerings were never conspicuously present in the campus literary magazine. She produced none of the one-act plays performed annually in heated class competitions. Being a campus big shot, a professional bright-girl-sure-to-heap-glory-on-all-of-us seemed as alien to slow-spoken, quiet-mannered Flannery as her stories and novels were later to the nice old ladies and other members of 'southern gentility' peopling her town and making up her earliest (and most embarrassed) public.

"... She was coming to see me, that fall day in 1944, in my capacity as faculty adviser to the student newspaper. But she wasn't bringing any literary piece clutched in any hot, little fist. She was bringing cartoons. Wonderful, merry cartoons. . . . Penetratingly conceived and skillfully executed, those cartoons were the most professional student work I have ever seen. . . .

"Her cartoons ill-prepared me for the fierce, elemental tragedies she was to set down in words within less than five years. But the economy of line and the swift, sure stabs were signposts of sorts, as were her small but telling rebellions against sacred systems and feminine foibles. . . .

"Flannery's family is *old* and proud and genteel—devoutly Catholic. Many of the friends of her mother and her aunt and of her friends' mothers and aunts are more proper than the properest Bostonians. . . . How then, as one elderly lady exclaimed, did Flannery O'Connor ever hear all the ugly words she wrote into her books—much less learn what they meant!

"... I was present at the first Author's Tea given for Flannery. It was held on the campus of the Georgia State College for Women (her first Alma Mater) in Milledgeville. . . . Having read her book, I understood perfectly the quandary that had befallen so many of the dressed-up visitors. Here was a hometown girl who with her first venture had made the big time. The critics were saying 'a remarkable accomplishment, remarkably precocious beginning' . . . 'taut, dry, economical and objective prose' . . . 'a good solid work' . . . 'introduces its author as a writer of power' . . . 'unusually mature, perceptive, and imaginative.' Regina Cline's daughter was evidently something of a genius—and at only twenty-six. . . . Flannery's book was about people who came to the back door if they came at all, people who made ugly noises on street corners and thought queer, godless thoughts, using ugly words to think them. What to do? Everybody liked the child. Everybody was glad that she'd got something published, but one did wish that it had been something ladylike. . . .

". . . When asked why she (along with certain other Southern writers) writes about freaks, she says, 'Because we can still recognize one. In the South where most people believe in original sin [Flannery does], our sense of evil is still just strong enough to make us skeptical about most modern solutions, no matter how we long to embrace them. We are still held by a sense of mystery, however much against our will. The prophet-freaks of Southern literature are not images of the man in the street. They are images of the man forced out to meet the extremes of his own nature. . . . '

". . . Thus, there is in Flannery—as in Flannery's works (cartoons, paintings, short stories, novels, speeches)—an arresting combination of a recognition of the ridiculous and the ironic, a strong feeling for the tragic, a sixth sense about human frailties, and an unwavering sense of responsibility for putting things as she sees them. . . .

"All in all, Flannery O'Connor is quite a person. For several years she has had a physical difficulty to put up with—a chronic crippling illness that forces the use of crutches. She bears it with equanimity and humor: 'The disease is of no consequence to my writing, since for that I use my head and not my feet. . . .'

"She writes regularly in the morning—three hours on schedule, then settles herself into a comfortable rocking chair on her front porch. 'If I waited for inspiration, I'd still be waiting.' She takes her talent as a vocation, close friends say, in the old Catholic sense of the term as set forth by Thomas Aquinas and others. . . .

"Flannery's correspondence is considerable. Important people come and go, but the community does not hear about them except most casually. The professor [Spivey] says that the town feels it has an important person—even a celebrity—on its hands and is curiously pleased; but few citizens really think she is much of a writer, and even fewer approve of what she writes about. . . .

"Undoubtedly, there are those citizens who raised bewildered or skeptical eyebrows at the words (if they saw them) of Orville Prescott, who found much he did not like about her latest novel *The Violent Bear It Away* and said so in his *New York Times* review, but who nevertheless had much to say about the ability of the author: 'Flannery O'Connor, whose talent for fiction is so great as to be almost overwhelming, is a sort of literary white witch. She writes with blazing skill . . . with dazzling verbal power that makes Miss O'Connor's short stories unforgettable. The language is . . . original and striking. The intricate shifts in time and point of view are . . . deftly and unobtrusively contrived. The smooth rush of the narrative is as compelling. These are great virtues. . . .'

"The day she sauntered along under the arching elms, I did not dream that in so short a while the quiet, somewhat withdrawn, unhurried girl would go so far. . . . Literary witch she may be; self-disciplined, friendly, good-humored, hard-working, wise, fun, she certainly is."[31]

Margaret Meaders, telephone interview by Suzanne Paulson, 1983:

Paulson: "What do you think about critics who see Flannery as a cruel satirist?

Meaders: "They don't understand her art. People who understand humor see it even in her most tragic stories because it is there. Her stories represent a sort of laughing at life. That's what she did with her own life. She took things very seriously but also had the light touch toward life. Many people wouldn't believe that unless they had known her. Probably the ability to see the light side made life possible for her in the last few years. She suffered a great deal [from lupus] and rarely ever mentioned it. She still could be a great humorist.

"Flannery had on campus a very close friend, Betty Boyd Love. And the two of them went into a special honors program as extraordinary young women. Both of them died relatively young. Flannery observed life and then wrote about it. Betty observed life and then did something about it. The two of them made interesting lives to observe. Flannery finished college in three years . . . would have graduated in 1946 but completed her program in 1945.

Paulson: "What were her interests in high school?

Meaders: "It was always literary for both of them. Flannery was more withdrawn. Betty was a campus leader. But they never missed a trick. They knew everything that was going on around them. Both were philosophical. Flannery wanted to *do* with words, Betty with action. They were remarkable.

Paulson: "How did O'Connor's mother affect her work?

Meaders: "Miss Regina [O'Connor's mother] never understood Flannery, but she was always willing to defend her and look after her. She was a typical Southern lady. Flannery was something of a problem to her family, but they did recognize that she had tremendous talent and were proud of her.

"Miss Regina especially dislikes commentators getting into the background of the Cline family. Her two oldest sisters were the most

professional Southern ladies I've ever known. There was a certain de-
corum to be maintained, and Flannery didn't fit into it. There have
been so many attempts by the critics at psychological interpretations
trying to explain Flannery in relation to her mother. There was a silly
thing explaining that everything grew out of Flannery's hatred of her
mother. That was perfectly ridiculous. That's one of the problems of
dying young. Conclusions are reached before the author has made
things clear.

"Flannery was one of the best observers of what was going on around
her that I've ever known. She didn't have to go far to find material to
suit her. What she did then was to understand it. It was a common
occurrence on Saturday afternoons for itinerant preachers to gather on
the courthouse square. This went on throughout Georgia and most of
the South. I can remember any number of very intense preachers, not
ordained at all, preaching to only three followers. Maybe as many as
twelve. Flannery didn't have to invent her characters or her plots. Remember 'A Late Encounter with the Enemy'? I was in charge of the
summer graduation ceremonies when that old man was brought back
by his daughter. Flannery with true genius turned his visit into a brilliant short story. . . .

Paulson: "Flannery's women characters more often rebel against
feminine foibles related to being a Southern lady. Is Sally Poker Sash's
reliance on her father for a sense of self-worth important in that story?

Meaders: "Yes, I think it was. But this story harkens back to a South
holding on to all the symbols of the Confederacy and then links them
with the future in the form of Sally Poker Sash's accomplishing what
she set out so many years before to accomplish. This old general
started off as a drummer boy, but with each passing year, the remaining
soldiers were promoted. It took Flannery's kind of genius to put a sociological touch to that story. And yet it identified something really
important in the lives of people far beyond the region of the South.
She was not writing about a decadent Southern aristocracy but about
the human condition. . . .

Paulson: "You mentioned O'Connor's rebellion against sacred systems. Paul Engle says that she never mentioned religion to him. How
closely did she adhere to her Catholic faith?

Meaders: "I never heard her in my entire experience with Flannery
ever mention anything religious. I never was made aware of whether
she did or did not adhere to the Catholic modes of behavior or whether
she ever missed mass. I would never have known her religious affilia-

tion if I hadn't known her family. I simply don't know how closely she adhered to her religious doctrine. Perhaps I should have said sacrosanct systems; I was referring to social standards, not religious creeds.

Paulson: "Her work does seem Catholic in the values it suggests. Given the Catholic emphasis on charity and humility, what do you think of critics suggesting that O'Connor's work is not comic and that she rails against the world because of her disease?

Meaders: "I wrote my article and let her read it because I knew she had been personally hurt by what people were saying about her illness and her art. I didn't want to write anything that would add to that unhappiness with the critical response to her work. She approved of my article ["Flannery O'Connor: Literary Witch", pp. 129–33 above].

Paulson: "Some critics suggest Flannery was somewhat racist. Does she have sympathy for the suffering of blacks?

Meaders: "She has sympathy for suffering wherever. I don't think race mattered to her. Nor any other category of humanity. The actuality of human life without categorizing it into any mold is what concerned her.

Paulson: "How can a biographer get her character right? She is so complex. Do you suppose Flannery's mother has autobiographical materials that would help us to define her?

Meaders: "Flannery did very little about Flannery. She never philosophized about her own life, made no effort to present Flannery to anybody. Her work is almost entirely symbolic, ironic. She was taken up with the battle of living and with the fact that life could be funny. That she was so subtle made it difficult for anyone to understand her work or her person. She herself was so subtle. Every breath she drew had meaning, but she never thought about herself. She never made any effort to being a big name on campus. Never. It never occurred to her. She had no interest in being recognized, in being important.

Paulson: "I think from reading the stories that she read a great deal of philosophical, sociological, and psychological stuff not represented in what is supposed to be her personal library on display at Georgia College. There is a great deal of such material in that library, but the collected letters indicate that she read even more. She seems to have read broadly the works of many different writers all over the world and in many different fields. Did O'Connor feel confined to her region?

Meaders: "A bright, young woman such as O'Connor must have felt some incompatibility with being limited physically to a rural area of the South. Many women students at Georgia College were chaffing against the strictures of the code. In the South, there was a definite pattern of behavior and of values among the people who considered themselves aristocrats. For Flannery, she would not chaff so much as just silently feel annoyed. She would have seen how silly and shallow being a Southern lady was. She wasn't really bothered by it, though, because she wasn't a social creature and wasn't called upon to be one for the most part. She was never a social butterfly. But the pressures to conform to the code were great. . . . In the old families, the greatest security still remained that code. The code was the platform on which their social importance rested. For those families, and the Clines were among them, failure to live by that code shook the security of the whole family. It's not that they would object to a career, however. Many Southern women were forced into careers. Mrs. O'Connor has been a very independent woman herself. She has been a good farm manager. She has managed to take care of Flannery and herself quite well. She's a dainty little woman, the last sort of woman you would expect to go out and be able to manage a big farm. But she did it. So there's been determination in the family. The Clines had a lot of determination, but they did have the code of living properly and maintaining the position of the family name. This caused some trouble for Flannery."

Caroline Gordon, writer friend and wife of Alan Tate, 1955: "This first collection of short stories by Flannery O'Connor exhibits what Henry James, in 'a partial portrait' of Guy de Maupassant, called 'the artful beauty of a master.' James added that Maupassant was 'a *case*, an embarrassment, a lion in the path.' The contemporary reviewer, called upon to evaluate the achievement of the young American writer, may well feel that a lioness has strayed across *his* path. O'Connor's works, like Maupassant's, are characterized by precision, density and an almost alarming circumscription. There are few landscapes in her stories. Her characters seem to move in the hard, white glare of a searchlight— or perhaps it is more as if the author viewed her subjects through the knothole in a fence or wall. . . . She is, like Maupassant, very much of her time."[32]

Ted R. Spivey, friend of the family and Georgia State University professor, 1972: "When I first visited Flannery O'Connor at her home just north of Milledgeville in the summer of 1958, she told me that she occasionally received letters from prison inmates. And she added that they seemed to understand what she was writing better than other people. She felt in 1958 that her stories were understood by very few. But

The Writer

early in the sixties a new understanding of her work seemed to appear in many quarters not only among university critics but also in the hearts and minds of an audience she was beginning to know in public appearances a few years before her death in 1964. This audience was the great body of American college students, who were reading her stories and novels in anthologies and in paperback volumes that were then appearing in increasing numbers.

"In teaching O'Connor's work for more than fifteen years, I have observed that an awareness of the affinity intelligent students have both for the author and for her stories becomes stronger every year. . . .

"The landscape of Flannery's South is at once fantastic and baroque. It represents a point of view and a way of life strange and yet familiar, remote and yet as new as tomorrow. And thinking back to the various discussions Flannery and I had together at Andalusia farm, I cannot account for that vision of the South contained in her work. Her mind was that of a modern intellectual of the sort found in universities, with the addition of a strong Christian faith. . . . Like the French, Flannery was open to many currents of thought, and in her conversation there was the urbanity of one acquainted with the intellectual world of her day. The strange South of her writing was not in her daily thought and conversation as far as I ever knew.

". . . Above all, I think that the dominant impression I always had of her was of a person deeply immersed in the profession of letters and of someone acutely knowledgeable about the serious writers of our times. As early as 1958, for instance, she seemed aware of the growing importance of James Dickey. For her, even then, he was one of the nation's important contemporary poets.

"From what I knew of her personally and from what I have read by others about her, I cannot find Flannery's South. Nor can I find it in the books and critical articles that are now appearing everywhere, most of them perceptive but none accounting for the strangeness of the world she created. Flannery herself gave no hints to me of the sources of her vision of the South. In fact some people who know her work but never met her have thought that she was a Southern conservative, like Caroline Gordon, for instance, with whom she was closely associated. In fact, I found her to be a Southern liberal, concerned with problems of integration and racism. Like a growing number of Catholics in our day, she did not see any incompatibility between her political liberalism and the practice of her religion. Her conversation on serious matters was thoughtful and penetrating, and often spiced with her surprising wit. But an author, especially an American author, as D. H. Lawrence points out in *Studies in Classic American Literature*, is usually not aware of the sources of his creative power. It is as if he has to keep his conscious mind darkened on certain matters in order to transmit a vision that is too strange to be accepted by the author and his own generation. It well may be that we will begin to discover O'Connor's South when we see it in the eyes of that generation born after World War II, which teachers now confront in the classrooms of our high schools and colleges.

". . . it is still much too soon to draw a psychic map of her South. . . . Yet my own speculations have led me to believe that it is the spirit of the Spanish Catholicism of an earlier day, summed up for me, at least, in the figure of Don Quixote, that haunts much of her best work. . . . When I say Spanish Catholicism I am thinking mainly of Spanish culture from the Renaissance to the present. Catholicism and Spanish culture are inseparable, and yet the two are best represented to the modern mind not by St. Teresa (the only saint I ever heard Flannery discuss with enthusiasm) but by that improbable knight Don Quixote of La Mancha. If one doubts the centrality of this knight to Spanish culture even today, let him sit for half a day, as I have done, in the little park in the center of Madrid which holds the statues of Don Quixote and Sancho Panza and study the faces of contemporary Spaniards as they gaze at these two figures.

"As I play around with the theory, it seems to apply to the whole Southern culture. Historians have traced the medievalism of antebellum Southerners to Romantic medievalism in general and to Sir Walter Scott's novels in particular. But possibly this medievalism only provided some of the trappings of Southern character; whereas, I believe, a deep stream of medievalism exists in Southern life from the seventeenth century forward that is related to an underground river of Spanish culture flowing undetected by most people through the life of the South. But why the South only? Maybe F. Scott Fitzgerald made a profounder statement than anyone knew when he had Nick Carraway say at the end of *The Great Gatsby*, speaking of the Long Island rich, 'I see it as a night scene by El Greco.' And Kazin in his statement about O'Connor speaks of 'something secret about America called the *South*.' Maybe there is a fantastic and baroque *South* in the soul of every American, partially submerged by our pragmatic, mechanistic civilization, now emerging in the lives of those no longer satisfied with the machine-dominated, man-isolating social *system* we have willed. Maybe Spain has been there all the time. If so, O'Connor might be a greater visionary than anyone has realized.

"Don Quixote is a man unable to live with the atomistic society of the post-medieval world, and if others are blind enough to accept social fragmentation, he refuses to live without those ideals that for him make true community possible. . . .

". . . Both Cervantes and O'Connor sympathize deeply with their characters because they are at least concerned with the individual and communal values, whereas the actions of people they encounter spring from selfishness. But both authors make it plain that even though the characters' hearts may be in the right place, they nevertheless are possessed by a fanatical madness, a gentle, humorous madness in Cervantes' work and a wilder, more destructive madness in O'Connor's writing, but still a madness.

". . . I think it is clear to the careful reader that Flannery's great subject is the person of *wise blood*, to use her phrase, who is driven to seek God even while fleeing Him. Flannery's South has at its center this person, who seems grotesque to those who have accepted our machine-dominated society in the belief that it is the only reality they can know. Her gift gave her the power to bring to life these strange modern Don Quixotes."[33]

Cecil Dawkins, letter to Suzanne Morrow Paulson, 1988: "Flannery O'Connor was indeed extraordinary, a true genius and, that rare being, a good person. Her comments on Mary Ann say clearly how well she knew the grotesquerie of sentimentality, and how it warps any picture of the human condition it touches. It is ironic that this author's lack of sentimentality has been seen as grotesque. I have always found her portraiture truly tender, especially as it clothes evil in her particular brand of humor."

The Critics and
O'Connor's Responses

Melvin J. Friedman, introduction to *Critical Essays on Flannery O'Connor*, 1985: "*The Habit of Being* is filled with O'Connor's ill-tempered responses to reviewers, critics, and even friends who she believed misunderstood her work. Yet except for early misreadings, unfounded accusations of her fiction shamefully indulging in the 'gratuitous grotesque,' she generally fared rather well with her commentators."[34]

Clara Claiborne Park, "Crippled Laughter: Toward Understanding Flannery O'Connor," *American Scholar*, 1982: "[Flannery O'Connor's stories] do not and cannot resolve as she would have them, but retain the murky hostility and anger out of which they grew."[35]

Flannery O'Connor, manuscript: "I can't defend the reasonableness of any and every freak in contemporary literature. There is a kind of grotesque fiction that is unacceptable. It comes about when the writer, without serious intentions, panders to the innate human desire to relish deformity and distortion for their own sakes. This never ends in high art because it is caused by a crippled view of life. It comes usually accompanied by the thesis that corruption lends zest to anything and that the writer has to be either evil or ill, preferably both, before his efforts can end in art."[36]

Flannery O'Connor, manuscript: "The fiction writer has to engage in a continual examination of conscience. He has to be aware of the freak in himself."[37]

Flannery O'Connor, letter to Thomas Stritch, 7 May 1962: "I'll just cherish what the dwarf said" [according to Sally Fitzgerald, Stritch "had told her that the motto of the complete New York edition of Joseph Conrad, taken from Grimm, is, 'Something human is dearer to me than all the gold in the world'"].[38]

Flannery O'Connor, manuscript: "No matter how well we are able to soften the grotesque by humor or compassion, there is always an intensity about it that creates a general discomfort, that brings with it a slight hint of death to the ego, a kind of momento [*sic*] mori that leaves us for an instant alone facing the ineffable."[39]

Josephine Hendin, *The World of Flannery O'Connor,* 1970: "While Flannery O'Connor was by any standard Southern, perhaps even a Southern lady, in a literary sense she is that and something more. . . . O'Connor abandoned the traditional concerns of Southern fiction for her own peculiar obsessions, obsessions which sprang from the unique circumstances of her life. . . . Her reductive, leveling impulse may be part of the demythologizing process in American fiction, a process usually associated with Northerners like William Carlos Williams or the more urbane Wallace Stevens."[40]

Flannery O'Connor, letter to "A," 24 September 1955: "To have sympathy for any character, you have to put a good deal of yourself in him. But to say that any complete denudation of the writer occurs in the successful work is, according to me, a romantic exaggeration. A great part of the art of it is precisely in seeing that this does not happen. . . . Everything has to be subordinated to a whole which is not you."[41]

Irving Howe, *New York Review of Books,* 1965: "[*Everything That Rises Must Converge* is] lacking in that resonance Miss O'Connor clearly hoped it might have. Why? One clue is a recurrent insecurity of tone, jarring sentences in which Miss O'Connor slips from the poise of irony to the smallness of sarcasm, thereby betraying an unresolved hostility to whatever it is she takes Julian to represent. . . . One can only assume it is a hostility rooted in Miss O'Connor's own experience and the kind of literary education she received (intellectuality admired but intellectuals distrusted). . . .

"In thus shaping her materials Miss O'Connor clearly intends us to savor a cluster of ironies; her sensibility as a writer of fiction was formed in a milieu where irony took on an almost totemic value. But there can be . . . a deep failure of ironic perception in a writer's unequivocal commitment to irony. Mustered with the regularity of battalions on parade, complex ironies have a way of crystalizing into simple and even smug conclusions."[42]

Flannery O'Connor, manuscript: "This is the land of dear old elegant grandmothers, of bright well-adjusted boys and girls, of waterproof coffins, of progressive education, of churches which offer the best in recreational and fellowship facilities. It's little wonder that a serious grotesque literature is not well received."[43]

John Hawkes, "Flannery O'Connor's Devil," *Sewanee Review,* 1962: "Though he died in 1940 [Nathanael] West is the one writer who, along with Flannery O'Connor, deserves singular attention as a rare American satirist. . . . They are very nearly alone in their employment of the devil's voice as vehicle for their satire. . . . Both West and Flannery O'Connor write about the devil . . . but seem to reflect the verbal mannerisms and explosively reductive attitudes of such figures in their own 'black' authorial stances. . . . As a writer [O'Connor is] on the devil's side."[44]

Flannery O'Connor, letter to "A," 16 September 1961: "The thing I am writing now is surely going to convince Jack that I am of the Devil's party. It is out of hand right now but I am hoping I can bring it into line. It is a composite of all the eccentricities of my writing and for this reason may not be any good, maybe almost a parody. . . . I am thinking of changing the title to 'The Lame Will Carry off the Prey.' Anyway that analysis of yours about why Jack argues the way he does sounds pretty right to me. Entirely subjective."[45]

Flannery O'Connor, letter to John Hawkes, 28 November 1961: "You haven't convinced me that I write with the Devil's will or belong in the romantic tradition. . . . I think I would admit to what Hawthorne called 'romances,' but I don't think that has anything to do with the romantic mentality."[46]

Flannery O'Connor, letter to John Hawkes, 6 February 1962: "In ['The Lame Shall Enter First'] I'll admit that the Devil's voice is my own."[47]

Flannery O'Connor, letter to John Hawkes, 24 November 1962: "[At the University of Southwestern Louisiana], a Prof. Wagner introduced me by quoting extensively from your essay in the *Sewanee*. It sounded good to me."[48]

Flannery O'Connor, letter to Dr. T. R. Spivey, 27 January 1963: "[The *Sewanee*] published one thing about me and the devil which was pretty off-center as far as I am concerned."[49]

Time, review of *A Good Man Is Hard to Find*, 1955: "These ten witheringly sarcastic stories come from a talented Southern lady whose work is highly unladylike. . . . Her instruments are a brutal irony, a slam-bam humor and a style of writing as balefully direct as a death sentence. The South . . . simpers, storms and snivels in these pages. . . .

"Nobody is noble in these stories. . . . Only in *The Displaced Person* does Ferocious Flannery weaken her wallop by groping about for a symbolic second-meaning—in this case, something about salvation."[50]

Flannery O'Connor, letter to "A," 11 November 1961: "You will have found Christ when you are concerned with other people's suffering and not your own."[51]

Joe Lee Davis, review of *Wise Blood, Kenyon Review,* 1953: "When the contemporary literary imagination, in all the anxious sensitivity and honesty of youth, explores the problem of what has happened in the modern world to belief, the result is likely to be bizarre, oblique, tortured, and ambiguous. A deeply tragic sense of the human condition will wear the mask of an irresponsibly sportive nihilism. Compassion will wield a whip. Awareness of the need for grace will vent itself in the evocation of obscenity and violence. So it seems to be in Miss O'Connor's first novel. . . .

". . . Like many first novels, [this is] pretty obviously derivative. . . . Miss O'Connor has perhaps followed too many and too diverse models for her own salvation. Onto the naturalistic farce of Erskine Caldwell she has grafted the satire of Evelyn Waugh. . . . Her sharp-eyed and saucy similes and metaphors indicate she may have been reading Raymond Chandler as well as Caldwell. Her allegory is Kafkaesque. . . . Farce, satire, and allegory are all modes that sacrifice empathy to detachment, that involve radical distortions and simplifications of character, reality, and experience, and that impose on the writer the most rigorous requirements of tonal consistency. It takes the maturest skill to combine their effects into a sustained unity. Miss O'Connor's skill is not yet that mature, although she makes a good run for the money."[52]

Flannery O'Connor, manuscript: "I don't believe any serious writer approaches a subject or a scene with the intention of creating a grotesque effect. I don't believe Kafka did this, and if our supposed predecessor Mr. Poe did it, I presume he was intoxicated at the time."[53]

John W. Simons, *Commonweal,* 1952: "This is the first novel of a twenty-six-year-old Georgia woman. . . . An important addition to the grotesque literature of Southern decadence."[54]

Flannery O'Connor, letter to "A," 25 November 1955: "I did fail myself. Understatement was not enough."[55]

Flannery O'Connor, letter to "A," 10 June 1961: "Anybody who writes anything about me is going to have to read everything I have written in order to make legitimate criticism, even and particularly the Mary Ann piece."[56]

Harold Bloom, ed., Modern Critical Views, 1986: Her pious admirers to the contrary, O'Connor would have bequeathed us even stronger novels and stories, of the eminence of Faulkner's, if she had been able to restrain her spiritual tendentiousness.[57]

Flannery O'Connor, introduction to *A Memoir of Mary Ann,* 1961: "Stories of pious children tend to be false. This may be because they are told by adults, who see virtue where their subjects would see only a practical course of action; or it may be because such stories are written to edify and what is written to edify usually ends by amusing. For my part, I have never cared to read about little boys who build altars and play they are priests, or about little girls who dress up as nuns, or about those pious Protestant children who lack this equipment but brighten the corners where they are.

"Last spring I received a letter from Sister Evangelist, the Sister Superior of Our Lady of Perpetual Help Free Cancer Home in Atlanta. 'This is a strange request,' the letter read, 'but we will try to tell our story as briefly as possible. In 1949, a little three-year-old girl, Mary Ann, was admitted to our Home as a patient. She proved to be a remarkable child and lived until she was twelve. Of those nine years, much is to be told. Patients, visitors, Sisters, all were influenced in some way by this afflicted child. . . . Now Mary Ann's story should be written but who to write it?' Not me, I said to myself. . . .

"It is always difficult to get across to people who are not professional writers that a talent to write does not mean a talent to write anything at all. I did not wish to imbibe Mary Ann's atmosphere. I was not capable of writing her story. Sister Evangelist had enclosed a picture of the child. . . . I continued to gaze at the picture long after I had thought to be finished with it.

"After a while I got up and went to the bookcase and took out a volume of Nathaniel Hawthorne's stories. The Dominican Congregation to which the nuns belong who had taken care of Mary Ann had been founded by Hawthorne's daughter, Rose. . . . In *Our Old Home,* Hawthorne tells about a fastidious gentleman who, while going through a Liverpool workhouse, was followed by a wretched and rheumy child, so awful-looking that he could not decide what sex it was. The child followed him about until it decided to put itself in front of him in a mute appeal to be held. The fastidious gentleman, after a pause that was significant for himself, picked it up and held it. Hawthorne comments upon this:

Nevertheless, it could be no easy thing for him to do, he being a person burdened with more than an Englishman's customary reserve, shy of actual contact with human beings, afflicted with a peculiar distaste for whatever was ugly, and, furthermore, accustomed to . . . the tendency of putting ice into the blood.

So I watched the struggle in his mind with a good deal of interest, and am seriously of the opinion that he did a heroic act and effected more than he dreamed of toward his final salvation when he took up the loathsome child and caressed it as tenderly as if he had been its father.

What Hawthorne neglected to add is that he was the gentleman who did this. . . .

"The work of Hawthorne's daughter is perhaps known by few in this country where it should be known by all. She discovered much that he sought, and fulfilled in a practical way the hidden desires of his life. The ice in the blood which he feared, and which this very fear preserved him from, was turned by her into a warmth which initiated action. . . .

"Toward the end of the nineteenth century, she became aware of the plight of the cancerous poor in New York and was stricken by it. Charity patients with incurable cancer were not kept in the city hospitals but were sent to Blackwell's Island or left to find their own place to die. In either case, it was a matter of being left to rot. Rose Hawthorne Lathrop was a woman of great force and energy. . . . With almost no money of her own, she moved into a tenement in the worst section of New York and began to take in incurable cancer patients. . . .

". . . I congratulated myself on having minimized the possibility of a book about Mary Ann by suggesting that the Sisters do it themselves. . . . Their manuscript arrived the first of August. After I had gathered myself together, I sat down and began to read it. There was everything about the writing to make the professional writer groan. Most of it was reported, very little was rendered; at the dramatic moment—where there was one—the observer seemed to fade away, and where an exact word or phrase was needed, a vague one was usually supplied. Yet when I had finished reading, I remained for some time, the imperfections of the writing forgotten, thinking about the mystery of Mary Ann. They had managed to convey it. . . .

". . . The creative action of the Christian's life is to prepare his death in Christ. It is a continuous action in which this world's goods are utilized to the fullest, both positive gifts and what Père Teilhard de Chardin calls 'passive diminishments.' Mary Ann's diminishment was extreme, but she was equipped by natural intelligence and by a suitable education, not simply to endure it, but to build upon it. She was an extraordinarily rich little girl.

"Death is the theme of much modern literature. There is *Death in Venice, Death of a Salesman, Death in the Afternoon, Death of a Man*. Mary Ann's was the death of a child. It was simpler than any of these, yet infinitely more knowing. When she entered the door of Our Lady of Perpetual Help Home in Atlanta, she fell into the hands of women who are shocked at nothing and who love life so much that they spend their lives making comfortable those who have been pronounced incurable of cancer. . . .

"This opened up for me also a new perspective on the grotesque. Most of us have learned to be dispassionate about evil, to look it in the face and find, as often as not, our own grinning reflections with which we do not argue, but good is another matter. Few have stared at that long enough to accept the fact that its face too is grotesque, that in us the good is something under construction. The modes of evil usually receive worthy expression. The modes of good have to be satisfied with a cliché or a smoothing down that will soften their real look. When we look into the face of good, we are liable to see a face like Mary Ann's, full of promise. . . .

"One of the tendencies of our age is to use the suffering of children to discredit the goodness of God, and once you have discredited His goodness, you are done with Him. . . . Ivan Karamazov cannot believe, as long as one child is in torment; Camus' hero cannot accept the divinity of Christ, because of the massacre of the innocents. In this popular pity, we mark our gain in sensibility and our loss in vision. If other ages felt less, they saw more, even though they saw with the blind, prophetical, unsentimental eye of acceptance, which is to say, of faith. In the absence of this faith now, we govern by tenderness. It is a tenderness which, long since cut off from the person of Christ, is wrapped in theory. When tenderness is detached from the source of tenderness, its logical outcome is terror. It ends in forced labor camps and in the fumes of the gas chambers."[58]

Flannery O'Connor, letter to Janet McKane, 30 January 1963: "[*A Memoir of Mary Ann*] . . . says something about the mystery of suffering."[59]

Notes

1. Sally Fitzgerald, ed., *Letters of Flannery O'Connor: The Habit of Being* (New York: Random House, 1979), 157.

2. Sally Fitzgerald and Robert Fitzgerald, eds., *Mystery and Manners* (New York: Farrar, Straus & Giroux, 1969), 45.

3. The unpublished manuscripts are housed in the Ina Dillard Russell Library, Georgia College, Milledgeville, Georgia, and are cited by file folder number (i.e., *FO* 219c, 13 in this instance). I am indebted to Professor Sarah Gordon of Georgia College, who generously shared with me a list of quotes she herself mined from the files (subsequently cited "Gordon").

4. "Of Ultimate Things," *Time* 85, 4 June 1965, 92.

5. Fitzgerald and Fitzgerald, eds., *Mystery and Manners*, 153; the dates of particular passages in these essays are hard to determine because Sally Fitzgerald compiled them from lectures presented at different times but often repeating the same general idea. In fact, O'Connor admits to this tendency to be repetitive when she declares: "I think every writer ought to have at least one lecture like an old fur coat that he can drag out for every occasion. If you care to think of my lecture here as an old fur coat, you can visualize it as part mink, part skunk, and part O'Cedar mop" (*FO* 256a, 1).

6. "A Symposium on the Short Story," *Esprit* (University of Scranton) 3 (1959):9.

7. Fitzgerald and Fitzgerald, eds., *Mystery and Manners*, 68.

8. FO 259c.

9. "Visit to Flannery O'Connor Proves a Novel Experience," 29 May.

10. *Letters*, 437.

11. 13 February, 24.

12. *FO* 256a, 1.

13. *Motley Special* (Spring Hill College, Mobile, Alabama) 9:29–31; reprinted by Rosemary M. Magee, ed., *Conversations with Flannery O'Connor* (Jackson: University Press of Mississippi, 1987), 15.

14. 13, no. 3:454–55.

15. *FO* 256a; refers to *Wise Blood*, published in 1952.

16. *FO* 239a.

17. *FO* 217c.

18. *Letters*, 358.

19. *FO* 218b.

20. *Letters*, 554.

21. "Galley Proof" (Program filmed by WRCA-TV, NBC, New York, May), reprinted by Magee, *Conversations*, 7–8.

22. "The Regional Writer," 7 (Winter), excerpted by Melvin J. Friedman and Lewis A. Lawson, eds., *The Added Dimension: The Art and Mind of Flannery O'Connor* (New York: Fordham University Press, 1966), 239.

23. Fitzgerald and Fitzgerald, eds., *Mystery and Manners*, 133–34.

24. *FO* 6; Gordon.

25. *FO* 7; Gordon.

26. *Letters*, 456.

27. *FO* 264g.

28. *FO* 214.

29. 29 November, 87–88.

30. (New York: New Directions, 1964), 42.

31. Reprinted from "Flannery O'Connor: 'Literary Witch,'" *Colorado Quarterly* 10 (1962):377–86, by permission of the University of Colorado at Boulder.

32. "With a Glitter of Evil," *New York Times Book Review*, 12 June 1955, 5.

33. Permission to reprint this excerpt from "Flannery's South: Don Quixote Rides Again," *Flannery O'Connor Bulletin* 1 (1972), is granted by the editors.

34. Melvin J. Friedman and Beverly Lyon Clark, eds. (Boston: G.K. Hall, 1985), 4.

35. 51, no. 2 (1982):252.

36. *FO* 219c, 3; Gordon.

37. *FO* 219c, 13.

38. *Letters*, 472.

39. *FO* 218a, 15.

40. (Bloomington: Indiana University Press, 1970), 131–56.

41. *Letters*, 105.

42. "Flannery O'Connor's Stories," 30 September, 16.

43. *FO* 219f, 13; Gordon.

44. 70:396–400.

45. *Letters*, 449–50.

46. *Letters*, 456–57.

47. *Letters*, 464.

48. *Letters*, 500.

49. *Letters*, 507.

50. 6 June, 114.

51. *Letters*, 453.

52. "Outraged, or Embarrased," 15, no. 1:320–25.

53. *FO* 253d, 2; Gordon.

54. 27 June, 297.

55. *Letters*, 118.

56. *Letters*, 442.

57. (New York: Chelsa House Publishers, 1986), 8.

58. This excerpt from the introduction to *A Memoir of Mary Ann*, by Flannery O'Connor, © 1961 by Farrar, Straus & Cudahy, is reprinted by permission of Farrar, Straus & Giroux, Inc.

59. *Letters*, 507.

Part 3

THE CRITICS

Introduction

[Gregory Zilboorg's *Freud and Religion*] is a valuable study for anyone interested in Freudian theories and their compatability with Christian belief.[1]

This section provides a selective sampling of articles and books on Flannery O'Connor for the general reader, student, teacher, and critic familiar with *The Complete Stories* but just beginning a study of the criticism. My greatest wish is that this selection of excerpts might serve to reconcile some of the differences in the critical canon, demonstrating, for example, that the psychoanalytic critics may complement the theological critics and vice versa. Readers interested in a selection of reviews should consult Melvin J. Friedman and Beverly Lyon Clark's *Critical Essays on Flannery O'Connor*. As I worked my way through some very difficult choices while reviewing the criticism, I looked for thoughtful interpretations representing diverse judgments about O'Connor's short fiction generally. A few close readings of particular stories are offered as examples of critical approaches. I have provided the page references to *The Complete Stories* in those excerpts that used other texts.

I have not arranged these essays chronologically; in fact, very early judgments, nonetheless valuable, end the section. My method in this regard encouraged some revealing juxtapositions of radically different readings (such as those on "Parker's Back"), which, taken together, demonstrate the richness of possibilities when studying O'Connor's art. I also juxtaposed similar judgments, disregarding time and place, in order to show consistent lines of thought, for example, Sister M. Bernetta Quinn writing in the 1950s in America and Maurice Lévy writing in the 1970s in France. My primary goal has been to expose the reader briefly to a broad range of different critical approaches, ultimately encouraging him or her to develop original insights—not from any narrow perspective but by considering the complexity of O'Connor's art and the validity of more than one reading. I apologize to the critics represented here for being forced to abridge some very fine essays that should be read in full. I regret that the constraints of space have limited my selections and acknowledge that many fine articles and books are not represented here but are essential to a more in-depth study of O'Connor.

At the start of this section, Quinn explains O'Connor's work in relation to her Catholicism, as do Lévy, Dan Curley, and Leon V. Driskell and Joan T. Brittain. Robert Fitzgerald, David Eggenschwiler, and David A. Myers identify O'Connor's Christian concerns in relation to the modern, materialistic, "wasteland" world and modern philosophy, especially existentialism. Arno Heller comments on the value of O'Connor's stories as an emotional complex relating the struggles of sensitive human beings in a rationalist, nihilist, pragmatist world. M. A. Klug considers the Manichaean urge of the modern artist represented in O'Connor's depiction of intellectuals alienated from their community. Michel Gresset considers O'Connor in the "southern line (from Poe and Twain to Thomas Wolfe, Caldwell, and Faulkner)"; Sarah Gordon focuses on reasons O'Connor should not be read as a realist in the tradition of the Southern regionalists. Louis D. Rubin, Jr., emphasizes O'Connor's importance as a Southern writer and encourages alternatives to the exclusively theological slant of many early critics. Several critics are later represented as they provide insights from a psychoanalytic perspective—insights that enhance rather than detract from the theological perspective. André Bleikasten provides such a reading of "Parker's Back" and Bartlett C. Jones of "Good Country People." Preston M. Browning speaks of O'Connor's "clinical understanding" of neurosis. Louise Westling and Mary L. Morton consider O'Connor's women characters—the latter critic depending on a Jungian perspective.

As with many authors who die young and who offer a rich and varied canon, controversies continue to rage in the flood of criticism written in the 1980s. I have tried to represent both sides of the major controversies: Claire Katz [Kahane] writes of O'Connor's "sadistic wit" and Robert Drake of her compassion; J. M. G. Le Clézio defines her focus on the dark side of the modern world but also her love of life. Kahane and Le Clézio note the grotesque and disturbing subject matter of O'Connor's tragicomedy, and Dorothy Walters defends O'Connor against the charge that her work lacks a sense of the world's beauty.

Several selections treat O'Connor's craft—focusing on a particular aspect of the work itself: Frederick Asals points to O'Connor's rapidly shifting tone as he defines comic and melodramatic elements in her art; Sheldon Currie analyzes her comic imagery; Edward Kessler defines the force of her poetic metaphors; and Claude Richard depends on recent studies of narratology to analyze O'Connor's style.

Note

1. Leo J. Zuber, comp., *The Presence of Grace and Other Book Reviews by Flannery O'Connor*, ed. by Carter W. Martin (Athens: University of Georgia Press, 1983), 65.

The Critics

[Flannery O'Connor and the Catholic Writer]

Sister M. Bernetta Quinn*

Unambiguously, the term *Catholic* before *physician, teacher, butcher, engineer,* refers to the fact that each of these persons belongs to the Catholic Church. Yet if the adjective *Catholic* is prefixed to *writer,* ambiguity immediately results. Does the speaker mean someone who whether a Catholic or not presents a view of reality similar to or identical with that held by those within the Church, or a writer who happens to be a Catholic and who may or may not let this commitment be evident in what he writes? . . .

[Flannery] O'Connor has not been unmindful of the question "What is a Catholic writer?" Neither has she brushed off the label as one which she does not care to have associated with her. She has tried to present for public scrutiny the fruits of her meditations on the subject in at least two articles—"The Church and the Fiction Writer" and "The Fiction Writer and His Country. . . ." In these she proposes that the Catholic writer is one who is humble before reality, never manipulating it and never turning his eyes away from its ugly or unpleasant phases. True humility is based upon the recognition that God has given man whatever portion of the "good" he possesses; in the case of the writer it is his talent . . . with all its limitations as well as its powers. Before scenes that one writer can recreate in words another is helplessly inarticulate, since within the large vocation of writer there are more specialized vocations; indeed, as Miss O'Connor says in "The Fiction Writer and His Country," "a vocation is a limiting factor which extends even to the kind of material that the writer is able to apprehend imaginatively. . . . The Christian writer particularly will feel that whatever his initial gift is, it comes from God; and no matter how minor a gift it is, he will not be willing to destroy it by trying to use it outside its proper limits." Thus, though she hates the phrase *regional writer,* her settings are Southern, and though she does not disbelieve in joy, her characters are drawn from those who have crippled it within them.

The Catholic writer reveals reality. . . . It is not the artist's job to assure modern America that because she is the greatest nation on the

*Reprinted with permission from "View from a Rock: The Fiction of Flannery O'Connor and J. F. Powers," *Critique: Studies in Modern Fiction* 2, no. 2 (1958):19–27.

face of the globe, all shall be well. . . . If the grotesque is an important part of reality today, the Catholic writer must not only portray grotesquerie but make sure that readers are shocked into realizing it as such, in an age when the perverse is accepted as the normal. Actually, "a purely affirmative vision cannot be demanded of him [the Catholic writer] without limiting his freedom to observe what man has done with the things of God" ("The Church and the Fiction Writer").

Undoubtedly Flannery O'Connor . . . has often met this query: "But doesn't your religion inhibit you? Doesn't it restrict the freedom of your art?" Her reply is a straightforward, "Not at all; in fact, quite the contrary." Her reasons for making this denial show that she has penetrated the sense of the Biblical line, "Ye shall know the truth and the truth shall make you free." In the essay quoted above, she explains her position:

> I have heard it said that belief in Christian dogma is a hindrance to a writer, but I myself have found nothing further from the truth. Actually, it frees the storyteller to observe. It is not a set of rules which fixes what he sees in the world. It affects his writing primarily by guaranteeing his respect for mystery.

In other words, it gives him a vantage point in the universe, a "view from a rock," where, knowing exactly where he is, he can accept the materials brought him by his servant the eye and, transfiguring them in the light of his mind, fashion microcosm after microcosm as he pursues his craft. Moreover, it prevents his mistaking statistics for reality by insisting that he use the absolute and not the relative as criterion. . . .

But most crucial of all in understanding what constitutes a Catholic writer is the realization that for such a person history leads up to and away from what happened on Calvary the first Good Friday. The center of all Catholic fiction is the Redemption. However mean or miserable or degraded human life may seem to the natural gaze, it must never be forgotten that God considered it valuable enough to send His only Son that He might reclaim it; the old priest in ["The Displaced Person"] tries in vain to bring this divine mission home to the spiritually wizened Mrs. McIntyre, who on behalf of her world proclaims: "As far as I'm concerned . . . Christ was just another D.P." [*CS*, 229]. Contemporary society in recent years has made a business of denying its need of redemption, the advertising agencies being among its chief allies in this endeavor. . . . The Catholic writer, his apprehension of life informed by the cross and its cause, will expose the leprous sores and blinded eyes and withered hands of those to be found on the highways and byways, not omitting to record, as in "The Enduring Chill," . . . the moments when the saving Dove comes to rest upon the head of the sinner, while in the same spirit of integrity refusing to falsify the instances where this miracle does not occur. . . .

But more important than incidental touches is Miss O'Connor's whole world—*country* is the word she prefers—as mirrored in her fiction. The sacraments, by explication, or implication, are represented there: Baptism in "The River," Confirmation in "A Temple of the Holy Ghost," Matrimony in "A Stroke of Good Fortune," Extreme Unction in "The Displaced Person," Penance in "The Enduring Chill." The nature of man revolves around his possession of moral intelligence, as even unethical Mr. Shiftlet points out. Prayer is a real force, and hell a certainty, its entrance symbolized by the opening to sewer passages on the streets of Atlanta. . . .

Flannery O'Connor pities the poor and afflicted denizens of the rural South who people her [fiction]. They are largely warped in spirit, a warping which becomes increasingly evident as their tales unfold; but somehow the shriveling of their souls has taken them by surprise and one cannot help feeling sympathy for their abortive efforts to break through the cocoon of ice that surrounds them —despite all barriers, to reach some sort of fulfillment. The evangelical religion of her area holds out to them little promise for communion either with the Deity or with each other.

Maurice Lévy

[Catholic Writing and Universal
Themes of Suffering]

*Maurice Lévy**

If the specific Catholic traits of a literary text are usually readily dis-
cernible in the works of authors who posit their religious faith as an
underlying assumption (think of writers like Bernanos, Mauriac, Graham Greene or Evelyn Waugh), still it must be admitted that nowhere
in the work of Flannery O'Connor is such transparency in evidence.
Far from treating certain problems of conscience peculiar to Catholics
(if there are any such), or (as sometimes happens) taking dogma as the
subject of a story, she places the drama in a context that is to all appearances completely foreign to her fundamental choices, which are,
nonetheless, reaffirmed over and over again. Explicit references to Roman Catholicism are rare, portraits of priests or nuns are neither well-
developed nor very edifying, and the opinions of her characters on a
religion still full of absurdities and unexamined for one thousand years
do not reflect the author's convictions on the subject. It would be futile
to look in her novels or short stories for any trace of Christian marvels:
no miraculous cures as Graham Greene has, no demons capering on
country paths, as Bernanos has. Everything in her work is determined
by necessity—the natural, cruel, and immutable order of things.

   A decision to show such discretion on the level of the imaginary and
by a woman who states her views of life so unreservedly in real life—
might be surprising if it were not related to a particular kind of writing,
which perhaps deserves to be analyzed. Her discourse on man is no
doubt just as moral or eschatological and just as Catholic as those of
Bernanos or Greene, but it does not have the cultural tenor of a language nourished by the sources of old European traditions. Being
Catholic and writing novels right in the middle of the "Bible belt"
almost necessarily implies the ambiguities inherent in minority writing,
which is torn between the need to speak out and a desire to conceal,
affirming an identity under the many masks of the background.

   It would thus be a mistake to see, in the portraits of these lost prophets who people Flannery O'Connor's world, any censure of the re-

*Excerpts reprinted with permission from "L'écriture catholique de Flannery O'Con-
nor," *Revue française d'études américaines*, 1976, 125–33. Translated by C. Frederick
Farrell, Jr., and Edith R. Farrell.

formed faith, or even of its aberrations. Obsessed as they are by baptism, they proclaim in words and gestures understood in the area, truths that the author believes to be universal. Baptist folklore in fact serves to transmit articles of Catholic faith. . . .

Ever since Paul, the humblest country priest has known and preached [that] baptism is first of all a death, the burial of the old man in the waters, followed only after a time, by resurrection and life: *sit fons vivus, aqua regenerans, unda purificans* [let the fountain be living, water regenerating, the waters purifying]. And there is something deeply shocking . . . about seeing Flannery O'Connor violate the symbol. On at least two occasions in her work, baptism is associated with the real, physical death (definitive as far as we can tell) of a child (Harry/Bevel in "The River" and Bishop in *The Violent Bear It Away*). Now this is a cruel irony that makes the story, which up to that time had been carried high on the crest of symbolic waters, crash on the reefs of the literal! What modern reader—who has lost his illusions but like Rayber has a taste for end-of-the-century positivism, or, like Hulga, is haunted by the void—would not applaud, thinking that he has discovered a naturalistic masterpiece? He would, nevertheless, be wrong, perhaps, if he were to limit himself only to this level of interpretation. For the irony that makes nature triumph, far from being a reducing factor, is inscribed in a dynamics that displaces the plot line. The writing traps the reader and forces him to go beyond the absurd to encounter mystery: a Catholic *writing* worth more than all the *thematic structure* built on the sacristy, since it integrates the richness and the weight of reality—the opaque necessity of things. . . .

Every short story or practically every one (except for a few near parodies that are simply stylistic exercises) has its own epiphany, its specific *coup de grace*: in "The Life You Save May Be Your Own," it is the instant when Shiftlet "felt that the rottenness of the world was about to engulf him." In "A Temple of the Holy Ghost," it is the recognition of the hermaphrodite's human dignity, its status changing from that of a curiosity seen at a fair to that of a temple of the Holy Ghost. In "A Circle in the Fire," it is when Mrs. Cope, in shock over the fire, drops the mask of rigid self-righteousness, thus revealing an expression that her daughter had never noticed before. . . . In these special moments in which the characters' experience is made pure and universal, there is no place for either the ironic or the grotesque, and God Himself seems to live again. Not the triumphant, security-giving God that

Dan Curley

societies need and constantly restore for their own particular ends, but He who is an open wound. . . .

This is Catholic writing, moreover, since, at the end of the journey, it places universal agony once more at the center of the human condition.

[Flannery O'Connor and Moral Relativism]

*Dan Curley**

Whatever else may be obscure in Flannery O'Connor's work, her opposition to moral relativism is clear and unchanging from first to last. Time after time she points out the inappropriateness of applying the ideas of progress, advance, and reform to eternal truths. A comparison of past and present with implications of progress comes invariably from a character who is, at least at that time, blind to unchanging realities and points to a character who is in harmony with these same realities. For example, Sarah Ham in "The Comforts of Home" says of Thomas' saintly mother, "She's just about seventy-five years behind the times!" [*CS*, 391]. In "The Displaced Person," Mrs. Shortley sees a picture of a concentration camp and reflects, "This was the kind of thing that was happening every day in Europe where they had not advanced as in this country" [*CS*, 196]. Later when she sees a group of Catholics with their priest she is "reminded that these people did not have an advanced religion. There was no telling what all they believed since none of the foolishness had been reformed out of it" [*CS*, 197–98]. When the old woman in "The Life You Save May Be Your Own" is told "The monks of old slept in their coffins," she replies "They wasn't as advanced as we are" [*CS*, 149]. In "Good Country People," Mrs. Hopewell is of the opinion that philosophy "ended with the Greeks and Romans" [*CS*, 276]. . . .

What Flannery O'Connor is still doing that people have stopped

*Reprinted with permission from "Flannery O'Connor and the Limitless Nature of Grace," *Revista de letras* 7 (1970):371–84.

159

doing is setting up the tension of her stories in terms of justification by faith. If her books had been published in the 1750's rather than the 1950's, no scholar could have missed it. . . . According to St. Paul, justification [by faith] cannot come about through any act of man himself. No amount of living by the law of the prophets can bring down divine grace. The initiative rests purely with God. To Paul, this is, in fact, the essence of the distinction between the Hebrew way based on the law and the Christian way based on faith. Paul, further, in his teaching concentrates on the vital moment in which faith comes to a man and changes his life and saves his soul. . . .

The Pauline moment is of great use to Flannery O'Connor because it has the basic form of fiction with all the fascination of a preoccupation with evil and all the excitement of a sudden reversal of fortune. The trouble is that the Pauline theory makes Flannery O'Connor's fiction look immoral in its system of rewards and punishments and grotesque in its emphasis on the morally and physically corrupt. The point, however, is that any one can be saved, even the storm trooper Paul in the very act of persecuting the Jews, but the problem for the reader is to learn to locate the signs and symbols which reveal the workings of salvation. For example, in many writers physical imperfection is an outward mark of spiritual imperfection, but in Flannery O'Connor physical imperfection is a sign of potential grace. This idea of grace through imperfection is an outgrowth of Miss O'Connor's belief that the true communion of saints is not a communion of love but a communion of suffering. . . .

The pattern of communion-of-suffering and salvation-by-agony can be carried over into virtually any of the stories. "A Circle in the Fire" amplifies the concept by saying "[the misery] might have belonged to anyone, a Negro or a European" [*CS*, 193]. The word *European* occurs in two other stories, "The Displaced Person" and "Revelation," in conjunction with references to box-cars and gas ovens and with exactly the same implications of universal suffering; and *Negro*, as we have seen, occupies the same position in "The Artificial Nigger." These are the wretched of the earth, and for them there is only one hope—the mercy of God—a hope which is in fact denied to many of the prosperous, who think all is well with them. . . .

Intimately connected with that condition of grace called the communion of suffering is the sign of grace to be seen in physical imperfection. Explicit connections are frequently made between imperfection and grace. Clubfooted Rufus Johnson is described as

Robert Fitzgerald

being "as touchy about the foot as if it were a sacred object" [*CS*, 459]. This would be striking enough in itself but it is much more so when we remember that Joy-Hulga in "Good Country People" is "as sensitive about [her] artificial leg as a peacock about his tail" [*CS*, 288]. The peacock, as is clear, especially in "The Displaced Person," has constant implications of divinity. . . . Imperfection is the basis for the suffering which is an approach to God. . . . Sarah Ham is described as representing "blameless corruption—the most unendurable form of innocence" [*CS*, 390]. Rufus carefully maintains the cross-eyed Norton in a sinless state until his death. Powell, in "A Circle in the Fire," is also cross-eyed and is specifically included in the communion of suffering. . . . The very effigy of the Negro in "The Artificial Nigger" is described as having one entirely white eye. In "A Temple of the Holy Ghost," there is even an hermaphrodite who speaks what may be the key speech for all of them: "God made me thisaway. . . . This is the way He wanted me to be and I ain't disputing His way. I'm showing you because I got to make the best of it. . . . I never done it to myself nor had a thing to do with it but I'm making the best of it. I don't dispute hit" [*CS*, 245].

In addition to the mark of physical imperfection, there is one other outstanding sign of potential grace in a character. This sign is what I would like to call the Doubting Thomas syndrome. What this means is that the louder a character proclaims his rebellion against God, the stronger is his desire to believe in God.

[Flannery O'Connor and the Modern Consciousness]

*Robert Fitzgerald**

A catchword when Flannery O'Connor began to write was the German *angst,* and it seemed that Auden had hit it off in one of his titles as the "Age of Anxiety." The last word in attitudes was the Existentialist one,

*This excerpt is from the introduction by Robert Fitzgerald to *Everything That Rises Must Converge,* by Flannery O'Connor; copyright© 1965 by the Estate of Mary Flannery O'Connor. Reprinted by permission of Farrar, Straus & Giroux, Inc., and Robert Giroux, literary executor.

161

resting on the perception that beyond any immediate situation there is possibly nothing—nothing beyond, nothing behind, *nada*. . . . Flannery O'Connor felt that an artist who was a Catholic should face all the truth down to the worst of it. . . .

In *Wise Blood* she did parody the Existentialist point of view . . . but the parody was very serious. In this and in most of her later writing she gave to the godless a force proportionate to the force it actually has: in episode after episode, as in the world, as in ourselves, it wins. We can all hear our disbelief, picked out of the air we breathe, when Hazel Motes says, "I'm going to preach there was no Fall because there was nothing to fall from and no Redemption because there was no Fall and no Judgment because there wasn't the first two. Nothing matters but that Jesus was a liar."

Note the velocity and rightness of these sentences. Many pages and a number of stories by this writer have the same perfection. . . . I am speaking now of merits achieved in the reader's interest: no unliving words, the realization of character by exquisitely chosen speech and interior speech and behavior, the action moving at the right speed so that no part of the situation is left out or blurred and the violent thing, though surprising, happens after due preparation, because it has to. Along with her gifts, patient toil and discipline brought about these merits. . . . What was the standard to which the writer felt herself answerable? In 1957 she said:

> The serious fiction writer will think that any story that can be entirely explained by the adequate motivation of the characters or by a believable imitation of a way of life or by a proper theology, will not be a large enough story for him to occupy himself with. This is not to say that he doesn't have to be concerned with adequate motivation or accurate reference or a right theology; he does; but he has to be concerned with them only because the meaning of his story does not begin except at a depth where these things have been exhausted. The fiction writer presents mystery through manners, grace through nature, but when he finishes, there always has to be left over that sense of Mystery which cannot be accounted for by any human formula.

This is an open and moving statement of a certain end for literary art. . . . similar to those of another Christian writer who died recently, T. S. Eliot. . . . [O'Connor and Eliot] were similarly moved toward serious art, being early and much possessed by death as a reality, a strong spiritual sensation, giving odd clarity to the appearances they saw through or saw beyond. In her case as in his, if anyone at first found the writing startling he could pertinently remind himself how startling it was going to be to lose his own body. . . .

When it comes to seeing the skull beneath the skin, we may remark that the heroes of both O'Connor novels are so perceived within the first few pages, and her published work begins and ends with coffin dreams. Her *memento mori* is no less authentic for being often hilarious, devastating to a secular world and all it cherishes. The O'Connor equivalent for Eliot's drowned Phoenician sailor ("Consider Phlebas, who was once handsome and tall as you") is a museum piece, the shrunken corpse that the idiot Enoch Emery in *Wise Blood* proposes as the new humanist jesus. . . . And there is a classic exchange in "The Life You Save May Be Your Own":

> "Why listen, lady," said Mr. Shiftlet with a grin of delight, "the monks of old slept in their coffins."
> "They wasn't as advanced as we are," the old woman said.

The state of being as advanced as we are had been, of course, blasted to glory in *The Waste Land* before Flannery made her version, a translation, as it were, into American ("The Vacant Lot"). To take what used to be called low life and picture it as farcically empty, raging with energy, and at the same time, *sub specie aeternitatis*, full of meaning: this was the point of *Sweeney Agonistes* and the point of many pages of O'Connor. As for our monuments, those of a decent godless people, surely the asphalt road and the thousand lost golf balls are not a patch on images like that of the hillside covered with used car bodies, in *The Violent Bear It Away*:

> In the indistinct darkness, they seemed to be drowning into the ground, to be about half-submerged already. The city hung in front of them on the side of the mountain as if it were a larger part of the same pile, not yet buried so deep. The fire had gone out of it and it appeared settled into its unbreakable parts.

Death is not the only one of the Last Things present in the O'Connor stories; Judgment is there, too. On the pride of contemporary man, in particular on flying as his greatest achievement, Tarwater in *The Violent*

Bear It Away has a prophet's opinion: "I wouldn't give you nothing for no airplane. A buzzard can fly."

Christ the tiger, a phrase in Eliot, is a force felt in O'Connor. So is the impulse to renounce the blessed face, and to renounce the voice. In her work we are shown that vices are fathered by our heroism, virtues forced upon us by our impudent crimes, and that neither fear nor courage saves us (we are saved by grace, if at all, though courage may dispose us toward grace). Her best stories do the work that Eliot wished his plays to do, raising anagogical meaning over literal action. He may have felt this himself, for though he rarely read fiction I am told that a few years before he died he read her stories and exclaimed in admiration at them.

[Wholeness, Incompleteness, and Estrangement: Flannery O'Connor and Christian Humanism]

*David Eggenschwiler**

The modern mind sees only half of the horse—that half which may become a dynamo, or an automobile, or any other horse-powered machine. If this mind had much respect for the full-dimensioned, grass-eating horse, it would never have invented the engine which represents only half of him. The religious mind, on the other hand, has this respect; it wants the whole horse, and it will be satisfied with nothing less.[1]

Many theologians [realize] that religion must not be separated from other concerns. . . . M. C. D'Arcy and Romano Guardini use Freudian and Jungian psychology in their studies of Christian love. And existentialism has had an enormous influence on both Protestant and Catholic commentators. Of course, these secular disciplines must undergo a sea-change for the ends of a God they were not intended to serve; otherwise, religion . . . would be left only with a horsepowered machine

---

*Reprinted from "The Whole Horse," in *The Christian Humanism of Flannery O'Connor* (1972), by permission of Wayne State University Press.

David Eggenschwiler

called "social ethics." The best of the eclectic theologians have emphasized the incomplete views of the disciplines they have incorporated. . . . D'Arcy denies Freud's pessimism by denying his biological determinism; Tillich claims that existentialism gives much to theology by analyzing the human situation but that the answers to its questions must come from outside the situation itself. They are quite aware that these disciplines have been used idolatrously to cut existence down to manageable size, to stuff it completely within the knowable and systematic. But they also know that one can be so afraid of idolatry that one retreats to another false extreme, refusing to admit the religious value of natural understanding. . . .

Assuming that such intellectually synthetic approaches are not only valuable but necessary at the present time, I have appropriated whatever I have found pertinent and enlightening in various disciplines for use in studying Flannery O'Connor. Such an approach seems especially helpful when applied to this author, who had a great respect for the whole horse, who saw life from many perspectives, but who also believed that what she saw was a whole that demanded complex and integrated responses from the writer. Throughout her essays and lectures O'Connor repeatedly claimed that the novelist writes "with the whole personality" and that "great fiction involves the whole range of human judgment" [*MM*, 156]. She insisted that the ultimate concerns of her art transcended the natural but that her art was primarily of the concrete world in which the transcendent was manifested. To paraphrase Maritain, I believe she sought a more than worldly knowledge, not by knowing the world badly but by knowing it well, by seeing more of it than we usually permit ourselves to see. . . . What Maritain calls the "theo-centric humanist" . . . considers man in his finite and infinite extensions, as a creature of religious, psychological, and social depths. And, since he considers existence to be a whole, he finds these dimensions necessarily related.[2]

In O'Connor's lectures on her writing, two subjects occur more than any other, and they are complementary concerns of the Christian humanist. First, she insisted that the fiction writer needs to have "anagogical vision," the ability "to see different levels of reality in one image or one situation," and she wrote that "the Catholic sacramental view of life is one that sustains and supports at every turn the vision that the storyteller must have if he is going to write fiction of any depth" [*MM*, 72, 152]. Even a casual reader must become aware of these "added dimensions" in her work. . . . One does not have to

165

know her comments on Hawthorne and romance to recognize that the often extreme stylization of her work suggests allegory. . . .

The second of her two main prescriptions shows that, at least in theory, she knew the dangers inherent in such allegory. She repeatedly warned students that stories do not begin with problems or issues that the writer feels a need to illustrate in some way; they begin with concrete situations, and the author's beliefs will determine *how* he sees the situation but they should not determine *what* he sees [*MM*, 90–91]. Thus, she cited the impressionistic Conrad . . . as often as she did the allegorical Hawthorne. There seems to be a conflict here between the allegorist's use of the natural to signify something beyond it and the impressionist's concern for the natural itself. But for the Christian humanist this is a false conflict arising from a false dualistic understanding of existence, from an inability to see the whole horse. If one saw only half a horse (either spirit or matter) or, at best, a schizophrenic horse (of irreconcilable spirit and matter), one would not understand how anagogical vision reconciled allegory and impressionism. One would see allegory as only a rhetorical means of signifying the spiritual or of representing conceptions about the natural. One would not consider allegory as a way of seeing. For the anagogical writer, however, especially the writer whose religious faith is centered on the Incarnation, the natural and the supernatural contain each other; the different levels of meaning are intrinsic to the image. The allegory of such a writer is more than a technique of discourse; it is a way of seeing the concrete situation most fully. He or she does not try to find more meaning in the situation created, for that would suggest that the situation contained hidden kernels of meaning and that the reader's job was to husk the story to get the messages out of it—an attitude against which O'Connor often warned her readers. Instead, the religious humanist writes allegory to see more of the situation. . . . [This] requires a wholeness of vision which theologians have associated with prophecy and which literary critics, following Blake and Coleridge, have associated with the poetic imagination at its highest, with the ability to represent multeity in unity. . . .

If O'Connor's fiction is successfully anagogical, as her critical comments show she intended it to be, then some form of anagogical reading of it would be necessary. The reader who responded to a single level of meaning would be responding not only partially but wrongly; he would be denying her central assumptions about existence. For example, it would be a basic distortion not to realize that in her work to be estranged from God is necessarily to be estranged from one's essential self, which involves a form of psychological imbalance and neurotic compulsion. This spiritual and psychic estrangement also causes an estrangement from other men, thus some form of anti-social, or more precisely "anti-communal," behavior. . . . As we assume temporarily the point of view of any one discipline, it must be to see more of the fictional work by moving around it and seeing it in new relationships. . . .

. . . Romano Guardini [whom] . . . O'Connor read, has developed all of his work about a similar assumption: that "to view the pattern of Christian existence as a whole" one must resist the modern tendency to divide and isolate areas of knowledge. . . . "Augustine draws no methodological division between philosophy and theology or, in philosophy, between metaphysics and psychology, within theology, between theoretical dogma and practical application to life, but his mind proceeds from the whole of Christian existence to consider the total pattern and its different parts."[3] If one believes that existence is basically unified, one cannot adequately approach it from any one separate discipline. The mind must begin with the "whole of Christian existence" and move to the parts of the pattern: wisdom, which is supernatural, revealed, and universal, must precede understanding, which is natural and therefore partial. . . . The critic, if he [or she] is more interested in the literature than in method, must not convert that literature into another discipline or even into several other disciplines. He [or she] must not assume that accumulating enough theological, philosophical, social, and psychological significances would explain the work. . . . These significances are not separable but they each describe the wholeness of the author's vision while being themselves less than it. In this way the critic would be both analytic and synthetic . . . thus demonstrating both the extensiveness and the oneness of the author's view.

. . . [O'Connor's] respect for the whole horse not only affected the form of her fiction, giving it that strange combination of mystery and manners . . . but it also provided her most important themes. . . . her preoccupations with original sin, grace, and freedom—she wrote about wholeness and incompleteness, subjects that are enormously complex. . . . For the Catholic, this wholeness . . . was lost in the Fall but is vouchsafed to man through the sanctification of grace. Correspondingly, many modern theologians approach the question of sinfulness in terms of broken harmony, of estrangement or alienation. . . . It is quite possible, then, to use the general concepts of unity and estrangement as a means of approaching the central Christian subjects of man's essential nature, his fallen state, and his redemption; and it is possible to use them to examine man from three perspectives, as a religious, psychological, and social being. . . .

According to this view, if man is in a proper relation to God . . . he has psychological wholeness. In a frequently quoted statement, O'Connor said that "to be able to recognize a freak, you have to have some conception of the whole man" [*MM*, 44]. . . .

. . . man's estrangement from his essential self, his whole, unfallen, eternal self, is necessarily estrangement from God. To the Christian humanist, since God is the ground of man's being, the center of his essential self, He is not the "other," not what Blake attacked as the completely external Nobbodaddy; He is the "Centre of centres." When one works from this point of view and explores the psychological correspondences, one finds new meaning in the basic Christian belief that man's freedom is obtained in accepting the will of God, his bondage in rebellion. O'Connor worked from such beliefs to show the demons of the mind by which man enslaves himself *and the means of salvation* by which he is freed and made whole.

1. Allen Tate, "Remarks on the Southern Religion," in *I'll Take My Stand* (New York: Harper & Brothers, 1930), 157.

2. See *Integral Humanism: Temporal and Spiritual Problems of a New Christendom*, trans. Joseph W. Evans (New York: Charles Scribner's Sons, 1968). The original French edition was published in 1936.

3. *Freedom, Grace, and Destiny*, trans. John Murray (London: Harvill Press, 1961), 9.

David A. Myers

[Fragmentation and Angst in "The Displaced Person"]

*David A. Myers**

In a spate of monographs that have appeared on the fiction of Flannery
O'Connor during the nineteen seventies, her work has been defini-
tively placed outside the limiting context of the Southern Gothic. She
is now seen as a Christian humanist who has inherited the spiritual
anguish and the anagogical vision of Melville and Dostoevsky, but who
consciously affirms religious faith and religious humility as antidotes to
the pride and the angst of the existential agnostics, as she explores
through her short stories the absurd dilemma of *homo dei*. She is also
now proven to be a scholar of theology and mysticism, and a composer
of tragic art. . . . Although the settings, characters and idiom of her
stories are limited in the sense that they are invariably Southern and
rural, her true range is "vertical and Dantaesque" [according to Robert
Fitzgerald] insofar as any spiritual rising or transcendent convergence
in God that is hinted at in the epiphanies of *Everything That Rises Must
Converge* is achieved only after tragic suffering. . . .

These epiphanies are always moral or spiritual in nature: an abrupt
illumination reveals to the characters how mistaken their way of life
and their self-assessment has been up until that moment. The epiphany is not a joyous revelation of God in all his glory but an anguished
and often paradoxical glimpse of some indirect evidence that God has
interfered with and guided the affairs of man. Such epiphanies are the
expression of an individual's transcendence of the empirical world and
his momentary achievement through anagogical vision of an approxi-
mation to God's view of human affairs. The inspirational moment is
inevitably preceded by a crushing awareness of one's unworthiness and
by a shedding of self-sufficiency. The penitent yearns for *unio mystica*
and achieves this state, though often in ambivalent form. . . .

Patrick White's *A Woman's Hand* and O'Connor's "The Displaced
Person" present characters who are obsessed with their private visions
of God and the devil and who experience bewilderment and terror in
their single-minded pursuit of this vision.

*Reprinted from "A Galaxy of Haloed Suns: Epiphanies and Peacocks in Patrick
White's *A Woman's Hand* and Flannery O'Connor's *The Displaced Person*," *Literatur in
Wissenschaft und Unterricht* 14, no. 4 (1981):214–24.

. . . Mrs. Shortley is convinced that she is one of the righteous, in contrast to the priest whom she sees as "the Whore of Babylon" [*CS*, 209] because he indirectly thwarts her social ambitions. Her religious zealotry is so bizarre that the reader needs no comment from the author to savour the full irony of such statements as "before long she had come to a deeper understanding of her existence" [*CS*, 209]. This seems to be one of the few stories by O'Connor where she satirizes rather than sympathizes with one of her primitive visionaries.

Mrs. Shortley had pretended to look down on "unreformed" Europe for its mass murders of Jews and Slavs, but here she equals Hitler and Stalin in her zeal for blood: "'The children of wicked nations will be butchered,' she said in a loud voice. 'Legs where arms should be, foot to face, ear in the palm of hand. Who will remain whole? Who will remain whole? Who?'" [*CS*, 210]. The irony of these words is that when Mrs. Shortley dies of a seizure a few days later it is she who seems dismembered as she grabs at "Mr. Shortley's elbow and Sarah Mae's foot at the same time and began to tug and pull on them as if she were trying to fit the two extra limbs onto herself" [*CS*, 213]. Flannery O'Connor comments further on Mrs. Shortley's grotesque lack of spiritual wholeness by having her see clouds as dead white fish and the force of the sun disintegrated into a jetsom of submerged "pieces" [*CS*, 210].

[The Parent's Fear of Death in Modern Civilization]

*J. M. G. Le Clézio**

For a religious person there is something worse than an atheist—a false prophet. Superstition, lies, the exploitation of credulity are truly the devil's work, while indifference is man's. The illusion-merchant, the sorcerer . . . degrades and dishonors. . . . If the world that Flannery O'Connor has created shocks us, it is not so much because it is confused and brutal, but because it is true. With its harsh, plain, intuitive

*Reprinted by permission from the preface to *Et ce sont les violents qui l'emportent*, © Editions Gallimard, 1965. Translated by C. Frederick Farrell, Jr., and Edith R. Farrell.

and demanding truth, it is there to uproot our illusions, to convince us, to make us question what our senses and our minds tell us, and to make us love lucidity. The civilization of which we are so proud belongs only to the few. All around us, if we open our eyes and look, is the domain of barbarity, lies, and cruelty, in which ethics and religion are merely alibis.

. . . Human evil has become universal; savagery and hatred have put their stamp on nature as if all living creatures were communicating in a kind of grandiose and demonical orchestration. . . .

A prisoner in an accursed world, man cannot be anything but a fanatic. His ideas are more important than his everyday actions. They provide his motivation, often on a very profound level; they are the person himself; they are what allow him to live and survive. At this point, reality is no longer so very important. What really counts are the changes that come from within, unknown impulses that rise up from the very depths of our being. The world splits irrevocably in two, and its dark instinctive face emerges. We witness the rebirth of myths and deceptions in a strange atmosphere of impotent terror—the one we know from nightmares.

The earth is peopled with prophets. Here everyone puts forth his God, his Truth, and seeks to impose it on others. Everyone has his own system. The adult world is inflexible, a tragic and pathetic world where solitude and suspicion reign. The prize in the struggle . . . is . . . the child soon to become a man. Only he counts. He is still receptive and must be won over, imprisoned at all costs in a system of ideas—conquered, entered, and possessed. Adults pay him pitiful and pitiless court; his mind is female, and the harsh powers of faith, ideas, and doctrines must impregnate it. This is the ritual course of nature that abhors a vacuum. . . . Whether to exploit or to save him, the prophet/parent needs the child. . . .

. . .Death is a constant obsession—an obsession which is not despair, but simply a recognition of the catastrophic cycle of life. Nature, human acts, the most intimate thoughts relate to this. Nothing is unconnected. Each [of the two men/enemies] knows that he carries within himself this ultimate defeat, and he accepts it. And he does not forget it; rather, he comes into close contact with death naturally, every day. The casket becomes a bed, and the costume one will wear in death is prepared long in advance. Once emptied of life, the body is treated casually, buried summarily near the fig tree. . . .

To struggle against this deadly atmosphere, men turn toward youth, childhood, birth, and try to make the child their own. Baptism, blasphemous or sacramental, is the most important of all. It is the proprietary act *par excellence*, the one that eradicates the void . . . and causes them to be born anew. A response to the obsession with death and decay, the obsession with baptism gives concrete form to man's fanaticism.

Hate, love, jealousy, doubt, and faith are the rules of life. There is no lasting truth or enjoyment. Relationships among men are master/slave relationships, and each one is both master and slave: dominated by other people's ideas, led by his own destiny, shaped, directed, acted upon and acting from birth to death. . . .

Such a book [as *The Violent Bear It Away*], in all of its despair and its cruelty, in its language that talks endlessly of persecution, hatred and death, can only be the work of someone who loves life passionately. Loving it as it is, with both joy and pity. To understand this, one need only follow the terrible conflicts that men's spirits undergo in the conquest of immortality. Within their systematic madness, these men struggle, suffer, blaspheme—because there is within them the very essence of existence. If their actions are sometimes mad, it is because life requires violence and is not dull. Revolt is active. It involves progress. It is a victory over death.

[The Developing Self in the Modern World]

Arno Heller*

O'Connor's fascination with the violent, the demonic, and the destructive that disrupts well-tempered, provincial quotidian life . . . and the withering satire directed at the normal, the conventional, and the rational support the assumption that for her the act of writing had the same exorcising effect she offered her "hostile audience." . . . [O'Connor's] religious beliefs and images make up the mythic-mystic dimen-

*Reprinted with permission from "'Experienced Meaning': Wirkungsästhetische Betrachtungen zur Kurzprosa Flannery O'Connor," in Sonja Bahn et al., eds., *Forms of the American Imagination*, Innsbruck, 1979, 165–79. Translated by Walter Hölbing, Graz, Austria.

sion that, together with her regional microcosm, she needs for the creative expression of her artistic self. On the other hand, these tales also appeal to the non-religious audience because the concepts illustrated in them are, finally, "fictions," that is, metaphorical concretizations of elementary psychic experience. Taken out of its specific religious context, the essence of this experience involves the rebellion of a sensitive human being against a rationalist and basically nihilist pragmatism that leaves no ground for creative human development. The controlled and restrained emotional intensity of O'Connor's contradictory thoughts and feelings is the unmistakable trademark of her stories. The intentional incongruence of language and subject evokes an illusionary sense of reality in the reader's mind, only to explode it with stunning effect. To put it succinctly, she creates illusion in order to destroy it. . . . The final purpose of her stories is not to provide meaning but to communicate feeling in a very comprehensive sense; that is, the stories strive to transmit the state of emotion out of which they have been created. As she herself put it: "Some people have the notion that you read the story and then climb out of it into the meaning, but for the fiction writer himself the whole story is the meaning, because it is an experience, not an abstraction" [MM, 73].

Flannery O'Connor and the Artist

*M. A. Klug**

O'Connor declares "strict" naturalism a "dead end in fiction" [MM, 68] and concentrates her assault on the perverse romanticism of the modern novel. She begins by condemning the romantic idealization of the modern writer as a sensitive loner. The myth of the lonely writer is "pernicious and untruthful" [MM, 52]. It makes a virtue of alienation, converting what "was once a diagnosis" into an ideal that dominates "much of the fiction of our time" [MM, 52]. For O'Connor, the artist's assumption of superiority to ordinary people and his or her willful cultivation of alienation are symptoms of the Manichean urge to escape from material creation in order to take up residence in the

*Reprinted with permission from "Flannery O'Connor and the Manichean Spirit of Modernism," *Southern Humanities Review* 17, no. 4 (1983):303–13.

purely spiritual realm of one's own mind [*MM*, 158]. Once secure from the intrusion of finite things, romantic artists can undertake the true work of forging their own souls, creating their own immortality through their vision or their work. In opposing this notion that artists achieve or fabricate their own essential selves, O'Connor takes her stand against one of the basic postulates of the modern American writer. . . .

. . . the imagination, the intellect, or the will . . . sets the hero apart from common folk. A familiar version of this modern quest for the essential self might be called the aesthetic heresy. The soul is equated with aspiration, with the urge to self-perfection that realizes itself in immortal creation or some other transcendent experience. The prototype of the spiritual hero becomes a kind of artist whatever the hero's occupation might be. The hero is a romantic artist of the self, furiously laboring to give birth to his or her own perfected being through the achievement of a personal destiny.

In refusing the inherent soul in favor of one that must be achieved, the spiritual hero of modern fiction faces mortal consequences that are familiar to every reader, since they supply many of the motifs of the literature of alienation. They are also precisely those consequences that O'Connor laments as the effect of the Manichean compulsion to try to "approach the infinite . . . without any mediation of matter" [*MM*, 68]. . . . The typical spiritual heroes of our fiction usually forsake their homes early in their careers. They have to be free to begin making themselves, but on a deeper level their rejection of home is an unconscious denial of that familiar world in which all persons are endowed with a soul and share a common spiritual inheritance and kinship. This act of denial leads to an irreconcilable conflict between such heroes and their environments. . . . In the most extreme cases, the hero is caught in a landscape of death and beset by vampires who thirst after the hero's being. Beneath this estrangement is the total failure of spiritual understanding. Heroes of modern fiction cannot locate their reflections in the eyes of ordinary humanity that surround them. The symptoms of the hero's loss of spiritual vision show up all across our fiction—in the frozen objectivity of the early realists and naturalists, in the paranoid fear of being watched which haunts so many of the central characters of recent fiction, and again in the constant preoccupation with voyeurism and the theme of blindness which shows up in the work of such writers as Bellow, Hawkes, Ellison, Plath, Malamud, Percy, and James Dickey. It is small wonder that modern heroes, surrounded by a hostile environment that threatens their very souls, characteristically retreat or try to retreat into a safe place in the hopes of preserving their spiritual beings. . . .

. . . [O'Connor] rejects alienation as a necessity, much less as an ideal, and her rejection of it goes much deeper than a commitment to a purely social or secular responsibility. It grows out of her belief in the inherent human spirit. She insists that there can be no need for the individual to create his soul; it is given once and for all to each. The soul can never be the basis of an exclusively personal distinction, just as it can never serve the ego or sublimate the ego's demand to some transcendent end. The burden is exactly the opposite. The soul is the destruction of a merely personal self, the defeat of any hope of an individual distinction that might justify being; for it is the inherent image of God upon each man, binding him to the mystery of creation and to all other men in kinship under God. While the individual has infinite worth, it does not rest upon that which separates him from others but upon that which joins him to the Universal.

. . . [O'Connor] has been accused of using religion as a spiritual retreat from material reality, but to the contrary she insists that all retreats are futile, whether they be spiritual or material. Indeed her conflict with the modern consciousness, especially as it expresses itself in literature, springs from her conviction that modernism commits the spirit or mind to perpetual flight from creation. For O'Connor the sense of alienation so pervasive in our time inevitably results from the Manichean urge to find a refuge in the enclosed mind. . . . She does not offer the consolations of a theology or even of religion, so much as she seeks to melt the modern glance, frozen in objectivity, detachment, indifference. To share her vision we must be willing to look for the spirit and the flesh orbiting together in the familiar circles of the idiot's eye.

[Flannery O'Connor and the South]

Michel Gresset*

In literature, the South gave to the United States approximately what Ireland gave to England: a vein of rich, striking, often black humor, which in its most highly developed form—a macabre burlesque—can include both feeling and tenderness. If we were to distinguish a northern line (the great writers of the nineteenth-century, Dreiser, Crane, Hemingway, et al.) and a southern line (from Poe and Twain to Thomas Wolfe, Caldwell, and Faulkner), we would notice that it is perhaps to the latter that the United States owes some of its best present-day writers: William Goyen, William Styron, and Flannery O'Connor, among others. . . .

It is, I think, in this double perspective (southern tradition and painful contemporary awareness) that we must see this Catholic novelist, Flannery O'Connor, whose opus, though relatively small, is perhaps beneath a restrained, seemingly modest appearance, one of the most powerful and also the most somber that we have ever had the good fortune to read. . . .

Flannery O'Connor's characters, in fact, make up a small world of Negroes, farm workers, and petty employees over whom looms the heroic but withered shadow of a few scattered old Southern figures: two or three widows who own once-prosperous plantations, a dissolute 104-year-old general, etc. These people are also a living museum of stupidity and all kinds of imperfections, perversions, repressions, infirmities, idiocies, and follies. Her first collection starts with a story about the assassination of a whole family by a "Misfit" who had escaped from jail and closes on the horrible death . . . of a hard-working Polish Catholic. . . . This is a world that is jarring, even incredible, where we cannot fail to recognize the setting and the climate that we have long associated with Faulkner. The same South is there: beaten down by the sun (which makes a deadly "little hole" in the general's skull and which describes Flannery O'Connor's art exactly . . .). Sinister buzzards fly overhead, and her South is peopled with poor white trash whose adolescence is marked by an initiation into the archetypal world of Blacks. It is, above all, a geographical South, the unique *place*

**Reprinted from "Le Petit Monde de Flannery O'Connor," *Mercure de France*, série moderne (January 1964), 141–43. Translated by C. Frederick Farrell, Jr., and Edith R. Farrell.

fostered by the old plantation, the dual sign of Order and of degeneration.

But what gives this voice its unique tone is the *inevitable*, almost obsessive, quality of the themes and the images: the Sun (which, as in Stephen Crane, is compared to a "bloody host," a very relevant symbol of that caricature of a world where the crucifixion is still going on); the sewer, in whose mouth the grandfather puts his grandson, as if to initiate him into the sickening substrata of existence; in a word, the whole grotesque and fantastic ballet of mutilated, diminished, obsessed people choreographed by death, always death by violence. . . . One thinks of Bosch, Poe, or even Beckett.

Nevertheless, it is not irony that governs the work. It is humor, but a terrible, macabre, grimacing, caricatural humor that sometimes carries the reader to the very edge of the unbearable and to the limits of tragicomic ambiguity. This is how it is with the affair of the young and intellectual one-legged woman and the innocent, cynical, and monstrously perverted, petty Bible salesman. What the author invites us to share is this concentrated, hard, implacable *vision*, one that has no trace of oneiric sponginess or fluidity, but where, under the sun's pitiless glare, there rise up images of which we might say (as the author says of one character's eyes), that "All the vision in them might have been turned around, looking inside her" [*CS*, 213]. The author's own words also furnish the best definition of this vision, "I don't have illusions. I'm one of those people who see *through* to nothing" [*CS*, 287].

In the depths of the void, there still shines a feeble ray: "[Mr. Head in 'The Artificial Nigger'] understood that [mercy] grew out of agony, which is not denied to any man and which is given in strange ways to children" [*CS*, 269]. In its "strange way," Flannery O'Connor's Catholicism is naked, tragic, and painful.

[Flannery O'Connor and Realism]

*Sarah Gordon**

Flannery O'Connor's fiction begins in the familiar, recognizable world that we know. Whether we've been in a *Southern* doctor's office or, more precisely, in Dr. Fulghum's office in Milledgeville is beside the

*Permission to reprint this excerpt from "Flannery O'Connor and the Common Reader," *Flannery O'Connor Bulletin* 10 (1981), is granted by the editors.

point. We've all sat in waiting rooms, perhaps crowded ones, in which in order to feel real at all we've sharply separated ourselves from those bodies, the mottled flesh of human frailty, surrounding us. And so does Mrs. Ruby Turpin in "Revelation," except for Mrs. Turpin such separation is made all the more difficult by the fact of her own enormous size; we note the first sentence of the story: "The doctor's waiting room, which was very small, was almost full when the Turpins entered and Mrs. Turpin, who was very large, made it look even smaller by her presence" [*CS*, 488]. Images of enormous size pervade this story, eventually harnessing Ruby Turpin to the old sow, her double, whom she hoses down in the fierceness of her pride and revelation.

We must feel free to laugh at Mrs. Turpin, from the very first sentence of the story. She is, on one level, the Fat Lady in the circus, and she is, on another, the deadly sin of pride. But let us dwell a while on our initial reactions. We must not feel inhibited by fear of laughter, of sneering, of just plain fun. We *know* Mrs. Turpin. And we feel comfortable in that doctor's waiting room, interestingly enough, because, while Ruby Turpin establishes her difference from the other patients, *we* are experiencing our own superiority to Mrs. Turpin. . . . O'Connor's technique distances the reader from this "stout," happy lady and her fatuous, self-congratulatory attitude. In a manner of speaking, then, it is the reader who "throws the book" at Mrs. Turpin through the agency of the intellectually superior (and fat) Mary Grace, just as, even more significantly, it is the reader's dangerous smugness and self-congratulation which are hit squam in the eye by O'Connor.

Flannery O'Connor achieves this reader involvement and reader indictment primarily through her ability to draw us into a world we *think* we know. To this extent, O'Connor is a realist. However . . . we must hasten to add that in the final analysis Flannery O'Connor takes us far away from the familiar world. In fact, to read O'Connor as a realistic writer, to see her primarily in the tradition, for example, of the regional humorists, is to limit severely the author's scope and, indeed, to invite difficulty and misunderstanding. Furthermore, comparisons of O'Connor with Faulkner and Welty are useful—to a point. But O'Connor's "plain folk"—her poor folk—bear only slight resemblance to the poor whites of other Southern writers. When we make too much of such similarity . . . we are, it seems to me, engaging in just another form of critical reductionism. To acknowledge the "Southern-ness" of setting and dialogue created by O'Connor's good eye and fine ear should not be the end of our discussion of "Revelation." And yet classifying

O'Connor as a Southern regionalist . . . may be tempting to those of us who, as literary critics, are a bit embarrassed by the theological implications of fiction. If O'Connor has lived and breathed the air of the Middle Georgia humorists, she has also read Hawthorne, François Mauriac, and Nathanael West. The form of Flannery O'Connor's fiction is unique in Southern letters: it is not Southern realism, though each of her stories begins in the familiar world. . . .

Flannery O'Connor's fiction is and is not the world we know, though we are not free to "interpit" it any way we want to—as Common Readers at whatever level. And contrary to the doctrine preached by Onnie Jay Holy [a character in *Wise Blood*], the reader of O'Connor may indeed be led to a place that is disturbing in its unfamiliarity. Onnie Jay is not describing the revelation of Ruby Turpin when he argues, "You don't have to believe nothing you don't understand and approve of." Onnie Jay continues by saying, "If you don't understand it, it ain't true, and that's all there is to it." As she stands scooting down the hogs with her hose, Ruby Turpin comes to know that there is Truth beyond her understanding, beyond the limits of her own scheme of things ("good order, common sense, and respectable behavior"). Questioning the Almighty in the straightforward manner of Job himself, Mrs. Turpin is finally vouchsafed a vision of her own vulnerability in the face of ultimate mystery: "like a monumental statue coming to life, she bent her head slowly and gazed, as if through the very heart of mystery, down into the pig parlor at the hogs. They had settled all in one corner around the old sow who was grunting softly. A red glow suffused them. They appeared to pant with a secret life" [*CS*, 508]. Ruby Turpin, at whom we directed our laughter at the beginning of the story, to whom we have believed ourselves superior, is here likened to "a monumental statue coming to life" and, implicitly, to the hogs before her. She, and they, experience a "secret life." And, in spite of the distance O'Connor creates between the voice of the narrator and Mrs. Turpin's experience, it is clear that we are to take Mrs. Turpin's revelation seriously. The comic absurdity of the "old sow's vision" in the pig parlor saves this story from sentimentality. . . .

. . . We must take to heart Flannery's admonition that "Many students confuse the *process* of understanding a thing with understanding it" [*MM*, 71]. If the fiction of Flannery O'Connor serves as a warning against any critical vice, that vice is excessive reliance on the understanding, the *reasonable* approach to things. Thus, those of us who read and who teach Flannery O'Connor have a difficult task. We must allow ourselves and our students to see in the form and the content of her fiction an immersion in the real so profound that it moves beyond realism to the final shapes and essences of our ultimate being. As Hopkins puts it, "To the Father through the features of men's faces."

[Flannery O'Connor and Southern Fiction]

Louis D. Rubin, Jr.*

[Flannery O'Connor's] fiction has been used principally as a weapon for belaboring the heathen—the heathen including most of us who must traffic with the post-Reformation world. . . .

. . . O'Connor criticism is usually not an expression of literary taste but of theological allegiance. It concentrates upon the religious authenticity of her fiction. It is thematic, not formal criticism. As such it sidesteps or obscures so much that is central to her literary art. Properly speaking, it is not really interested in the author's literary imagination at all. It is next to useless in helping the reader to understand the human texture of this intensely Southern author's work. So far as a great deal of the critical commentary on Flannery O'Connor's fiction is concerned, one might as well be dealing with *Pilgrim's Progress* or the book of *Jeremiah*. . . .

. . . The issue is further confused by the fact that when [O'Connor] herself wrote about the art of fiction as she saw and practiced it, it was most often in terms of its religious dimension. A statement such as "I have found, in short, from reading my own writing, that my subject in fiction is the action of grace in territory largely held by the devil"— such a statement is theological and not literary. Or more accurately, such a statement isolates from the complex entity of fiction a single aspect of the work of art, its thematic concern, and appears to assert that in writing her fiction [O'Connor] was exclusively concerned with its religious significance.

*Permission to reprint this excerpt from "Flannery O'Connor's Company of Southerners: or 'The Artificial Nigger' Read as Fiction Rather than Theology," *Flannery O'Connor Bulletin* 6 (1977), is granted by the editors.

The fact is, however, that that is not what the statement really says at all, and in other remarks she has made about her high art—remarks that I am sorry to say seem to be less heeded by many of her admirers than her strictly theological pronouncements—she has been at pains to indicate that to write good fiction is to concern oneself with people in time and place, not with religious revelation as such. . . .

What I propose to do is to speak out . . . for Flannery O'Connor as a Southern writer rather than as a theologian, to confront her as the master artist who has given us a powerfully concrete and tangible gallery of men and women and children with Southern accents and whose life and thought are deeply grounded in the regional experience. I want to try to demonstrate that the Southern milieu in which her art is set, rather than being a mere stage setting for theological concerns . . . is not only part and parcel of her fiction but significantly modifies and shapes the meaning, the theme, of her fiction. And by this I am not merely talking about Southern fundamentalist Protestant Christianity, but Southern secular society, human forms and political, social and moral interests. . . .

. . . Thus the notion, which so many critics of Flannery O'Connor's fiction seem to hold, that it is the religious allegiance that gives her work its principal thrust, while the specifically Southern regional material is little more than a setting in which religious concerns manifest themselves, is hardly valid.

Indeed, if anything it might appear to be the other way around: one might almost say that the religious concerns—the so-called "drama of salvation"—provided her with a thematic device for focusing a set of attitudes, secular rather than religious, toward the nature of man in human time and in society, that were deeply grounded in the life of her region, with tenacious historical underpinnings, and held in common with a galaxy of writers, few of whom shared her specific religious concerns. . . .

. . . It is true that she read Teilhard de Chardin and Maritain and Mauriac; she also read Ralph McGill and Joel Chandler Harris and Henry W. Grady. She wrote about primitive unlettered Fundamentalists; but she was herself a very sophisticated and widely read young woman who was not a Hardshell Baptist but a Roman Catholic communicant. The trouble with many of those who write about her fiction is that they over-simplify both it and her.

. . . [O'Connor] said something that I have always remembered. It was, "So many students approach a story as if it were a problem in

algebra; find X and when they find X they can dismiss the rest of it."
That is what I feel uncomfortable with about so much that has been
written about her stories. Find X—find the act of grace, find the religious theme, and nothing else matters. It may be good exegetical theology; it makes for wretched literary criticism, for it ignores the
richness and mystery in order to fasten upon the immediately usable.
It reduces the gallery of characters with whom the O'Connor fiction is
peopled, that magnificently motley company of Southerners, to the
level of one-dimensional figures in a latterday morality play. What we
need is criticism that will explore the complexity of the work, and not
merely seek to use it to make theological observations.

[Flannery O'Connor and the Bible]

*Leon V. Driskell and Joan T. Brittain**

[Parker's Back"] is a story of redemption and of rebirth expressed
through O. E. Parker's assuming a prophetic role; he becomes Obadiah
Elihue as a result of two "miracles" drawn directly from the Old Testament sources of his name. Both stories demonstrate Miss O'Connor's
reliance upon, and fidelity to, scriptural sources, but they are themat-
ically quite different.
    . . . At first O. E. Parker is ashamed of his Christian name. During
their courtship, when he had whispered "what them letters are the
short of" to Sarah Ruth Cates, "her face slowly brightened as if the
name came as a sign to her . . . 'Obadiah,' she said. The name still
stank in Parker's estimation. 'Obadiah Elihue,' she said in a reverent
voice. 'If you call me that aloud, I'll bust your head open,' Parker said"
[*CS*, 517]. Returning home after the tattooing, eager to show his "picture of God" to his fundamentalist wife and certain she will recognize
and understand it, Parker finds the door locked. Sarah refuses to open
it when he identifies himself as O.E. "I don't know no O.E.," she says.
Finally "Parker bent down and put his mouth near the stuffed keyhole.
'Obadiah,' he whispered and all at once he felt the light pouring
through him, turning his spider web soul into a perfect arabesque of

*Reprinted from *The Eternal Crossroads: The Art of Flannery O'Connor* by permission
of the publishers; © 1971 by the University Press of Kentucky.

colors, a garden of trees and birds and beasts. 'Obadiah Elihue!' he whispered. The door opened and he stumbled in" [*CS*, 528].

. . . The intuitive and compulsive selection of the "picture of God" to be [tattooed] on his back and the identification of himself as Obadiah Elihue indicate that he has accepted his role as prophet of the destruction of the Edomites, as recorded in the vision of Obadiah in the Old Testament. He has already shown his difference by fighting with his former cronies in the poolhall. As she frequently does, Miss O'Connor reinforces the biblical parallels here with numerous specific details, enriching the story for the Bible student or for those readers willing to accept her terms and pursue her hints. . . .

The book of Obadiah follows the book of Amos and contains a vision of the destruction of Edom, as prophesied in Amos 1:11. In the eighth chapter of Amos, the prophet is shown a basket of summer fruit and the Lord tells him: "The end is come upon my people of Israel; I will not again pass by them any more" (Amos 8:2). Later (verse II) the Lord says: "Behold the days come that I will send a famine in the land, not a famine of bread, nor a thirst for water, but of hearing the words of the Lord." O.E.'s occupation and his apparent thirst for the word of God, despite his denials, allude to these passages in Amos. In the city he meets mockery on all sides—in the tattoo artist's studio and in the poolhall. The destruction of Edom is the destruction of the sons of Esau, son of Isaac and older brother of Jacob. Esau says to his brother, "Behold, I am at the point to die, and what profit shall this birthright do to me?" (Gen. 25:32). Recalling that the birthright is the father's blessing, and consequently God's blessing, one is justified in comparing Esau's question with Job's question, as stated by Elihu: "For thou saidst, What advantage will it be unto thee [God]? and, What profit shall I have if I be cleansed from my sin?" (Job 35:3).

Esau means "the red," and *Edom* comes from a primitive root meaning "to make or do." Esau the hunter is apparently more concerned with his physical than with his spiritual needs; consequently, he relinquishes his birthright though he later wheedles a blessing of sorts from Isaac. According to the vision of Obadiah, Edom is destroyed for its "violence against thy brother Jacob," the chosen of *the Lord* (Obad. 1:10). Metaphorically, however, Esau's sin is secularism, or materialism—the elevation of the physical over the spiritual.

Apparently, Parker is associated with Edom in the early parts of the story; his Christian name also associates him with the prophet who reports the vision. Verses three and four of the book of Obadiah, for

The Critics

instance, allude to the mountain which Edom occupies and to the Edomites' efforts to associate themselves with the eagle ("thou that dwellest in the clefts of the rock" and "though thou exalt thyself as the eagle"). In Miss O'Connor's story Sarah Ruth Cates declares that she likes none of O. E. Parker's tattoos but admits that "the chicken is not as bad as the rest." "'What chicken?' Parker almost yelled. She pointed to the eagle" [*CS*, 515].

At first Parker's attitude toward being saved, expressed to Sarah Ruth and to the tattoo artist, reveals that he considers salvation purely physical. He tells Sarah Ruth that "he didn't see it was anything in particular to save him from" [*CS*, 518], and to the artist's mocking question, "Are you saved?" he says, "I ain't got no use for none of that. A man can't save his self from whatever it is don't deserve none of my sympathy." But his words "seemed . . . to evaporate at once as if he had never uttered them" [*CS*, 524–25].

The first verse of the book of Obadiah reads: "We have heard a rumour from the Lord, and an ambassador is sent among the heathen, Arise ye, and let us rise up against her in battle." Obadiah Parker also hears a rumor from the Lord, as he testifies with his cry "GOD ABOVE!" [*CS*, 520] when he crashes into the tree and sees his shoes eaten by the fire. He goes among the heathen, the blasphemers in the poolhall, and "rises up against them": "Parker lunged into the midst of them and like a whirlwind on a summer's day there began a fight that raged amid overturned tables . . . Then a calm descended on the pool hall as nerve shattering as if the long barn-like room were the ship from which Jonah had been cast into the sea" [*CS*, 527]. As usual, Miss O'Connor has not permitted her biblical source to limit her choice of images, but her allusion to Jonah makes explicit the prophetic role which descends upon Parker because of the "rumour from the Lord." The Bible student will recall that Jonah follows Obadiah and that the great storm at sea results from Jonah's disobeying the Lord. The sailors cast Jonah into the sea "and the sea ceased from her raging. Then the men feared the Lord exceedingly, and offered a sacrifice unto the Lord, and made vows" (Jon. 1:15, 16). Although Parker, like Jonah, does not fully realize it, he has already begun his vocation.

André Bleikasten

[Flannery O'Connor, Freud, and Lacan]

*André Bleikasten**

Flannery O'Connor's novels and stories . . . at some point verges on what Freud, in one of his essays, termed "the uncanny," *das Unheimliche*—that disquieting strangeness apt to arise at every turn out of the most intimately familiar, and through which our everyday sense of reality is made to yield to the troubling awareness of the world's otherness. Much of the impact and lasting resonance of O'Connor's work proceeds from its ability to *bewilder* the reader, to take him out of his depths and jolt him into a fictional environment which is both homely (*heimisch, heimlich*) and uncannily estranged.

"Parker's Back" is a case in point: homely, indeed, in its rural setting and characters, homely too in its action—a domestic tragicomedy pitting wife against husband—yet at the same time wildly extravagant, throbbing with violence, ablaze with madness and terror, *unheimlich*. . . .

What is it that makes "Parker's Back" so uniquely intriguing? Not its manner, assuredly, nor its subject. . . . "Parker's Back" belongs with O'Connor's most explicitly religious stories. The Old Testament names of the two central characters, the harsh fundamentalism of Parker's wife, the "burning bush" experience undergone by Parker in the farming accident, and the Byzantine Christ tattooed on his back are as many signposts, clearly pointing to the religious issues at stake in the text. . . .

. . . Nearly all readings of "Parker's Back" are merely elaborations of the religious meaning. . . . Other avenues of inquiry and interpretation . . . are not only possible, but legitimate. . . .

. . . What is it that startles and shocks us in reading a story like "Parker's Back"? Obviously, its most arresting feature, the one most likely to disturb a modern reader, is Parker's *tattooing*. The more surprising it is that in most discussions of the story it should have been given so little consideration. To be sure, all commentators refer to it, vaguely puzzled and perhaps even a bit disgusted (tattooing, in our "civilized" countries, has come to be considered an "unnatural" practice, associ-

*Reprinted by permission of *The Southern Literary Journal* from "Writing on the Flesh: Tattoos and Taboos in 'Parker's Back,'" *The Southern Literary Journal* 14, no. 2 (1982):8–18.

ated with either savagery or deviant behavior), yet, in their eagerness to convert it at once into a secular metaphor for Parker's supposed spiritual quest, they tend to overlook its complex and shifting implications in the story of his development.

Parker's obsession with tattoos, we are told, begins when he is fourteen (in many cultures the canonical age for initiation) and sees a circus performer tattooed from head to foot. . . . The youth is at once fascinated by the spectacle and undergoes a kind of illumination, after which the course of his existence will take a radically different turn. . . . [This] turning-point [prefigures] Parker's later conversion. One might see it too . . . as the beginning of an "identity crisis." And what seems to be at stake in this crisis is above all his *body*.

No sooner has Parker seen the tattooed man than he identifies with him. . . . What enthralls Parker is a body or, more precisely, a body *image*, the seductive spectacle of a pattern engraved on a human skin. The word "pattern" could not be more apropos, referring as it does to either an ornamental design or a model worthy of imitation. To Parker it is clearly both. Henceforth, he will not rest until he has equalled his model, driven on by the compulsion to collect tattoos on his own body, to have his whole skin covered with them, to become in turn a pattern made flesh. Each new tattoo, however, only leads to further frustration. . . . What Parker goes through during his encounter with the tattooed man is like a replay of that infantile experience: it is the unexpected meeting of a mirror self, the discovery of an ideal double. The man, as Parker sees him, is "one intricate arabesque of colors"; he has managed, that is, to achieve unity, integrity, and harmony, by making his body into an artifact, a work of art. . . . The sight of the tattooed man startles him out of his drooling stupor into awareness of a body not yet totally his, a body to be appropriated and made whole and beautiful. An "awakening" has indeed occurred, but not in any spiritual sense, since Parker's exclusive concern, once he has had his "revelation," is the individuation of his body through systematic adornment of his skin. His enthrallment with the tattooed man points to nothing else but his late awakening to the exorbitant demands of narcissism.

By tattooing his skin, Parker, one might argue, attempts to phallicize his body, to turn it into a living fetish. Significantly enough, most of his tattoos are either pictures of wild animals (eagles, falcons, tigers, panthers, serpents) or conventional symbols of love (hearts pierced with arrows, a royal couple), not to mention the "obscenities" scribbled on his belly [cf. *CS*, 514]. . . . they all illustrate his narcissistic fantasies and attest to his desire for sexual daring, sexual potency, and unrestrained sexual gratification. . . . After being tattooed, Parker sets out to assert his manhood according to established norms of manliness. . . . his self-fetishization transforms him into a successful seducer. . . .

Parker's tattooing, then, has most remarkable effects in his life. . . . Yet . . . the more tattoos on his skin, the deeper his internal disorder and distress. As might be expected, the narcissistic attempt to transfigure his body ends in a shambles. In looking at himself in the mirror, Parker realizes with dismay that the tattoos fail to cohere, and that their overall effect is "of something haphazard and botched" [*CS*, 514]. And, if his long overdue "mirror-stage" proves a total mess, his series of cheap sexual triumphs comes likewise to a sorry end when he meets his wife-to-be, Sarah Ruth Cates.

His encounter with her marks the second turning-point in his destiny, and what follows it is his daily confrontation with someone who, in all conceivable respects, is his very opposite. Daughter of a "Straight Gospel preacher" [*CS*, 517], Sarah Ruth is a fanatical fundamentalist. She finds Parker's cursing outrageous, his tattoos repulsive. . . . Why a man like Parker should court and marry a woman like Sarah Ruth is the more perplexing as the latter, apart from being a redoubtable shrew, is "plain, plain" [*CS*, 510]. . . . To Parker himself the implausible choice is an endless source of gloomy wonder and speculation. What drew him and still draws him to Sarah Ruth has assuredly little to do with ordinary sexual attraction; it has much to do, however, with her *otherness*—not, this time, the alluring otherness of a gaudy *doppelganger*, but the radical otherness of the Law, whose fiercely uncompromising representative she turns out to be. . . . Sarah Ruth destroys his dream of carefree philandering by insisting on lawful marriage. It is she, too, who coaxes him into owning his Christian name, Obadiah Elihue. . . . Sarah Ruth's immediate function in the story is to discipline the unruly male . . . and make him conform to the accepted standards of a cultural order, . . . in this role, she performs a socializing (or "civilizing") task often assigned to woman in American fiction. To point out these secular implications of "Parker's Back" is not to belittle its religious significance, but rather to emphasize the interrelatedness of the sacred and the profane in its densely woven texture. . . .

. . . The urge to adorn one's body reflects dissatisfaction with one's body in its natural state, as a mere given, a random and transient fragment of the world. As we have pointed out, Parker's tattooing rage, at least in its early phase, has no other source: he rejects his given body, even as he rejects his given name, because he wishes to become the sovereign shaper of his own gorgeous self. This wish is surely also the artist's, the writer's, and Parker, therefore, should be seen, . . . as a comically distorted projection of the writer.

[Flannery O'Connor and Depth Psychology]

*Bartlett C. Jones**

Flannery O'Connor has been received favorably by critics who consider her a keen analyst of the decadent South, following the Gothic tradition of Poe, and with some embarrassment by Catholics who have tried to explain away her interest in the grotesque by calling it the depiction of modern man in need of redemption. (One Catholic apologist states that "it is the typical and essential which interest her, not the unique of abnormal psychology.")[1] Neither of these approaches is very helpful in analyzing her controversial short story, "Good Country People," in which she presents Southern victims of a classic neurosis. . . .

. . . Both the main characters and the story's structuring owe much to a perversion first analyzed by Karl Abraham, M.D.

The noted psychoanalyst shows that scoptophilia (pleasure in looking) may produce photophobia (hatred of light). This type of neurotic particularly wishes to protect his eyes from the sun, which is a bisexual symbol for certain unpleasant things he wants to avoid. "It not only represented his father (i.e., his watchful eye or his shining splendour) but also his mother, whom he must not look at for fear of calling down upon himself his father's anger."[2] The fear of the sun is partially the result of the patient's desire to view his mother's genitals. Since this was prohibited, the patient's scoptophilia was directed to parts of the

*Reprinted from *Midcontinent American Studies Journal* 5, no. 2; © 1964 Mid-America American Studies Association. Used by permission of the editors and Bartlett C. Jones, Ph.D., J.D., Central Methodist College.

body far removed from the genitals, to the eyes and feet. According to Abraham:

> Even these parts of the body were not themselves permitted to play the role assigned to them through the process of displacement, but had to yield to accessory parts that did not belong to the body itself. Thus girls who wore glasses or who had a false leg would attract him most of all; and a lame gait which suggested a stiff leg or an artificial limb would have the same effect on him. (178)

We learn that one "of the patient's most pleasurable phantasies was the idea of taking away her glasses from a short-sighted girl, or, better still, a one-eyed girl, or of depriving a young woman of her artificial leg" (179). (The Bible salesman boasts of stealing a woman's glass eye through the same method he used to trick Hulga.) O'Connor transforms the patient's phantasies into the salesman's perverted acts. We must reject the view that stealing the leg is "a familiar 'comic' device which may have originated on the American frontier, where mutilation was common."[3]

The story's structural unity is based on this neurosis. It begins with a description of the intense gaze of Mrs. Freeman, the tenant's wife, whose eyes "never swerved to left or right" [*CS*, 271]. O'Connor thus introduces the image of the strong parental eye; Mrs. Freeman watches everything and everybody, particularly her two daughters. As the salesman makes his escape in the story's final scene, "Mrs. Freeman's gaze drove forward and just touched him before he disappeared under the hill" [*CS*, 291]. The story thus ends as it began, with the parental eye dominant. This image is reinforced by Mrs. Hopewell's close watch over Hulga. who is acutely aware of this scrutiny. When preparing breakfast, prior to keeping her tryst with the salesman, Hulga "perceived her mother's eye upon her" [*CS*, 282]. Disturbed as well by mention of the salesman, Hulga soon stumps from the room.

. . . Hulga and the salesman are drawn together because they have the same neurosis. . . . both have lost their father, he through a fatal accident while Hulga's parents were long ago divorced. And Abraham's patient, whose father was dead, "had the idea that his father was standing in heaven next to the sun and looking down upon him in order to observe what he did," indicating that the father was "being likened to the sun without as yet having been united with it into a single being" (186). Hulga is "squint-eyed" [*CS*, 276] and, in the loft scene, turns her head away from the sunlight. . . . Hulga's affinity for this particular youth, whose ignorance and stupidity would usually repel her, is described when "she was thinking that she would run away with him and that every night he would take the leg off and every morning put it on again" [*CS*, 289]. O'Connor surmises that the active desires of the male neurotic have passive female equivalents. Part of the salesman's pitch to Mrs. Hopewell was the claim that he would not live long because of a heart condition. Thinking of her daughter, Mrs. Hopewell was touched because both "had the same condition." This conclusion becomes highly ironic as we discover their similar neurotic afflictions.

Whatever final judgments are made concerning this virtually inexhaustible story, we should concede that the well-established perversion affects the characters, structure, action, irony, imagery, and meaning. It makes the story universal, but neither dictates nor excludes a religious affirmation. . . . The ideal critic is supposed to be an expert in all academic disciplines. Psychoanalytic insights may partially explain all artists, literary works, and aesthetic responses; but not exhaust literature which is greater than the sum of its parts.

1. P. Albert Duhamel, "Flannery O'Connor's Violent View of Reality," *Catholic World* 190 (1960):281. [The danger of relying too much on the author's own words taken out of context is evident in this judgment: cf. part 2, p. 125 above.]

2. Karl Abraham, *Selected Papers of Karl Abraham, M.D.* (New York, 1960), 177. Subsequent references are to this text.

3. J. Greene, "Comic and Sad," *Commonweal* 62 (22 July 1955).

4. Caroline Gordon, "Flannery O'Connor's *Wise Blood*," *Critique* 2 (Fall 1958):9.

Claire Katz [Kahane]

[Flannery O'Connor's Sadistic Wit]

Claire Katz [Kahane]*

In discussing the writer in America, A. Alvarez has noted that the ubiq-
uitous violence which threatens to devour us in this age has been in-
ternalized by the artist who works out in the microcosm of his self the
destructive potentiality of the time.[1] Certainly the times have provided
spectacular metaphors for the darkest side of the mind; the violence of
Dachau, Hiroshima, Mississippi too easily supports our most primitive
fears. But the writer does more than assimilate the other world to his
purposes; he also projects his own corresponding impulses onto the
macrocosm, shaping through his fictions a world which reflects his specific inner vision. For the writer, the inner and outer worlds merge in
an imaginatively extended country, and in the fiction of Flannery
O'Connor that country is dominated by a sense of imminent destruction. From the moment the reader enters O'Connor's backwoods, he
is poised on the edge of a pervasive violence. Characters barely contain
their rage; images reflect a hostile nature. . . .

Since O'Connor had identified her theme as Christian, it is no surprise to find critics discussing this prototypical pattern in religious
terms: the protagonist is humiliated in order to recognize his state of
sin and is thus open to grace and redemption. Characters are classified
anagogically, Christian symbols and biblical references noted, and what
emerges from these studies is the portrait of a writer tracing a timeless
moral schema instead of engaging imaginatively with her felt experience. Yet one might wonder at the readiness with which O'Connor's
anagogic intent is critically accepted as definitive. For although she
remarked that "violence is strangely capable of returning my characters
to reality and preparing them for their moment of grace" [*MM*, 112],
she unleashes a whirlwind of destructive forces more profound than
her Christian theme would seem to justify—murder, rape, mutilation—for ostensibly religious purposes. . . .

. . . conventional readings ignore the deeply private nature of
O'Connor's vision, the inner necessities which dominate her fictional
world. Her peculiar insistence on absolute powerlessness as a condition
of salvation so that any assertion of autonomy elicits violence with a

*Reprinted with permission from Claire Katz, "Flannery O'Connor's Rage of Vision,"
American Literature 46, no. 1 (1974):54–67; Copyright © 1974, Duke University Press.

vengeance, the fact that she locates the means of grace repeatedly in the sexually perverse as in Tarwater's rape, or in the literally murderous rage of characters like the Misfit, suggest that at the center of her work is a psychological demand which overshadows her religious intent, shaping plot, image and character as well as her distinctive narrative voice. . . .

Perhaps nowhere is her use of violence more sophisticated than in her narrative voice. For O'Connor as narrator plays the role of scourge. Using the weapons of wit, she derides the pretensions of personality in icily-wrought metaphors. . . . Ruby in "A Stroke of Good Fortune" appears carrying her groceries, her "head like a big florid vegetable at the top of the sack" [CS, 95]. Mrs. Freeman in "Good Country People," "besides the neutral expression that she wore when she was alone . . . had two others, forward and reverse, that she used for all her human dealings" [CS, 271]. One might surmise that O'Connor was a cartoonist, for here her eye is the eye of the caricaturist. . . .

. . . The sadism of the narrator exorcises the sadism of the characters, but both participate in the sadistic impulse. Indeed, narrator and protagonist are two aspects of one dynamic: the author's psyche, split into the punishing parent and the rebellious child. Thus, most of her protagonists, even when they are adults, seem fixed as children, acting out a drama of infantile conflict in a context strangely isolated from social realities. . . . Although O'Connor conceived of art as an adjustment of inner and outer worlds, the inner world predominates. Paradoxically, it is because the narrator functions as punishing parent that she can distance herself from the protagonist and express the fantasies and forbidden impulses of the rebellious child, punishing him simultaneously by both the resolution of plot and her acidic wit.

This authorial ambivalence causes the reader to respond to her work on two levels. The reader identifies with the narrator, enjoying the wit and the sadistic impulses behind it. . . .

. . . The reader also identifies with the protagonist to the extent that the violent confrontations arouse dread and anxiety even under the surveillance of wit. Indeed, wit itself originates in what was once feared but is now mastered; and security from danger, both internal and external, is a precondition of comic enjoyment. Yet O'Connor undermines the reader's sense of security, undermines comic elements by making the familiar world strange, by weakening our sense of reality through the distorting lens of an imagery that evokes archaic fears. A construction machine seems a "big disembodied gullet" which gorges itself on clay and then, "with the sound of a deep sustained nausea and a slow mechanical revulsion," turns and spits it up. The smile of a prostitute becomes a "mouth split into a wide full grin that showed her teeth. They were small and pointed and speckled with green and there was a wide space between each one." A cloud "shaped like a turnip" descends "over the sun, and another, worse looking, crouched behind the car." Trees "pierce out of the ground" or stand "in a pool of red light that gushed from the almost hidden sun setting behind them." Aggressive verbs make the landscape threatening: "the fields stretched sodden on either side until they hit the scrub pines"; "trains passing appeared to emerge from a tunnel of trees and, hit for a second by the cold sky, vanish terrified into the woods again." Sun, sky and woods constantly engage in violent interactions: the sun "was swollen and flame-colored and hung in a net of ragged cloud as if it might burn through any second and fall into the woods"; "the blank sky looked as if it were pushing against the fortress wall [of trees], trying to break through." This is an animistic world, fraught with images of infantile fears—of devouring, of penetration, of castration—in which the distinctions between physical and psychical reality blur. The comic vision has yielded to reveal its fearsome, uncanny origins.

Traditionally, it is this admixture of the uncanny and the comic which comprises the grotesque. While "grotesque" has been the word used to label O'Connor's world, it has not been used to explain it. In his essay "The Uncanny," Freud has provided a key to understanding that essential aspect of the grotesque. The uncanny exists "when repressed infantile complexes have been revived by some impression, or when the primitive beliefs we have surmounted seem once more to be confirmed."[2] As elements which compose the uncanny, he lists the castration complex, womb fantasies, the idea of the double, the animistic conception of the universe, the omnipotence of thoughts, and the primitive fear of the dead—all concepts of very early mental life which, when they emerge in the context of ordinary adult reality, have the effect of weakening our ego faculty. These elements, skillfully integrated into the imagery of O'Connor's fiction, are responsible for its disturbingly grotesque quality. . . .

The source of imaginative power in O'Connor's fiction, then, lies in her ability to evoke fearful primitive fantasies, fantasies made especially vivid by her use of uncanny imagery but countered both by a defensive wit which barely assuages the terror of her vision and by resolutions of plot which mitigate the provoked anxiety. In O'Connor's world the environment becomes a projection of sadistic impulses and fears so strong that the dissolution of the ego's power, ultimately death, is the only path to safety. Paradoxically, to be destroyed is to be saved.

To understand the psychoanalytic dynamics of this paradox, it is helpful to recall that initially a child conceives of himself as essentially omnipotent, the external world, including the parent, an extension of himself. As reality collapses that fantasy, every frustration is reacted to with a rage of destructive fantasies directed at the source of frustration, typically the mother. But the child's helplessness and his fears of retaliation cause him to project his aggressive wishes onto the environment. . . . the fates of O'Connor characters parallel these childhood fantasies. They are drowned ("The River"), engulfed by the rottenness of the world ("The Life You Save May Be Your Own"), raped or otherwise destructively penetrated (*The Violent Bear It Away*), blinded or otherwise symbolically castrated (*Wise Blood*). . . .

This regressive fantasy dominates O'Connor's fiction, appearing repeatedly in the situation of a rebellious child confronting a parent who exerts some form of control. In each case, the child perceives that control as violation of his integrity; but, although he angrily insists on his self-reliance, violence forces him into submission. . . .

The equation between independence and anarchic aggression is complicated by the child's unresolved relation to the father. Actual fathers rarely appear in O'Connor's fiction; when they do, they are usually sadistic figures, their aggressiveness associated with the sexual role of the male as penetrator. The child can identify with this role and with the father's power, as Thomas does in "The Comforts of Home"; but this story shows the awful consequences of that identification. Thomas shoots his mother; and, although the act is apparently accidental, the Sheriff's misconstruction of the crime as intentional is supported by O'Connor's textual ambiguities: she implies that Thomas's assumption of his father's role is responsible for his mother's death.

Or the child can choose to be the object of this aggression, equating it masochistically with love. Mary Fortune, in "A View of the Woods," about to be beaten by her father, "followed him almost ran after him," eager to accept the beating as an act of love. But because of the guilt evoked by this forbidden gratification, with its incestuous overtones, she ritually denies that her father beats her. Challenged by her grandfather on this very issue, she defensively identifies with her father—

"I'm pure Pitts"—and attacks her grandfather, whipping him in a vicious repudiation of her passive role. To act, O'Connor implies, is to assume the male role and the power associated with the father. . . .

What makes Flannery O'Connor's fiction so compelling to the contemporary imagination is that her personal conflict precisely reflects a major twentieth-century dilemma. The central struggle between parent and child, defined by the child's relative helplessness and anger, by his fear of engulfment by omnipotent figures, is paradigmatic. It parallels our subsequent struggle to assert the magnitude of the individual against the engulfing enormity of a technological society which fragments social roles, shatters community, and splits off those qualities of warmth, intimacy and mutual dependence which nourish a sense of identity. The violence in American life which punctuates and relieves the tension of that struggle is like a mirror projection of the violence with which O'Connor's characters respond to frustration.

1. A. Alvarez, "The Problem of the Artist," *Under Pressure* (Baltimore, 1965), 178.

2. "The Uncanny" (1919), rpt. in *On Creativity and the Unconscious*, ed. Benjamin Nelson (New York, 1958), 157.

[Feminine Identity]

Louise Westling*

The farm stories are some of [O'Connor's] most vivid and absorbing works, and all of them are concerned with the issues of feminine identity and authority. . . .

The main character of "A Temple of the Holy Ghost" is a sour twelve-year-old girl whose widowed mother runs a small farm. The child is never named, but her ugliness and her intelligence make her an unforgettable character. She is fat and clumsy, with a mouth full of braces that glare like tin, but she is a very serious child with relentlessly

*Reprinted by permission of the University of Georgia Press from, *Sacred Groves and Ravaged Gardens: The Fiction of Eudora Welty, Carson McCullers, and Flannery O'Connor*, by Louise Westling; © 1985 the University of Georgia Press.

acute perceptions of the people around her and a precocious moral awareness. Like Sally Virginia Cope in "A Circle in the Fire," Joy-Hulga Hopewell in "Good Country People," and numerous minor characters in other stories, she is a hilarious caricature of her creator. . . . Most of these fat, intelligent young women only slenderly know themselves and have few emotions besides rage and contempt. This unnamed girl, however, understands her faults and has a sense of humor, real intellectual curiosity, serious ambitions, and an intense religious faith like Flannery O'Connor's.

. . . The major elements of the mother-daughter pattern appear in "Good Country People." . . . In at least six of O'Connor's thirty-one published stories, the plot centers on a mother resembling Mrs. Hopewell and a daughter like Joy. The mother is a hardworking widow who supports and cares for her large, physically marred girl by running a small farm. The daughter is almost always bookish and very disagreeable. The mother is devoted to her nevertheless, but she is exasperated by her daughter's perversity. Most critics of O'Connor's fiction have noticed how often variations of this motif appear in the stories, but few commentators go beyond asserting that this material has autobiographical sources.

. . . In fully half the stories published in *A Good Man Is Hard to Find* and the posthumous *Everything That Rises Must Converge*, widowed or divorced mothers are central female characters who are tricked, deluded, or violently chastened. These stranded women have been left to raise bad-tempered sons or, more often, daughters, but they prove tough and resourceful in their dealings with the outside world and thus create modest little matriarchies where their sour children can lead comfortable lives. O'Connor satirizes the [matriarch's] stinginess, smugness, wariness of strangers, and determination to see things in a cheerful light, which are the side effects of the widow's struggle. In most of these stories the mother's pride is ultimately smashed by a vindictive male force, perhaps most extremely in "Greenleaf," "The Comforts of Home," and "Everything That Rises Must Converge," where she dies under assault.

Daughters have the same outrage at their mothers' smugness and the same resentment of her authority that sons express, but there the similarity ends. Almost every son wants to punish his mother or "teach her a lesson." Two actually kill their mothers, and The Misfit of "A Good Man Is Hard to Find" could be said to have the same instinctive reaction in shooting the grandmother when she reaches out to him saying, "Why, you're one of my babies!" Daughters, on the other hand, usually end up as allies of their mothers, forced by male deceit and violence into humiliating defeat.

. . . Southern legal traditions made it difficult for women to control property in the nineteenth century, and widows who attempted to manage their own affairs were regarded as arrogant. The carnage of the Civil War produced many widows who had to support their families alone through the terrible decades of Reconstruction. Although most succeeded, they did so in a hostile masculine business and legal environment. . . . O'Connor's stories show us a modern South where similar hardships exist for widows in muted form; her Mrs. Cope, Mrs. Hopewell, Mrs. MacIntyre, Mrs. May, and Mrs. Crater all preserve a fear of disaster hovering just at the borders of consciousness. This fear is a defensive understanding of the predatory forces they have only narrowly survived.

These women have maintained homes for their children against great odds, and have sacrificed to give them a chance in life, yet neither sons nor daughters mature successfully. Sons grow up to be intellectual drones who live at home, sullenly resentful of their mothers but unable to break away. In "Why Do the Heathen Rage?" a son snarls at his mother, "A woman of your generation is better than a man of mine" [*CS*, 485]. He sees this as a shameful reversal of normal masculine superiority, and O'Connor intends it to demonstrate his bitter understanding of his own failure. The daughters' situations are more specifically hopeless because they are not only physically unappealing but also too intelligent, well educated, and sourly independent to ever assume "normal" roles as wives and mothers. . . . the daughters of the stories are social misfits whom she is always contrasting to girls of both upper and lower classes who are immersed in courtship and reproduction. Nothing could be further from the beauty and grace of the Southern belle than the glasses, ugly braces, and extra pounds of O'Connor's twelve-year-old girls or the wooden legs, bad hearts, and fondness for the ridiculous sweat shirts and Girl Scout shoes of her mature daughters.

. . . Rebellion against the standards set by genteel mothers is typical for the daughters of the stories. . . . If we wish to know why the daughters resist so fiercely, we need only turn to "The Life You Save May Be Your Own." The story opens with a mother and daughter who live in a perfect harmony symbolized by their bearing exactly the same name—Lucynell Crater. That is their only resemblance, however, and their grotesque differences provide a caricature of their relationship. The mother is a hard-bitten, leathery, and toothless country widow whose toughness has enabled her to survive but has taken its toll. The daughter is a moron whose vapid beauty is, in Martha Chew's words, "a parody of the pink and white looks and facade of sweetness required of Southern women."[1] She has long pink-gold hair and "eyes as blue as a peacock's neck." In contrast to most of O'Connor's daughters, Lucynell Jr. is absolutely docile, serving as a strange and distorted symbol of spiritual innocence.

Lucynell's speechless imbecility must be the reason for her sweet nature. Female intelligence is a curse in the world of these stories, for it creates profound discontent. Frustrated in a society of hillbillies, religious fundamentalists, and snuff-dipping tenant farmers, most of these bright fat girls snipe away at the pretension and stupidity around them. In "A Temple of the Holy Ghost" . . . the twelve-year-old girl's proud and sour intelligence makes her see her cousins and their dates as "stupid idiots" and prevents her from participating in their normal adolescent activities. In "Revelation," the same kind of intelligence causes a rage of resentment verging on madness for the acne-faced college girl in the doctor's waiting room. Mary Grace grows more and more outraged as she listens to Mrs. Turpin's self-congratulatory remarks about her own virtuous place in Southern society. Although her genteel mother tries to placate her, the girl finally explodes, hurling her book across the room at Mrs. Turpin's head and then leaping after it and trying to strangle the object of her rage. . . . the strange intensity of her hatred and the unexpected violence of her action leave us with a shocked curiosity. Intelligence seems a curse which has unbalanced her, but at the same time the story's resolution bears out the rightness of her negative judgment upon Mrs. Turpin's pride. Ultimately, Mary Grace's presence in the story is too strong and troubling for the limited role she plays.

Most of O'Connor's daughters keep their intolerance under better control and try to maintain an aloofness from the world their mothers and people like Mrs. Turpin represent. Involvement with men eventually destroys their pretensions of independence, however, and forces them to share their mother's vulnerability.

1. Martha Chew, "Flannery O'Connor's Double-edged Satire: The Idiot Daughter Versus the Lady Ph.D.," *Southern Quarterly* 19 (1981):20.

Preston M. Browning, Jr.

[O'Connor's Clinical Understanding of Neurosis]

*Preston M. Browning, Jr.**

Wherever one turns in [O'Connor's second collection, *Everything That Rises Must Converge*], there is evidence of [her] sensitivity to the changes which her region was undergoing during the late 1950s and early 1960s.

As always, O'Connor brought to these subjects an intelligence keenly alive to the complexities of the human mind—its subterfuges, its self-deceptions, its seemingly inexhaustible capacity for rationalization. In her two novels and in such early stories as "Good Country People," "The Life You Save May Be Your Own," and "The Artificial Nigger," she has demonstrated an astonishingly mature grasp of the dynamics of human psychology. Yet something new (in degree if not in kind) seems to distinguish the stories of the second collection: an almost clinical understanding of certain forms of neurosis. The title story, for example, is a virtual case study of what psychoanalysts would describe as denial and projection. . . .

One critic offers a useful clue to the basis of these stories' commonly acknowledged excellence when he observes that "it is as though in the struggle against her illness [O'Connor] had come to locate grotesqueness and grace in the common life of men and that she had no more time or talent to waste on merely being odd or bizarre."[1] Here one may feel compelled to demur, since today most critics agree that even in her earliest fiction O'Connor spent little of her time on the *merely* odd or bizarre. Yet this reviewer has put his finger on something real and important in the development of O'Connor's talent: in the last stories she has apparently left behind the blatant melodrama of, say, "A Good Man Is Hard to Find." Her Misfits are no longer psychopathic killers or voyeuristic Bible salesmen. They are instead the ineffectual sons of well-meaning but exasperating mothers. Or they are the emotionally disturbed Wellesley student and the self-righteous Mrs. Turpin of "Revelation." . . . for the most part she [seemed] to find her imagination creating less extravagantly fanciful characters than Tom T. Shiftlet or Manley Pointer or Hazel Motes. More often than not, too, it is

*Reprinted with permission from *Flannery O'Connor* (Carbondale: Southern Illinois University Press, 1974), 99–131.

in the "common life of men" that she located the workings of grace. Which is not to say that there is anything commonplace or tame about the stories in *Everything That Rises*; on the contrary, here is abundant grotesquerie and violence. Instead of abandoning altogether her taste for melodrama, "she severely disciplined it to weigh the consequences of perverse will and crooked passions,"[2] the result being that in such a story as "A View of the Woods," what appears as a more or less harmless and humorous contest of wills detonates into a fury of destruction, and self-destruction, even as the comic surface is preserved almost to the very end. . . .

O'Connor's fiction projects an image of man who has lost so completely his capacity for apprehending true evil that he is equally incapable of recognizing true good. And his addiction to superficial and platitudinous conceptions of both good and evil seems the consequence of a loss even more profound—the experience of the self as grounded in being.

Both O'Connor's positivists and her positive thinkers, then, like the "faithless pilgrims" of Conrad's *Heart of Darkness*, suffer from a malaise which is, at bottom, ontological. Dispossessed both of their original innocence and of their postlapsarian knowledge, they seek, however unconsciously, a way back into being. But the way to being is fraught with peril, since it entails confronting the irrational and destructive aspects of the self, facing up to the ugliness and cruelty of life, exploring that foul "dungeon of the heart," which Hawthorne, Dostoevsky and other spiritual forefathers of O'Connor considered of the essence of human existence but which centuries of moralistic Christianity and Bourgeois culture have tended to deny or obscure. . . .

Flannery O'Connor, it might finally be argued, sought to recover the depth dimension of existence in order to adumbrate an answer to the "ontological void" posited by Ionesco and other contemporary artists and philosophers. But she recognized that the recovery of depth, or being, was possible only by stripping the masks from men whose fraudulent righteousness had rendered them too complacent even to be damned. Therefore, her strategy as a writer was to make as vivid as possible the reality of the demonic, to celebrate, as it were, "spiritual crime," to employ the shock of evil over and over again, in the hope that, finally, by plunging into those fearful psychic depths she might bring up some evidence that, in a time marked by moral chaos and ontological deprivation, it was yet being, not absurdity, which would have the last word.

1. Theodore Solotaroff, "You Can Go Home Again," New York *Herald Tribunes's Book Week*, 30 May 1965, 13.
2. Ibid.

[O'Connor and Jung]

*Mary L. Morton**

In an essay published in 1969, Robert Drake asks whether, in creating so many villainesses, Flannery O'Connor uses a spiritual double standard (440).[1] His question reflects a somewhat superficial assessment of the O'Connor canon. To begin, women predominate in her human comedy, doing something with percentages. Excluding five short stories eventually rewritten and integrated into the two novels, we find female protagonists in eighteen of the remaining twenty-six short stories. Next, erring males like Mr. Head or Mr. Shiftlet do populate her fiction. But because O'Connor used a large cast of females to satirize those beset with pride and an ensuing sense of superiority, anyone may think her a traitor to her sex. On the contrary, O'Connor's stories dramatize the ludicrosity of women who have denied the spirit of femininity, the *anima*. Such angular, ludicrous women in one archetypal class are the managerial women who scorn any beliefs in mystery or interest in creation. Their doubles are fat women of the earth. O'Connor's trick on some readers is to arouse sympathy with the lean, joyless women of the work ethic and rejection of the women akin to the "lilies of the field." A look at the doubling of the angular female with her obese counterpart in several of the stories shows the former possessed of *animus*, the latter of *anima*.

O'Connor records in her stories a period of cataclysmic change in the South. Three apocalyptic stories signifying a violent breakup of an old way of life feature the pairings of managerial women and their obese, chthonic doubles: "A Circle in the Fire," "Greenleaf," and "The Displaced Person." Mrs. Cope, Mrs. May, and Mrs. McIntyre are the respective managers; they are angular, careworn, joyless, humorless

---

*Reprinted from "Doubling in Flannery O'Connor's Female Characters: Animus and Anima," *Southern Quarterly* 23, no. 4 (1985):57–63, with permission from the editor.

women who lack any qualities associated with the *anima*. Indeed, they constantly mouth shallow beliefs in the Puritan work ethic: industry, cleanliness, reason, and righteousness. On the other hand, their doubles, sharecroppers' wives, are fat, indolent, fascinated with mystery, whether of reproduction or whatever, and show close affinities with mother earth. The managerial type in each story represents a woman who has abandoned the *anima* and consciously adopted a masculine ethic. At some point in each story, she assumes some of the characteristics of the chthonic archetype, with results varying from increased wisdom to total destruction—not only of self, but of a total way of life.

First of all, the managerial women who avow themselves rationalists and exhibit contempt for any belief in the supernatural and irrational are shown to be notoriously blind to their predicaments. Each fancies herself in control of a farm and of the people around her, but each story dramatizes the opposite in fact. Although Mrs. Cope of "A Circle in the Fire" derides "omens and signs" as "figments of the imagination," she nevertheless entertains "vague dreads" that she attempts to suppress. Because she is graced with enough intuition to realize that she may not totally control fate, she is spared to live a wiser woman than she was.

As the story opens, Mrs. Cope wears a sunbonnet originally identical to the one worn by her chthonic double, Mrs. Pritchard. Mrs. Cope's is still unfaded, representing the angular rigid woman who parries the prurient gossip of her double, whose bonnet is a sad victim of time. Mrs. Cope's frenetic attacks on the nut-grass contrast with Mrs. Pritchard's lackadaisical swings of the hoe. Mrs. Cope tries to deny or minimize the reality of suffering; she particularly wants to ignore the fact that a woman could conceive a child while in an iron lung, a fact which is a source of wonder to Mrs. Pritchard. Nor has Mrs. Cope any sympathy for the deaths of the mother and child—death has no place in her bright superficiality; Mrs. Pritchard, on the other hand, would go "thirty miles for the satisfaction of seeing anybody laid away." Her conversation establishes her chthonic affinities with human sexuality, irrationality, death—characteristic of the mythos of femininity, albeit in O'Connor's comedy of rural female manners.

Mrs. Pritchard recognizes the potential for irrational evil in the boys who visit the farm. Mrs. Cope, however, feels she can control the son of a former sharecropper on her place. The son and his friends represent a class of people who have moved from the country to the city, a phenomenon remarked upon in "Everything That Rises Must Converge" and in a letter O'Connor wrote to John Hawkes. The managerial woman fails to "cope" through her hypocritical and syrupy manners: "I think it was real sweet of you boys to visit me." When manners fail, she tries the law, which also fails.

When reason and logic fail, Mrs. Cope fastens her irritability on her daughter, Sally Virginia, telling her she should belong to Mrs. Pritchard. This wish for child-swapping found in many of the stories symbolizes a link between the fragmented selves, a combining of the *anima* and *animus*. Sally Virginia, the innocent recorder, knows that anything cheerful puts Mrs. Pritchard in a bad humor, yet she herself, unlike her mother who tries to ignore subconscious fear, is alive to "mysterious shrieks." Sally Virginia's is the balancing consciousness of the story.

Through her eyes we see the structural circle of the story. At the end, Mrs. Cope and Mrs. Pritchard have reversed roles. Initially, Mrs. Cope's bright hat and cheery outlook contrast with Mrs. Pritchard's faded hat and dark view. One's litany of thanksgiving is counterpointed by the other's catalog of woe. At the end, Mrs. Pritchard's lassitude disappears as she energetically attacks the fire while Mrs. Cope stands paralyzed. She, who had earlier denied kinship with the generation and death cycle of the woman in the iron lung, wears a look of "old misery." Following the archetypal pattern of a closed existence, having travelled the labyrinths of the interior self, she emerges an aged woman, resembling not only Mrs. Pritchard but all who have suffered, as Sally Virginia observes. The old order of the women's lives is purged by fire as their identities merge. The masculine Protestant work ethic that Mrs. Cope had adopted as her own, while attempting to deny feminine mystery and intuition, fails her. Mrs. Pritchard has, in her chthonic affinities, at least a sounder sense of what is real—the suffering that binds humankind together—even the sharecropping class seeking refuge from urban ills.

1. Robert Drake, "The Paradigm of Flannery O'Connor's True Country," *Studies in Short Fiction* 6, no. 4 (1969):433–42.

[The Terrifying, the Comic, and the Melodramatic]

*Frederick Asals**

[Flannery O'Connor] is quite capable, particularly in her later stories, of a rapid shifting of tone (demanding a comparable nimbleness in the reader), but her most characteristic voice is that of the ironist who speaks at a great emotional distance from her subject yet, paradoxically, with great intensity, as if, although her characters must be viewed as fools or worse, what happens to them *matters* enormously. . . .

The act of looking demands distance, sharp vision requires removal from the object viewed. If O'Connor's detachment implies anything but indifference, the severity of her act of perception *is* inextricable from the disconcerting laughter that sounds through her fiction. For her view of man is incorrigibly comic, comic with the piercing insight that can suddenly flip up the dark underside of human folly to reveal the matching grin of the memento mori. The grandmother of "A Good Man Is Hard to Find," for example, dresses elaborately for the family trip so that "in case of an accident, anyone seeing her dead on the highway would know at once that she was a lady" [*CS*, 118]. The wild disproportion of the terms, the vapid composure that summons up the ultimate violence only to treat it as a rare social opportunity, and the cool irony with which O'Connor presents the sentence make it both fearful and ludicrous.

. . . O'Connor's comic range is of course not limited to any single effect; she moves easily from paradoxical wit to the confusions of farce, from sharp satire to dialect humor, from subtle ironies to broad laughter. The stories are not monochromatic: they possess shadings of tone, degrees of distance and sympathy, and the later works in particular require complex responses throughout. . . .

The implicit violence in comedy is the hidden link between manner and matter in O'Connor, between the freeing of laughter and the freezing of fear. . . . the terrifying and the comic create a tension analogous to the recurrent motif of unrecognized double figures, or the repeated clashes between parents and children. Yet this fundamental doubleness

*Reprinted by permission of the University of Georgia Press from *Flannery O'Connor: The Imagination of Extremity*, by Frederick Asals; © 1982 the University of Georgia Press.

also makes itself felt in her pervasive use of that highly ironic narrative voice. The duality implicit in all irony is heightened and sustained in O'Connor's work. In insisting on the split between what the protagonist takes himself to be and what he actually is (which in turn is inseparable from what he takes his world to be as opposed to what *it* is), her narrator points not just to a misjudgment or incomplete awareness, but to a veritable chasm of self-deception. "You aren't who you think you are" ["Everything That Rises Must Converge," *CS*, 419], one of those protagonists smugly tells his mother (neither, of course, is he), and the remark might serve as a motto for all her central figures. That gap between the fabricated and deeply false persona and the true self . . . is already implied in the double consciousness of the ironic narrator, whose false speaking masks true knowing and who thereby creates a double consciousness in the reader as well.

Along with the poised distance of that ironic narrative voice and the sustained comic perception, the rigorous attention to craft and the sparely honed style help achieve in O'Connor's fiction . . . the powerful sense of discipline and control that seems at the opposite pole from—and so perhaps made possible—the unleashing of the dark unreasonable forces of the violent and terrifying. For at the heart of her imagination is an irremediable wildness, a deliberate pursuit of the "extreme situation" that for her seems to have demanded the craftsmanship and coolness and ironic comedy to bring her obsessive materials under control. She was clearly determined to make the violence she conjured up engage a larger meaning and thus point to a greater order, but much of the power of her work flows from the unimpeded intensity of deeply felt sources which she learned how to shape without suppressing. One of Flannery O'Connor's firmest convictions is that the vital centers of life, both within and beyond the self, are radically unreasonable, and in her fiction the nonrational expresses itself in violence.

As a result, the shocking climaxes of her stories are frequently appropriate to the action that precedes them without seeming entirely inevitable. O'Connor herself once described those moments as characterized by "an action or a gesture which was both totally right and totally unexpected" [*MM*, 111]. Almost inescapably her plots have a melodramatic cast, sometimes sensationally so. The number of accidents in her fiction alone is an index of the best of her imagination, from the overturned car of "A Good Man Is Hard to Find" to the runaway tractor that kills the displaced person, from the bull's goring of

Mrs. May in "Greenleaf" to Thomas's shooting of his mother in "The Comforts of Home." But despite the gratuitousness inherent in melodramatic action, O'Connor's climaxes grow out of an incipient violence of language, imagery, and emotion which creates explosive pressures. In "A Circle in the Fire," for example, the increasing fierceness of the landscape—from the opening "black wall" of trees behind which "the sun was a livid glaring white" to that sun "swollen and flame-colored and hung in a net of ragged cloud as if it might burn through any second and fall into the woods" [CS, 175, 184]—parallels the developing antagonism between the farm dwellers and the invading city boys. Yet this hostility is itself rooted in the obsessive fears and negations of the farm owner, Mrs. Cope—she tears at weeds "as if they were an evil sent directly by the devil to destroy the place" [CS, 175]—which in turn increasingly evokes the boys' latent destructiveness; and the atmosphere of impending violence is further heightened by dialogue given over to discussions of fires, hurricanes, European boxcars, iron lungs, guns, fighting, stealing, and poisoning. When the story bursts into the climactic fire, that outcome immediately seems right if not inescapable.

O'Connor's use of melodramatic action is central to her strategy to make available in fiction that realm of mystery beyond manners. "If art imitates life," Bentley has noted, "it should be added that while naturalistic art imitates the surfaces, 'melodramatic' art imitates what is beneath the surface."[1] Elsewhere he has elaborated on the capacity of melodrama to evoke fear, not the common-sense fear of the every day world, but the fear that "perhaps none too rationally is called irrational. Savage superstitions, neurotic fantasies, and childhood imaginings spring to mind, and equally outside the bounds of common sense is the fear of God."[2] Peter Brooks has recently gone further in terms directly relevant to O'Connor. Tracing the rise of stage melodrama in the late eighteenth and early nineteenth centuries to the "desacralization" of the universe, the final breakup of a widely shared belief in Christianity, Brooks sees melodrama as an attempt to recover not the realm of the sacred, which is "no longer viable," but "the ethical imperatives that traditionally depended on it." In this effort, melodrama becomes "an emblem of the cosmic ethical drama, which by reflection illuminates life here below." Necessarily, the world of melodrama is sharply dualistic: "What we most retain from any consideration of melodramatic structures is the sense of fundamental bipolar contrast and clash. The world according to melodrama is built on an irreducible Manichaeism, the conflict of good and evil not subject to compromise. . . . The middle ground and middle condition are excluded." The melodramatic mode, Brooks argues, is by no means an outdated, Victorian excess, but "a central fact of the modern sensibility."[3]

1. Eric Bentley, "The Psychology of Farce," in *"Let's Get a Divorce!" and Other Plays* (New York: Hill & Wang, 1957), ix.

2. Eric Bentley, *Life of the Drama* (New York: Atheneum, 1970), 201.

3. Peter Brooks, *The Melodramatic Imagination* (New Haven, Conn.: Yale University Press, 1976), 14–20, 54, 36, 21.

[Flannery O'Connor's Comic Imagery]

*Sheldon Currie**

Henri Bergson in his precise essay, "Laughter,"[1] reduces the comic to four essential characteristics: it is exclusively human, purely intellectual in that it requires absence of feeling, socially significant or corrective, and is the result of something mechanical encrusted on the living: we laugh when a person gives the impression of being a thing.

Although [O'Connor] says she never read Bergson [*Letters*, 518], a reader might suspect she had set out in her fiction to illustrate his theory of the comic. In "The Life You Save May Be Your Own," Mr. Shiftlet proclaims himself endowed with "a moral intelligence" [*CS*, 149]: he has meditated on the mystery of life and the potential of the human spirit: "Lady," he tells Mrs. Crater, "a man is divided into two parts, body and spirit . . . The body, lady, is like a house: it don't go anywhere; but the spirit, lady, is like a automobile: always on the move" [*CS*, 152].

Car imagery, whereby, in Bergson's terms, "something mechanical is encrusted on the living," and "a person gives us the impression of being a thing," is used to describe Mrs. Freeman in "Good Country People": "Besides the neutral expression that she wore when she was

*Reprinted with permission from "Freaks and Folks: Comic Imagery in the Fiction of Flannery O'Connor," *Antigonish Review* 62–63 (1985):133–42.

alone, Mrs. Freeman had two others, forward and reverse" [*CS*, 271], and the main character in this story, Joy, renamed Hulga, meaning ugly hulk, presumably, is "encrusted" by the mechanical in a fundamental way because she has become a thing. She stalks around her mother's house, pounding her wooden leg into the floor, defiant, hostile, and full of pride; she has "the look of someone who has achieved blindness by an act of will and means to keep it," [*CS*, 273] a woman who "looked at nice young men as if she could smell their stupidity" [*CS*, 276]; she considers herself superior; she has a Ph.D.; she is in love with her wooden leg.

A wooden leg is not comic, but a wooden soul is. A wooden leg makes a person "walk funny" because he appears to be a puppet, a robot, a mechanical thing, whereas we know the person by definition, to be a spirit. Henri Bergson explains: "To sum up . . . our imagination . . . in every human form . . . sees the effort of a soul . . . shaping matter, a soul . . . infinitely supple and perpetually in motion, subject to no law of gravitation. . . . This soul imparts . . . its winged lightness to the body it animates: the immateriality which thus passes into matter is what is called gracefulness. Matter, however, is obstinate and resists. . . . Where matter thus succeeds in dulling the outward life of the soul, in petrifying its movements and thwarting its gracefulness, it achieves, at the expense of a body, an effect that is comic" (78–79).

The makers of wooden legs do their best to keep their products from appearing "immersed and absorbed in the materiality of some mechanical occupation," and usually their clients cooperate and dress them up and direct them to appear to be vital and animated adjuncts of a spirited person, and we who watch hope the partnership succeeds, so we won't be tempted to entertain uncharitable thoughts, and perhaps even snigger behind our hands. Hulga, however, does not cooperate. Watching her graceless stomp, the maker of her leg would think himself a clumsy failure. Hulga is far from trying to incorporate her leg, to spiritualize it, to make it a vital and animated adjunct. She herself becomes the adjunct, and the leg becomes her center and she its satellite, like Mr. Shiftlet who, instead of making the car a part of his life, becomes part of the life of the car, which runs off with him to Mobile. . . .

O'Connor's short stories are full of characters like Hulga and Shiftlet, who have not developed into the animated beings nature intended. The relationship between body and soul is defective; the body is not, as it should be, the satellite of the soul; so the person appears not as a

Edward Kessler

body animated by spirit, but rather as spirit trying, unsuccessfully, to overcome the animal, vegetable or mechanical aspects of its nature.

O'Connor sees the human as a defeated spirit, dominated either by the mind or by the body; that is, by being too much like the angels whose mental nature man shares, or by being too much like the animals whose corporeal nature he shares.

1. Henri Bergson, "Laughter," in *Comedy*, ed. Wylie Sypher (New York: Doubleday, 1956), 61–146; subsequent references appear parenthetically.

[Flannery O'Connor's Poetic Metaphors]

*Edward Kessler**

Because I see O'Connor in the company of apocalyptic poets like Blake and T.S. Eliot, I do not attend closely to the "materials" of her fiction, the phenomenal reality that seems only a vocabulary for a poetry that aspires to reach beyond both time and space. Her "realism"—her characters' recognizable speech and behavior—resembles the piece of meat that Eliot said the burglar-poet tosses to the watchdog, so that he can go about his business. The outer reality presented seems unreliable, perhaps even misleading, as an entry into the interior life. Like any poet, O'Connor re-creates the world by means of figures of speech that often violate the plain sense of ordinary prose discourse. Representational language could not mirror a hunger that refuses to be satisfied by the food at hand. In an early television interview, O'Connor said that Northerners might appreciate her fiction more readily than Southerners since they would be less distracted by its "accident" (its regional aspects) and would not confuse it with "reality."[1] She continually met with resistance from readers expecting the assurances of verisimilitude: *people aren't like that; things don't happen in that way.* Only through poetic metaphor could she shatter the mirror held up to external nature and declare that fiction is neither true nor false—but fiction.

*Excerpts, pp. 7–14, reprinted from *Flannery O'Connor and the Language of Apocalypse*, by permission of Princeton University Press; Copyright © 1986.

The Critics

In calling the reader's attention to O'Connor's use of language, I intend to show how metaphor transforms, if not transfigures, the phenomenon of straightforward, referential prose. Never merely decorative, O'Connor's metaphors constitute verbal strategies for engaging the unknown, for making what Eliot called "raids on the inarticulate." Because her metaphors are more allied with feeling than with ideas, they sometimes appear, like feelings themselves, illogical, incoherent, and pervasively ambiguous. . . . In alienating her readers from the world they already know, she offers them in metaphor not a copy but an imitation, in the classical sense: whereas a copy represents and is consequently subordinate to the already made, an imitation re-creates, joining man's creating power with the creating power of nature. Rather than demonstrating a preconceived "truth," O'Connor's stories show that contriving a fiction and discovering a truth are not antithetical.

Because language exists in time, its reconciliations must be temporal, and though believing in the final reconciliation that religion provides, O'Connor nevertheless knew that her "true country" could be seen only from the threshold where metaphor has its being: looking backward at the given world while at the same time looking beyond it. As with Blake, belief, in any theological sense, appears in the work as a way of *seeing* and manifests itself obliquely. It is metaphor that informs the work and only on those rare occasions when O'Connor resorts to direct statement (e.g., when she identifies the Displaced Person with Christ or a waterstain with the Holy Ghost) does she weaken her fictional contract. To argue that her stories proclaim dogmatic beliefs is to ignore the equivocal nature of metaphor, in effect to deny its invigorating power and to arrest the process of language whereby belief is in the making. Metaphor as lie—the bringing together of two incongruous entities *as if* they were one—remains the poet's only means of pointing toward the true, and in O'Connor's act of writing fiction, it supersedes all other shapes for human experience.

O'Connor's noted satire and irony, moreover, are less dependent on moral norms external to her fiction than on her compelling need to rescue her readers from a closed linguistic order. When metaphor hardens into cliché or into concept, it no longer retains its power to evolve a new consciousness. Showing how satisfaction with an accepted language parallels self-satisfaction, O'Connor ridicules the platitudes that block her characters from any genuine understanding of themselves. . . . a stock language limits all of us to stock responses. On the

210

other hand, we are reminded that every dead metaphor or cliché masks a genuine emotion that can be awakened. In "The Comforts of Home," Thomas knows that even though his mother's "conversation moved from cliché to cliché there were real experiences behind them." Irony exposes both vulgarity and banality, in the interest of liberating our "real experiences."

Because metaphor is a way of seeing, and not the object seen, we can detect O'Connor's world-view in how her characters react to their surroundings. Many of them possess what Blake called "single vision"; they see objectively, that is, only what meets the eye. They take the world and language at face value. . . . Hulga in "Good Country People" . . . has "the look of someone who has achieved blindness by an act of will and means to keep it." She ignores her natural surroundings, the ground of metaphor. . . .

O'Connor's intolerance of dead metaphors probably influenced as well her attitude toward genre, preordained literary forms. The poets Robert Lowell and Elizabeth Bishop claimed O'Connor as one of their own, and she herself praised Hawthorne for attempting to steer the novel "in the direction of poetry." By displacing history and community as primary subjects for fiction, and disparaging "social or economic or psychological forces," she chose to elevate poetic metaphor beyond its usual position in customary prose. As a consequence, the interplay of ways of seeing overrides the beginning-middle-end of conventional form. She could easily begin a novel by presenting a character in an unstable situation, and she could remove that instability through the intervention of an outside force, but she struggled to create sustaining middles. . . .

Much closer to poetry in its condensation, the short story remained O'Connor's congenial form. Its single moment made possible her escape from the trap of time, the cause and effect of conventional narrative, and allowed her to assume a position from which initial action and denouement connect, necessitating little intermediate traffic with the quotidian. Resembling the Biblical parable, the short story intimately combines narrative with a metaphorical process. Thus any single metaphor is a microcosm: the ever-present, ever-varying conjunction of the known and unknown.

In describing Coleridge's "doctrines" of imagination, I. A. Richards could well have been talking about Flannery O'Connor, who shares the poet's discoveries about the natural world and about himself:

The Critics

1. The mind of the poet at moments, penetrating "the film of familiarity and selfish solicitude," gains an insight into reality, reads Nature as a symbol of something behind or within Nature not ordinarily perceived.

2. The mind of the poet creates a Nature into which his own feelings, his aspirations and apprehensions, are projected.[2]

Although both writers project a world of words, within which they can read and know themselves, they also apprehend a power external to the self that provides the cure for solipsism. For both Coleridge and O'Connor the "something" behind or within nature should more accurately be labeled a "someone" or a "presence," to use her recurring word. All self-comforting fictions dissolve when one is alone on a wide wide sea, isolated from "ordinary sights." . . .

O'Connor's metaphors are rarely simple resemblances (or compressed similes) that connect us with the natural order. They both rescue us from things as they are, and free us from the confines of "ordinary" discourse. . . . Figurative language is the poet's only evidence of things not seen, her only promise of "redemption" for her suffering characters, who, like most people, resist having to endure the birth-agony of a new consciousness. Flannery O'Connor's characters develop *in spite* of themselves, for to see what resides "behind or within" nature requires painful displacement from the material world, and from *words* as they correspond to *things*. In *The Violent Bear It Away*, Tarwater would ignore the process of his interior life and substitute a mere objective existence:

> He tried when possible to pass over these thoughts, to keep his vision located on an even level, to see no more than what was in front of his face and to let his eyes stop at the surface of that. It was as if he were afraid that if he let his eye rest for an instant longer than was needed to place something—a spade, a hoe, the mule's hind quarters before his plow, the red furrow under him—that the thing would suddenly stand before him, strange and terrifying, demanding that he name it and name it justly and be judged for the name he gave it. He did all he could to avoid the threatened intimacy of creation.

Projecting one world while revealing another, O'Connor would turn her reluctant hero into original man, naming the things of God's creation. However, after his fall, he must painfully *reenter* the originating metaphoric process that refuses to allow things, even a spade or a hoe, to

212

Claude Richard

remain unspirited. In effect, Tarwater's thoughts mirror O'Connor's personal struggle with a literal or representational language that accompanies the understanding. Her metaphoric language, on the other hand, was her means of sharing the mysterious and threatening "intimacy of creation." As with Blake, Coleridge, Eliot, in their differing ways, creative power can make the already-made terrifying, a threat to the established selfhood. "Human kind / Cannot bear very much reality."

1. A print of the Harvey Breit-O'Connor television interview (NBC "Galley-proof," May 1955) is in the O'Connor Collection at Georgia College.
2. I. A. Richards, *Coleridge on Imagination* (Bloomington: Indiana University Press, 1960), 145.

[Flannery O'Connor and Narratology]

Claude Richard*

The grandmother didn't *want* to go to Florida. She *wanted* to visit some of her connections in East Tennessee. [*CS*, 117]

The repetition of the verbal root, *want*, in the two statements with which the description of the "omniscient" narrator opens, focalizes the theme of desire in the character of the grandmother; moreover, the word-by-word contrast introduced by the juxtaposition of the affirmative and the negative forms establishes a real geography of desire.

The narrator's speech reveals from the very beginning the valorizations of the grandmother's desire in geographical terms—geography considered in both its literal and figurative meanings. The desire for Tennessee is contrasted with the non-desire for Florida, a contrast more marked because, if the grandmother has a *relationship* with Tennessee through her relatives (connections) she appears by contrast (un-

*Excerpts reprinted from "Desire and Destiny in Flannery O'Connor's 'A Good Man Is Hard To Find,'" *Delta* 2 (1976):61–74, with permission by Université Paul Valéry, Montpellier, France. Translated by C. Frederick Farrell, Jr., and Edith R. Farrell.

derscored by the complete absence of qualifiers in the first statement) as a complete stranger to Florida.

This first statement (the radical opposition of Florida and Tennessee on the grandmother's map of desires) authorizes—even encourages—us to look carefully at references to Florida and Tennessee that may come up in the parts of the story told from the grandmother's viewpoint.

Now, from the first time that the grandmother's own words are quoted, Florida is given not as a place, but as a *direction*: "The Misfit is aloose from the Federal Pen and headed toward Florida. . . . I wouldn't take my children *in any direction* with a criminal like that aloose in it" [*CS*, 117].

Syntactically, the pronoun *it* refers to the direction, not to Florida: Florida, then, first appears in the grandmother's frame of reference, as an "orientation," insofar as the very ambiguity of the word *direction*, as it emerges from the wording of the specific context, authorizes our reading it figuratively: . . . [Going to Florida] is the path which the grandmother would not encourage her children to pursue. Crime stalks that path, that "direction with a criminal . . . aloose in it." Thus, the grandmother appears from her first speech as the adversary of the criminal path—or as the pilgrim pursuing the path of conscience: "I couldn't answer to my conscience" [*CS*, 117].

By way of contrast, in the system of opposing desires that the narrator attributes to her, and which her speech patterns reveal, Tennessee appears as the place of conscience, with which the grandmother maintains a close relationship (*her connections*). Now, in her secret value system, Tennessee would contribute, as it should, an ethical and intellectual broadening: the children "would see different parts of the world and *be broad*. They have never been to East Tennessee" [*CS*, 117].

In the grandmother's system of references, Tennessee will be revealed more and more as a "cultural place," which will explain the contrast with Florida—a natural place. This cultural place is defined, in her mind, by a certain number of historical values belonging to the traditional South: elegance, worldly pleasures represented by the "Tennessee Waltz" that makes her want to dance [*CS*, 121]. The elegant and courtly world found in the plantations of a by-gone era (with their white columns and little intimate bowers) with which she is obsessed and will remember at the very last minute is not found in Geor-

gia but as a matter of fact in Tennessee. The horrible thought she had
[before the accident] was that the house she had remembered so vividly was not in Georgia but in Tennessee [*CS*, 125]. In her view, this
world stands in opposition to Florida as the place par excellence for
"educational" values: "It would be very *educational* for them" [*CS*,
123].

Thus, from the very beginning of the story, the grandmother seems
to belong exclusively to the cultural order, an idea on which we need
to elaborate, but one that she uses systematically to justify her desires. . . .

. . . She is the one who, thanks to her historical sense ("In my time"
[*CS*, 119]) is the repository of class cultural values: "In the case of
accident, anyone seeing her dead on the highway would know at once
that *she was a lady*" [*CS*, 118].

A cruel irony for anyone who knows the story's denouement results
from a careful comparison between the grandmother's foretelling of her
own death and the sight of her actual death as it is described in "objective" terms (from the narrator's viewpoint) at the end of the story:

Grandmother's death from her viewpoint (internal monologue: narrative level)	Grandmother's death as told by the narrator (omniscient narrator's speech: diegetic level)
In case of an *accident*, any one *seeing her*	. . .ACCIDENT [CS, 125]. Hiram and Bobby Lee [. . .] *looking* down at the grandmother
dead	who *half sat and half lay in a puddle of blood* with her legs crossed under her
on the *highway* would know at once that she was a *lady* [*CS*, 118].	[over *the ditch*] like a *child's* [CS, 132].

[This] comparison . . . brings out even more clearly the cultural va-
lorization of the grandmother through her own speech. The hypothet-
ical diegetic elements are realized (an accident with witnesses), but
certain factors of the imagined decor undergo a shift to a lower level
that destroys the grandmother's image of herself: the abstraction

"dead," is given concrete form in the sprawled posture and the puddle of blood; the highway is now merely a ditch. . . .

. . . It seems, then, not inappropriate to posit that the grandmother's story can be defined as a passage from the cultural order (lady) to the natural order (child). . . . This transmutation through death is prefigured, on the diegetic level, by another passage emphasizing the physical and once more prophetically representing the enthroning of the grandmother in another world, but this time without irony. The text in effect gives "her figure," a structure that both underlies and illustrates it, by giving the actors different places within the car at the time of the accident when "the old lady was thrown into the front seat" [*CS*, 124].

Now a retrospective reading of the story's opening passages allows us to perceive that the organization of the car's interior space represents, in a figurative mode, the text's ideological space.

But to do this, we must go back to try to determine the relative positions of the actors who will occupy this privileged place of preparation for the mystical revelation that the automobile represents in Flannery O'Connor's work ("The Life You Save May Be Your Own").

The "children's mother" [*CS*, 117]—deprived of a personality of her own by having no name and reduced to a maternal function by this expression, the only one ever used to describe her—seems, by virtue of this reduction, to belong to the natural order already. This is supported by the fact that she is constantly associated with natural objects—vegetables and animals: "her face was broad and innocent *as a cabbage* and was tied around with a green head-kerchief that had two points on the top *like a rabbit's ears*" [*CS*, 117].

We can . . . understand better [the grandmother's] hostility toward Florida, the land of *flowers* (natural) and *flowering*, that is, the land of a wilderness that she challenges, confident in her Old South cultural background [which includes] . . . *Gone With the Wind*. This last-named ambivalent allusion—to an historical fact and a novel, which is itself a vehicle of all the tawdry myths of the old South—along with the humorous play with the initials of her old beau, Mr. Teagarden . . . allows us to affirm that—for the grandmother—"culture" is basically in the province of language.

Through the use of language, she is the one who shows what to see, read and discover: "She pointed out" [*CS*, 119]; [exclaimed] "Oh look . . . I'd paint that picture" [*CS*, 119] and "'Look at the graveyard' . . . pointing it out" [*CS*, 120]. As a matter of fact, the exercise of power by means of language, or, in other words, the accomplishment of desire by words, yields the key to the story's organization, which is under the sign of the inevitable confrontation of the sinner and the dragon referred to in the epigraph from St. Cyril of Jerusalem [which begins the collection of short stories with the same title]: "The Dragon is by the side of the road, watching those who pass. Beware lest he devour you—we go to the father of souls, but it is necessary to pass by the dragon."

. . . The grandmother will be forced . . . to reveal the ideological sub-strata beneath her notion of Good: "I know you're a good man," she says after she recognizes The Misfit "at once" [*CS*, 127], but the magic formula does not work because, in the face of danger, the grandmother reveals the purely social nature of her concept of Good to a character whose very name (Mis-fit) defines him as a-social: "You're a good man. You don't look a bit like you have common blood" [*CS*, 127]; "I just know you're a good man. . . . You're not a bit common" [*CS*, 128]. Here she is downstage, in direct contact with a destiny that has no connection with the cultural order.

[The Misfit's] crime is not a social crime attacking someone else's property (as the grandmother thought)—"You must have stolen something," says the grandmother, faithful to her social values. "Nobody had nothing I wanted," answers The Misfit [*CS*, 130]—but a "natural" crime, parricide. The Misfit is thus placed outside the realm of cultural desires; his crime arises from the natural order because it is produced by his destiny, the "natural" situation of the child in his relations with his father and mother.

When she is alone with this creature of nature, a victim of society and more especially society's *language* ("They had the papers on me" [*CS*, 130; repeated *CS*, 131]), the grandmother loses her cultural attributes: here, language. When the grandmother is alone with The Misfit, she has "lost her voice" [*CS*, 131]. Then and only then, after the beginnings of a process of "naturalization," does the grandmother reach a form of expression that is no longer an attempt to dominate the world but rather the basic and multi-faceted language of invocation: "'Jesus, Jesus,' meaning Jesus will help you, but the way she was saying it, it sounded as if she might be cursing" [*CS*, 131].

The verb clauses, "the grandmother found . . . she found herself" [*CS*, 131], clearly demonstrate that the grandmother has progressed from the order of desire (active) to the order of destiny (passive).

She is thus ready to receive the revelation, for it is by reaching the order of nature from which Grace springs that man can receive revelations. . . . By attaining the language of invocation, that is, the realm of Christ . . . , the grandmother attains the realm of God, previously defined by Red Sam's wife as a green place: "It isn't a soul *in this green world of God* that you can trust" [*CS*, 122].

Thus, by reaching the consciousness of Jesus beyond prayer (social and verbal), the grandmother, at the very moment of her death, receives the revelation of the *natural order* of God.

This revelation is expressed to the fullest by her last remark, which takes on its full meaning only in relation (opposition) to an indication that the narrator gave us (but which could perfectly well be expressed from the grandmother's point of view) at the very beginning of the story: "Bailey was *the son* she lived with, her *only* boy" [*CS*, 117]; "Why you're one of my *babies*. You're *one of my own children*" [*CS*, 132].

From a cultural conception of love and goodness inscribed in the reductive structure of the family (a cultural notion), the grandmother passes on, thanks to her encounter with the dragon, to a consciousness of the universal love that God has inscribed in the order of nature.

And The Misfit understands his special role as the agent of Destiny perfectly when he says to Bobby Lee that only death (destiny) could teach this person defined by desire the true meaning of the word *goodness*: "She would have been a *good* woman . . . if it had been somebody there to *shoot* her every minute of her life" [*CS*, 133].

[Flannery O'Connor's Compassion]

*Robert Drake**

Perhaps a final word may be in order here about the lack of tenderness or compassion with which Miss O'Connor has sometimes been charged—especially toward those characters of hers who seem headed for damnation. Miss O'Connor *is* a "tough" writer, but she is not an inhumane one. . . . Her damned characters prepare their own ends: they *do* choose this day whom they will serve. And she refuses to let them off the hook by interfering with the consequences of their actions, which *are* inevitable. (Thomas Hardy, though he did not share

*Reprinted by permission of the publisher from *Flannery O'Connor: A Critical Essay* (William B. Eerdmans, 1966); copyright © 1966 by William B. Eerdmans.

Miss O'Connor's Christian persuasion, has often been accused of the same inhumanity simply because he insists, again and again, that, once a choice has been made, the game must be played all the way out.) But, for Miss O'Connor, the wages of sin is *still* death; and she is powerless to intervene in the Hellish consequences which overtake her prideful and self-justified villains.

For her, such "tenderness," very much touted in a modern world that likes to believe there is *always* a second chance and indeed often encourages man to believe that he is a creature more sinned against than sinning, would not only have been unrealistic: it would have been downright sentimental—or even sinister. . . .

. . . in "A Temple of the Holy Ghost," the natural order itself seems gone haywire. Two giggling convent-school-girls and their "big dumb Church of God ox" escorts attend a side show at the fair and see a hermaphrodite. But the hermaphrodite's words, spoken in turn to each section of the sexually segregated audience, are, for Miss O'Connor, right on key. "God made me thisaway and if you laugh He may strike you the same way. This is the way He wanted me to be and I ain't disputing His way" [*CS*, 245]. It would seem that the hermaphrodite's very existence violates the natural order and presumably calls into question belief in an all-good, all-loving God and His whole Creation, which, we are told, He looked on and found good. But Miss O'Connor doesn't "dispute it" either. . . .

The natural world is mysterious and strange, Miss O'Connor implies, sometimes baffling, ugly, even disgusting. In any case, it's surely a "fallen" one. And it is for her very much as it was for Hopkins: bleared and seared by man, wearing his smudge and sharing his smell. But always over this brown bent world there broods the Holy Ghost, with His warm breast and bright wings, blessing and sanctifying our smudged world and lightening our darkness, whether in rest and quietness or in the blinding revelation of the Damascus Road.

Perhaps, to sum it all up, no sentence Miss O'Connor ever wrote better embodies her attitude toward the Creation than one Robert Fitzgerald has pointed out in "A Good Man Is Hard to Find": "The trees were full of silver-white sunlight and the meanest of them sparkled" [*CS*, 119]. Surely, surely the operative word here is *meanest*. Miss O'-Connor's view then of both man and nature is thoroughly sacramental. If man's body, no matter how warped or deformed, is a temple of the Holy Ghost, the earth also is the Lord's and the fullness thereof. And man violates neither with impunity.

[The Lack of Beauty in Flannery O'Connor's Work]

*Dorothy Walters**

[Some readers protest] the apparent absence in [O'Connor's] work of a sense of natural beauty. True, we seldom turn from her creations refreshed by a sense of the transcendental beauty of natural forms. More often, the atmosphere reflects the characters' dispositions—"sour," "dull," "sullen." The landscape—though it seldom reinforces our sense of the esthetic attractions of the surroundings—serves very well its intended purpose: to set the emotional tone of the narrations. Her characters—themselves so frequently marred inwardly or outwardly by self-imposed spiritual deprivation—are for the most part oblivious to the beauties about them. They pay no heed to the stars over Taulkingham or to the peacock's splendor. Mr. Fortune three times moves to the window to discover the mystery of the "view" his granddaughter praises, but, blind to the beauty before him, he matter-of-factly concludes that "a pine trunk is a pine trunk" [*CS*, 348].

The sun itself is the most important element of O'Connor's natural settings, and it is most often employed in one of two typical moments, both of major importance in establishing psychological setting. In the first of these, the sun at midday burns the sky into a brilliant blankness to provide an absolutely neutral backdrop for dramatic action. . . . Such episodes are like sudden shifts into intense black-and-white movie sequences, where the tension of the action is reinforced by the sharp delineation of the characters in closeup. Furthermore, the whitening of the sky . . . suggests a purification and removal of all inconsequential, accidental features of earthly experience into an essential reality. . . . God as pure spirit does not manifest Himself in accidents of color, shape, or texture. He is the essence—the seeming nothingness which remains when all phenomenal accidents have been removed.

Against such radiance, Mrs. May encounters her fatal lover, the grandmother is struck down after her brief moment of grace, and Mrs. Turpin confesses her humiliation to the uncomprehending audience of black helpers. These blazing scenes depict moments of absolute truth,

*Reprinted from *Flannery O'Connor*, by Dorothy Walters, copyright © 1973, with permission of Twayne Publishers, a division of G.K. Hall & Co., Boston.

when one at last confronts the undeniable realities of self which have so long been ignored.

A second major emblematic use of the sun occurs when, at sunset, the brilliant reds of the Georgia sky become dramatic reminders of the Passion of the Cross. To the child contemplating the mysteries of divine perfection incarnate in the imperfect human vessel, the sun over the dark woods is "like an elevated Host drenched in blood" [CS, 248]. Mr. Fortune, viewing the trees "bathed in blood" as if "someone were wounded behind the woods," feels himself held by "an uncomfortable mystery" [CS, 348]. And Mrs. Turpin, gazing at the crimson curtain of the evening sky, perceives a "vast swinging bridge extending upward from the earth through a field of living fire" [CS, 508]. The "beauty" of such scenes goes beyond external splendor to reveal the agony by which man joins Christ in the suffering of Calvary.

The natural setting is invariably fitted to the action. Mr. Shiftlet's hypocritical prayer to the Lord to "Break forth and wash the slime from this earth" [CS, 156] is voiced beneath an angry, roiling sky. But Mr. Head, returning home to experience a second action of mercy, is met by a scene of delicate moonlit beauty: "the moon, restored to its full splendor, sprang from a cloud and flooded the clearing with light. As they stepped off, the sage grass was shivering gently in shades of silver and the clinkers under their feet glittered with a fresh black light. The treetops, fencing the junction like the protecting walls of a garden, were darker than the sky which was hung with gigantic white clouds illuminated like lanterns."

[Some readers also object] that O'Connor's works are depressing because of her over-emphasis on "morbid" and "bizarre" aspects of experience. To this objection, we can only say that Flannery O'Connor is seeking to reach precisely that audience which would resolutely contemplate only the "smiling aspects of life." Like Melville, she insists that the sharks hidden in the depths are as much of the scene as the gilded sea surface which lulls the viewer into a dangerous serenity. Her vision is apocalyptic; and, of those who prefer to shrug off such serious visions of man's destiny, she would doubtless say that they suffer "the blindness of those who don't know that they cannot see."

. . . certain elements in her work link her undeniably with the mainstream of Southern literature both traditional and modern. The frontier writers, in particular, are famed for their vivid couplings of humor with violence—a trait that has continued to characterize the Southern writer down to our own age.

Mark Twain also mixed the laughable and the terrible. . . . Twain's awareness of the casual yoking of the absurd and the deplorable in everyday life is epitomized in Huck's offhand answer to Mrs. Phelp's query about the steamboat wreck ("Anybody hurt?" "No'm. Killed a nigger").

In our own time, Faulkner [fuses] violent and comic elements. This trait is amply illustrated in *The Hamlet* when Mink Snopes murders Jack Houston and then frantically attempts to dispose of the body. Mink first laboriously deposits the corpse in a hollow trunk, returning later to retrieve the body with an ax. He then dumps the cadaver in the river, only to observe that it is disappointingly minus a limb, which he inadvertently detached in the process of installing the body in the tree. He returns to the mangled tree stump and there doggedly probes for the missing member. Throughout the scene, the humor aroused by Flem's furious efforts is leavened by a rising horror at the actual occupation in which he is engaged. The double focus of the grisly comedy parallels the dual thrust of the novel toward the rarefied regions of myth on the one hand and coarse country realism on the other.

Katherine Anne Porter, Erskine Caldwell, Truman Capote, Carson McCullers—all discover a comic residue in disaster. Even Eudora Welty occasionally weds terror and laughter, as in "Clytie," where she leaves her unfortunate heroine up-ended in a rain barrel. The Southerners' irreverent refusal to separate the comic and the catastrophic in airtight compartments lays them open to the chronic charge that they deliberately seek sensational effects. Yet, much of their undeniable success is attributable to their emphatic insistence on the inherent complexity of human experience, one in which comic and tragic moments do not group themselves in orderly arrangement around conveniently isolated poles, but often interfuse and in fact help to establish by their very presence the essential timbre of the antithesis. Likewise in the work of Flannery O'Connor, comedy modulates tragedy, and laughter is tempered by impending disaster.

Though her contrapuntal manipulation of comic-serious elements allies Flannery O'Connor closely to many of her regional predecessors and contemporaries, she is assuredly much more than just a "Southern" writer. . . . many of her major preoccupations are those which define the main currents of twentieth-century literature. Her concern for violence, for example, is shared by many writers of the last half-century, from Franz Kafka to Alain Robbe-Grillet.

Her acute awareness of the essential absurdity which characterizes much of daily experience finds numerous analogues in Samuel Beckett, Eugene Ionesco, or, in modified form, Albert Camus, who poses the doctrine of the absurd at the center of his ideology. The banal exchanges of O'Connor's characters are frequently like regional renderings of Ionesco's pointless dialogues. But the grotesque mode, traditionally associated with the Southern school, is, in fact, a prominent feature of much of modern American and world literature. Sherwood Anderson, Kafka, Edward Albee are but representatives of the vast group which rely on grotesquerie as a prime instrument in conveying their world vision.

And, although O'Connor's controlled artistry is far removed from the ostensibly unstructured creations of the Surrealists, her drama moves at times surprisingly close to the Surrealistic moment. The unanticipated catastrophe involves a violent dislocation of the normal frame of experience, and the victims seldom find rational explanations to account for the irrational event. Furthermore, the agents and circumstances of the disaster frequently suggest nightmare visions thrown up from the very depths of the unconscious. The homicidal maniac appearing on the horizon above the vacationing family, the son who becomes his mother's inadvertent executioner, the farm trio watching in paralyzed horror as the tractor grinds the helpless Pole to death before their eyes—these seem terrible extensions of a reality gone amuck, the tragic consequence of a sudden collapse of rational structures.

In O'Connor's fiction, we begin invariably in the seemingly "safe" world of the normal and familiar, but we proceed inevitably to the dire moment when the scaffolds of reality collapse into the perilous chaos of the unlooked-for peripety. The consequent fall is not merely from "good fortune" to bad but from rational forms of consciousness into Surrealistic realms where all prior assumptions are challenged and threatened with annihilation. Even the stories of revelation partake of this nonrational aspect. Basically, O'Connor's emphasis on violence and absurdity, her insistence on the grotesque evidence and the Surrealistic moment, fuse in a vision which is simultaneously comic and tragic. This blending of disparate modes to produce a single effect is typical of many modern writers. The choice is not—for these writers or for O'Connor—one of either-or. Life does not seal its subject into neat categories, easily identifiable for purposes of evoking an appropriate emotional attitude. The serious and the absurd, the laughable and the deplorable, constantly overlap in life—and in the art of the present century.

Chronology

1925   25 March, Mary Flannery O'Connor born, an only child of Edward Francis and Regina Cline O'Connor, Savannah, Georgia.

1937   O'Connor's father develops disseminated lupus.

1941   February, father dies; moves to Atlanta and attends North Fulton High School for a short period before moving to mother's hometown of Milledgeville, Georgia.

1942   Graduates from Peabody High School, Milledgeville.

1942–1945   Attends Georgia State College for Women, Milledgeville; starts as an English major but earns B.S. in sociology in three years by taking courses during the summer (two summers of four courses each and one summer of two courses); editor of the literary quarterly, the *Corinthian*, and arts editor of the student newspaper, the *Colonnade*; publishes cartoons in the Georgia State College journal and newspaper.

1945–1948   University of Iowa Writer's Workshop; stays an extra year to write; drops "Mary" from her name.

1946   Summer, "The Geranium," her first publication, appears in *Accent*; this is one of six stories comprising her thesis (the others were "The Barber," "Wildcat," "The Crop," "The Turkey" also entitled "The Capture," and "The Train," which was revised and incorporated into her first novel, *Wise Blood*).

1947   Receives master of fine arts degree, University of Iowa.

1948   June, Elizabeth McKee begins a professional relationship as O'Connor's agent—a relationship that develops into friendship and lasts until the author's death.

1948   Brief residence at Yaddo, a writer's colony in New York; "The Train" is published in the *Sewanee Review* and "The Capture" in *Mademoiselle*.

1949 Rents an apartment in New York City for a short period and then returns home for an extended visit with her mother. Robert Lowell introduces O'Connor to Robert Giroux, who becomes her publisher when she signs a contract for *Wise Blood* in 1950; rents a room above the garage of Sally and Robert Fitzgerald's farm in Connecticut for approximately one year and a half; "The Woman on the Stairs" (revised as "A Stroke of Good Fortune") is published in *Tomorrow*, "The Peeler" and "The Heart of the Park" (revised for *Wise Blood*) published in *Partisan Review*.

1950 December, first major attack of lupus; in and out of Emory Hospital, Atlanta, Georgia, for nine months.

1951 Establishes permanent residence with mother in Milledgeville; mother relocates her personal belongings from second floor of their town residence to a first-floor room at Andalusia, the family dairy farm on the outskirts of Milledgeville.

1952 "Enoch and the Gorilla" is published in *New World Writing*, then revised as chapters 11 and 12 of *Wise Blood*, her first novel, which is also published the same year by Harcourt-Brace.

1953 "The Life You Save May Be Your Own" is published in the *Kenyon Review* and *Prize Stories 1954: The O. Henry Awards*; "A Stroke of Good Fortune" published in *Shenandoah*, "The River" in *Sewanee Review*, "A Late Encounter with the Enemy" in *Harper's Bazaar*, and "A Good Man Is Hard to Find" in *The Berkeley Book of Modern Writing* (ed. William Phillips and Phillip Rahv); receives the *Kenyon Review* Fellowship in Fiction.

1954 "A Circle in the Fire" published in the *Kenyon Review*, "A Temple of the Holy Ghost" in *Harper's Bazaar*, and "The Displaced Person" in *Sewanee Review*; reappointed Kenyon Fellow; receives O. Henry Award, second prize, for "The Life You Save May Be Your Own."

1955 Harcourt-Brace releases first collection of short stories, *A Good Man Is Hard to Find*; "The Artificial Nigger" published in the *Kenyon Review*, "Good Country People" in

Harper's Bazaar, and "You Can't Be Any Poorer than Dead" (revised and incorporated into second novel) in *New World Writing;* receives O. Henry Award, second prize, for "A Circle in the Fire."

1956 "Greenleaf" published in the *Kenyon Review;* receives O. Henry Award for "The Artificial Nigger"; first of many lecture trips to colleges and universities.

1957 Grant from the National Institute of Arts and Letters; "A View of the Woods" published in *Partisan Review;* receives O. Henry Award for "Greenleaf."

1958 Travels to Lourdes with mother and friends; receives O. Henry Award for "A View of the Woods"; "The Enduring Chill" published in *Harper's Bazaar.*

1959 Ford Foundation Grant.

1960 Farrar, Straus & Giroux releases second novel, *The Violent Bear It Away;* "The Comforts of Home" published in the *Kenyon Review.*

1961 "Everything That Rises Must Converge" published in *New World Writing* and "The Partridge Festival" in *Critic;* edits and writes introduction for *Death of a Child* by the Dominican Nuns of Our Lady of Perpetual Help Home (New York: Farrar, Straus & Cudahy).

1962 Honorary Doctor of Letters, St. Mary's College, Notre Dame; "The Lame Shall Enter First" published in the *Sewanee Review;* "Everything That Rises Must Converge" published in *The Best American Short Stories of 1962; Wise Blood* reissued with an introduction by O'Connor.

1963 Farrar, Straus & Giroux releases second collection of short stories; Honorary Doctor of Letters, Smith College; receives O. Henry Award for "Everything That Rises Must Converge"; "Why Do the Heathen Rage?" published in *Esquire.*

1964 3 August, dies in a coma, Baldwin County Hospital, Milledgeville, Georgia, when lupus is reactivated by abdominal surgery for a benign tumor; Henry Bellaman Foundation Award; "Revelation" published in the *Sewanee Review;* Farrar, Straus & Giroux releases *Three by O'Connor,* which contains *Wise Blood,* the first collection of stories, and *The Violent Bear It Away,* and is reissued in 1983 (the second collection of stories then replaces the first).

1965　Farrar, Straus, & Giroux releases *Everything That Rises Must Converge,* the second collection of short stories; "Revelation" receives the O. Henry Award; "Parker's Back" published in *Esquire.*

1966　National Catholic Book Award to *Everything That Rises Must Converge.*

1969　O'Connor's lectures selected and edited by Sally and Robert Fitzgerald, the published as *Mystery and Manners: Occasional Prose of Flannery O'Connor* by Farrar, Straus & Giroux.

1970　"The Barber" (written for her 1947 master's thesis) is published in *The Atlantic* with the permission of her literary executor, Robert Fitzgerald, a Harvard professor, translator, and poet; also, "Wildcat" (again from the thesis) published in *The North American Review.*

1971　Farrar, Straus & Giroux releases *The Complete Stories,* which wins the National Book Award; "The Crop" (from the thesis) published in *Mademoiselle;* O'Connor's mother establishes the Ina Dillard Russell Library, Georgia College; this richly decorated room contains O'Connor's oil paintings, cartoons, family photographs, manuscripts, letters, and part of O'Connor's personal library.

1979　Farrar, Straus & Giroux releases *The Habit of Being: Letters of Flannery O'Connor,* ed. Sally Fitzgerald.

Bibliography

Primary Sources

A Good Man Is Hard to Find. New York: Harcourt, Brace, 1955.

Introduction to *A Memoir of Mary Ann*, by the Dominican Nuns of Our Lady of Perpetual Help Home. New York: Farrar, Straus & Cudahy, 1961.

Three by Flannery O'Connor. New York: Signet, 1962.

Everything That Rises Must Converge. New York: Farrar, Straus & Giroux, 1965.

Mystery and Manners—Flannery O'Connor: Occasional Prose. Edited by Sally Fitzgerald and Robert Fitzgerald. New York: Farrar, Straus & Giroux, 1969.

Flannery O'Connor: The Complete Stories. New York: Farrar, Straus & Giroux, 1971.

The Habit of Being: Letters of Flannery O'Connor. Edited by Sally Fitzgerald. New York: Random House, 1979.

Unpublished Manuscripts. The Flannery O'Connor Collection. Ina Dillard Russell Library, Georgia College, Milledgeville, Georgia.

Secondary Sources

Archer, Jane Elizabeth. "This Is My Place: The Short Films Made from Flannery O'Connor's Short Fiction." *Studies in American Humor* 1, no. 1 (1982):52–65.

Asals, Frederick. *Flannery O'Connor: The Imagination of Extremity.* Athens: University of Georgia Press, 1982.

———. "Flannery O'Connor's 'The Lame Shall Enter First.'" *Mississippi Quarterly* 23 (1970):103–20.

———. "The Mythic Dimensions of Flannery O'Connor's 'Greenleaf.'" *Studies in Short Fiction* 5 (1968):317–30.

Blackwell, Louise. "Humor and Irony in Flannery O'Connor." *Recherches anglaises et americaines* 4 (1971):61–68.

Bleikasten, André. "Writing of the Flesh: Tattoos and Taboos in 'Parker's Back.'" *Southern Literary Journal* 14, no. 2 (1982):8–18.

Booth, Wayne. "Ready-made Values: 'Everything That Rises Must Converge.'" In *The Rhetoric of Irony*. Chicago: University of Chicago Press, 1974.

Brooks, Cleanth. *The Language of the American South*. Athens: University of Georgia Press, 1985.

Browning, Preston M., Jr. "Flannery O'Connor and the Demonic." *Modern Fiction Studies* 19 (1973):29–41.

———. *Flannery O'Connor*. Carbondale: Southern Illinois University Press, 1974.

Burns, Stuart L. "'Torn by the Lord's Eye': Flannery O'Connor's Use of Sun Imagery." *Twentieth Century Literature* 13, no. 3 (1967):154–66.

Byrd, Turner F. "Ironic Dimension in Flannery O'Connor's 'The Artificial Nigger.'" *Mississippi Quarterly* 21 (1968):243–51.

Carlson, Thomas M. "Flannery O'Connor: The Manichaean Dilemma." *Sewanee Review* 77 (1969):254–76.

Cheney, Brainard. "Miss O'Connor Creates Unusual Humor Out of Ordinary Sin." *Sewanee Review* 71 (1963):644–52.

Coale, Samuel Chase. *In Hawthorne's Shadow: American Romance From Melville to Mailer*. Lexington: University Press of Kentucky, 1985.

Curley, Dan. "Flannery O'Connor and the Limitless Nature of Grace." *Revista de letras* 7 (September 1970):371–84.

Currie, Sheldon. "Freaks and Folks: Comic Imagery in the Fiction of Flannery O'Connor." *Antigonish Review* [Canada] 62–63 (1985):133.

Desmond, John F. "The Shifting of Mr. Shiftlet: Flannery O'Connor's 'The Life You Save May Be Your Own.'" *Mississippi Quarterly* 28 (1975): 55–59.

———. "Flannery O'Connor's Sense of Place." *Southern Humanities Review* 10 (1976):251–59.

Drake, Robert. *Flannery O'Connor: A Critical Essay*. Grand Rapids, Mich.: William B. Eerdmans, 1966.

Driskell, Leon V., and Joan T. Brittain. *The Eternal Crossroads: The Art of Flannery O'Connor*. Lexington: University Press of Kentucky, 1971.

Edelstein, Mark G. "Flannery O'Connor and the Problem of Modern Satire." *Studies in Short Fiction* 12 (1975):139–44.

Eggenschwiler, David. *The Christian Humanism of Flannery O'Connor*. Detroit: Wayne State University Press, 1972.

Esprit [University of Scranton] 8, no. 1 (1964):1–84.

Farmer, David. *Flannery O'Connor: A Descriptive Bibliography*. New York: Garland Publishing, 1981.

Feeley, Sister Kathleen. *Flannery O'Connor: The Voice of the Peacock*. New Brunswick, N.J.: Rutgers University Press, 1972.

Fitzgerald, Robert. "The Countryside and the True Country." *Sewanee Review* 70 (1962):380–94.

———. Introduction to *Everything That Rises Must Converge*. New York: Farrar, Straus & Giroux, 1965.

Flannery O'Connor Bulletin 1–15 (1972–88).

Folks, Jeffrey J. "The Mechanical in *Everything That Rises Must Converge.*" *Southern Literary Journal* 18, no. 2 (1986):14–25.

Foster, Shirley. "Flannery O'Connor's Short Stories: The Assault on the Reader." *Journal of American Studies* [Norwich, England] 20, no. 2 (1986):259–72.

Friedman, Melvin J., and Lewis A. Lawson, eds. *The Added Dimension: The Art and Mind of Flannery O'Connor.* New York: Fordham University Press, 1966.

Friedman, Melvin J., and Beverly Lyon Clark, eds. *Critical Essays on Flannery O'Connor.* Boston: G.K. Hall, 1985.

Getz, Lorine M. *Flannery O'Connor: Her Life, Library, and Book Reviews.* New York: Edwin Mellen Press, 1980.

Golden, Robert E., and Mary C. Sullivan. *Flannery O'Connor and Caroline Gordon: A Reference Guide.* Boston: G.K. Hall, 1977.

Gordon, Caroline. "Heresy in Dixie." *Sewanee Review* 76 (1968):263–97.

Gresset, Michel. "Le Petit Monde de Flannery O'Connor." *Mercure de France,* série moderne (January 1964), 141–43.

Heller, Arno. "'Experienced Meaning': Wirkungsästhetische Betrachtungen zur Kurzprosa Flannery O'Connor." In Sonja Bahn and others. *Forms of the American Imagination.* Innsbruck, 1979, 165–79.

Hicks, Granville. "A Cold, Hard Look at Humankind." Review of *Everything That Rises Must Converge. Saturday Review,* 29 May 1965, 23–25.

Holsen, Ruth M. "Flannery O'Connor's Good Country People." *Explicator* 42 (Spring 1984):59.

Humphries, Jefferson. *The Otherness Within: Gnostic Readings in Marcel Proust, Flannery O'Connor, and François Villon.* Baton Rouge: Louisiana State University Press, 1983.

Hyman, Stanley Edgar. *Flannery O'Connor.* University of Minnesota Pamphlets on American Writers, no. 54. Minneapolis: University of Minnesota Press, 1966.

"Interview with Flannery O'Connor and Robert Penn Warren." *Vagabond* [Vanderbilt University] 4, no. 1 (1960):14.

Jones, Bartlett C. "Depth Psychology and Literary Study." *Midcontinent American Studies Journal* [University of Kansas] 5, no. 2 (1964):50–56.

Kahane, Claire [Katz]. "Flannery O'Connor's Rage of Vision." *American Literature* 46 (1974):54–67.

———. "The Artificial Niggers." *Massachusetts Review* 19, no.1 (1978):183–98.

———. "Comic Vibrations and Self-Construction in Grotesque Literature." *Literature and Psychology* 29 (1979):114–19.

———. "Gothic Mirrors and Feminine Identity." *Centenary Review* 24, no. 1 (1980):43–64.

Kessler, Edward. *Flannery O'Connor and the Language of Apocalypse.* Princeton: Princeton University Press, 1986.

Bibliography

Klug, M. A. "Flannery O'Connor and the Manichean Spirit of Modernism." *Southern Humanities Review* 17, no. 4 (1983):303–13.

Le Clézio, J. M. G. "L'Univers de Flannery O'Connor." *La nouvelle revue française*, September 1965, 488–93.

Lévy, Maurice. "L'ecriture catholique de Flannery O'Connor." *Revue française d'etudes americaines*, April 1976, 125–33.

Magee, Rosemary M., ed. *Conversations with Flannery O'Connor.* Jackson: University Press of Mississippi, 1987.

May, John R. "Flannery O'Connor and the Critical Consensus." *Renascence* 27 (1975):179–92.

Mayer, Charles W. "The Comic Spirit in 'A Stroke of Good Fortune.'" *Studies in Short Fiction* 16 (1979):70–74.

Mayer, David R. "Outer Marks, Inner Grace: Flannery O'Connor's Tattooed Christ." *Asian Folklore Studies* 42 (1983):117–27.

McKenzie, Barbara. *Flannery O'Connor's Georgia.* Athens: University of Georgia Press, 1981.

Meaders, Margaret. "Flannery O'Connor: Literary Witch." *Colorado Quarterly* 10 (1962):377–86.

Merton, Thomas. "The Other Side of Despair: Notes on Christian Existentialism." *Critic* 24 (1965):12–23.

Montgomery, Marion. "Of Cloaks and Hats and Doublings in Poe and O'Connor." *Southern Carolina Review* 11 (1978):60–69.

Morton, Mary L. "Doubling in Flannery O'Connor's Female Characters: Animus and Anima." *Southern Quarterly* 23, no. 4 (1985):57–63.

Muller, Gilbert H. *Nightmares and Visions: Flannery O'Connor and the Catholic Grotesque.* Athens: University of Georgia Press, 1972.

Myers, David A. "A Galaxy of Haloed Suns: Epiphanies and Peacocks in Patrick White's *A Woman's Hand* and Flannery O'Connor's "The Displaced Person," *Literatur in Wissenschaft und Unterricht* 14, no. 4 (1981):214–24.

Nisly, Paul W. "The Prison of the Self: Isolation in Flannery O'Connor's Fiction." *Studies in Short Fiction* 3 (1980):49–54.

Oates, Joyce Carol. *New Heaven, New Earth: The Visionary Experience in Literature.* New York: Fawcett Crest Books, 1974.

O'Connor, William Van. *The Grotesque: An American Genre and Other Essays.* Carbondale: Southern Illinois University Press, 1962.

Oreovicz, Cheryl Z. "Seduced by Language: The Case of Joy-Hulga Hopewell." *Studies in American Fiction* 7, no. 2 (1979):221–28.

Orvell, Miles. *Invisible Parade.* Philadelphia: Temple University Press, 1972.

Pachmuss, Temira. "Dostoevsky and America's Southern Women Writers." In *Poetica Slavica*, edited by J. Douglas Clayton and Gunter Schaarschmidt. Ottawa: University of Ottawa Press, 1981.

Quinn, Sister M. Bernetta. "View from a Rock: The Fiction of Flannery O'Connor and J. F. Powers." *Critique: Studies in Modern Fiction* 2, no. 2 (1958):19–27.

Richard, Claude. "Desire and Destiny in 'A Good Man Is Hard to Find.'" *Delta* 2 (1976):61–74.

Rosenfield, Claire. "The Shadow Within: The Conscious and Unconscious Use of the Double." *Daedalus* 92 (1963):326–44.

Rubin, Louis D., Jr. *The Faraway Country: Writers of the Modern South.* Seattle: University of Washington Press, 1963.

———. "Southerners and Jews." *Southern Review* 2 (1966):697–713.

Schleifer, Ronald. "Rural Gothic: The Stories of Flannery O'Connor." *Modern Fiction Studies* 28, no. 3 (1982):475–85.

Shields, John C. "Flannery O'Connor's 'Greenleaf' and the Myth of Europa and the Bull." *Studies in Short Fiction* 18, no. 4 (1981):421–31.

Spivey, Ted. R. "Flannery O'Connor's View of God and Man." *Studies in Short Fiction* 1, no. 3 (1964):200–206.

———. "Religion and the Reintegration of Man in Flannery O'Connor and Walker Percy." In *Spectrum: Monograph Series in the Arts and Sciences.* Vol. 2, *The Poetry of Community: Essays on the Southern Sensibility of History and Literature*, edited by Lewis P. Simpson, 67–79. Atlanta: Georgia State University, 1972.

———. "O'Connor, Joyce, and the Southern City." *Studies in the Literary Imagination*, Winter 1988.

Walters, Dorothy. *Flannery O'Connor.* Twayne United States Author's Series, no. 216. New York: Twayne Publishers, 1973.

Westarp, Karl-Heinz, and Jan Nordby Gretlund. *Realist of Distances: Flannery O'Connor Revisited.* Aarhus, Denmark: Aarhus University Press, 1987.

Westling, Louise. *Sacred Groves and Ravaged Gardens: The Fiction of Eudora Welty, Carson McCullers, and Flannery O'Connor.* Athens: University of Georgia Press, 1985.

Zuber, Leo J., comp. *The Presence of Grace and Other Book Reviews by Flannery O'Connor.* Edited by Carter W. Martin. Athens: University of Georgia Press, 1983.

Index

"A" (anonymous correspondent):
O'Connor's letters to, 4, 126–27,
140, 141, 142
Abnormal psychology, 125
Abraham, Karl, 105, 188–90
Albee, Edward, 223
American romance tradition, 12, 86,
141
Anderson, Sherwood, 223
Anima/animus, 32–33, 201–3
Aquinas, Saint Thomas, 4–5, 131
Asals, Frederick, 31, 33–34, 40, 152–
53, 204–7
Atlanta Journal and Constitution, 125
Auden, W. H., 161
Augustine, Saint, 85, 97, 167

Bachelard, Gaston, 78
Ballif, Algene, xiv
Baptism, 158
Becker, Ernest, 38
Beckett, Samuel, 177, 223
Bellow, Saul, 174
Bentley, Eric, 206
Bergson, Henri, 207–9
Bernanos, Georges, 157
Bishop, Elizabeth, 211
Blake, William, 112, 166–68, 209,
210, 211, 213
Bleikasten, André, 107, 152, 185–88
Bloom, Harold, 143
Book reviews, 151, 153
Booth, Wayne, 109
Brittain, Joan T., and Driskell, Leon
V., 152, 182–84
Brooks, Cleanth, 7–9, 11–12
Brooks, Peter, 206–7
Browning, Preston, M., 152, 199–
201

Caldwell, Erskine, 142, 152, 176,
222
Calvinism, 86, 202–3
Campbell, Joseph, 29
Camus, Albert, 145, 223
Capote, Truman, 222
Cartoons, 130, 131
Carver, Catherine, 127
Catholicism. *See* Roman Catholicism;
Spanish Catholicism
Cervantes, Miguel de, 138
Chandler, Raymond, 142
Chekhov, Anton Pavlovich, 127
Christian humanism, 164–68, 169
Coleridge, Samuel Taylor, 211–13,
166
Comic, the, ix–xi, 36, 53, 56, 87,
91–92, 103, 108–11, 122, 153,
177, 192–93, 200, 204–9, 222
Conrad, Joseph, x, 139, 166, 200
Crane, Stephen, 176, 177
Curley, Dan, 152, 159–61
Currie, Sheldon, 153, 207–9

Dante, 76, 169
D'Arcy, M. C., 164–65
Davis, Joe Lee. *See Kenyon Review*
Dawkins, Cecil, 5–6, 32, 121, 138
Dickey, James, 136, 174
Divided self, 5, 11, 13–14, 24, 29,
32, 39, 52–53, 55, 61, 76, 85, 103–
6, 170, 207
Don Quixote, 137, 138
Dostoyevski, Fyodor, x, 125, 127,
169, 200
Double figure, 5, 11, 13, 16, 55, 67,
70, 74, 92, 178, 187, 193–95, 201–
3, 204–5
Drake, Robert, 152, 218–19

Dreiser, Theodore, 176
Driskell, Leon V., and Joan T.
  Brittain, 152, 182–84

Eggenschwiler, David, 152, 164–68
Eliade, Mircea, 41
Eliot, T. S., 7, 16, 40, 112, 162–65,
  209, 213
Ellison, Ralph, 174
Empson, William, 7–9
Engle, Paul, 121, 129, 133
Epiphany, 85, 96, 158, 169
Erikson, Erik, 46–48, 52, 105
Esprit, 127
Eucharist, 102–3
Existentialism, 13–27, 106, 109, 152,
  161–62, 164–65, 169

Fall, the, 123
Faulkner, William, x, 125, 143, 152,
  176, 178, 222
Feminism, 28–45, 195–98, 201–3
Fitzgerald, Robert, 152, 161, 169,
  219
Fitzgerald, Sally, 3, 139
Freud, Sigmund, 4–7, 15, 21–22, 28,
  32, 38, 42, 48–49, 54, 71, 77, 88,
  90, 105, 151, 164–65, 185–86,
  193, 199–201
Friedman, Melvin J., 121, 139, 151

Giroux, Robert, 121, 129
Gogol, Nikolai Vasilievich, 127
Goodman, Mary Ellen, 68–69, 75
Gordon, Caroline, 9, 82, 121, 135,
  136
Gordon, Sarah, 152, 177–80
Gothic, American, 124
Goyen, William, 176
Grady, Henry W., 181
Greene, Graham, 157
Gresset, Michel, 152
Grotesque, 96, 140, 142, 155, 188,
  193, 199–200, 223
Grotesque tragicomedy, 122
Guardini, Romano, 164, 167

Hardy, Thomas, 219
Harris, Joel Chandler, 181
Hawkes, John, 122, 128, 140–41,
  174, 203
Hawthorne, Nathaniel, 72, 76, 106,
  141, 143–44, 166, 179, 200, 211
Heidegger, Martin, 106
Heller, Arno, 152, 172–73
Hemingway, Ernest, 129, 176
Hendin, Josephine, 10, 69, 107, 140
Hopkins, Gerard Manley, 180, 219
Howe, Irving, 140
Hudson Review, 126
Humor, 177–80, 200; popular
  American, 92–94; of frontier
  writers, 221

Imagery, 11–12
Incarnation, the, 68, 85–111
Ionesco, Eugene, 223

James, Henry, 123, 135
Jansenism, 85, 100
Jones, Bartlett C., 152, 188–90
Joyce, James, 9–10, 11, 40, 85
Jung, Carl, 5–6, 28–45, 112, 152,
  164, 201–3

Kafka, Franz, x, 38, 107, 142, 222–
  23
Kahane, [Katz], Claire, 10, 18, 30,
  71, 152, 191–95
Karamazov, Ivan, 145
Kenyon Review, 142
Kessler, Edward, 153, 209–13
Kierkegaard, Søren, 13
Klug, M. A., 152, 173–75
Kovel, Joel, 68–69, 75, 78
Krieger, Murray, 8
Kubie, Lawrence S., 68–69, 75, 79–
  80

Lacan, Jacques, 185–88
Lawrence, D. H., 137
Le Clézio, J. M. G., 152, 170–72
Lévy, Maurice, 151, 157–59

Index

Lone Ranger, the, ix
Love, Betty Boyd, 132
Lowell, Robert, 211

McCown, Father J. H., 123
McCullers, Carson, 222
McGill, Ralph, 181
Malamud, Bernard, 174
Manichaeanism, 85, 106, 152, 173–75, 206–7
Maritain, Jacques, 98, 116, 165, 181
Mauriac, François, 157, 179, 181
Meaders, Margaret, 121, 129–35
Melodrama, 204–7
Melville, Herman, 169, 221
Memoir of Mary Ann, A. See Flannery O'Connor
Mercier, Vivian. *See Hudson Review*
Merton, Thomas. *See Time*
Metaphor, 20, 209–13
Modernism, ix–xi, 4–5, 12, 48, 109–10, 122, 136–38, 164–68, 170–75, 222
Morton, Mary L., 152, 201–3
Myers, David A., 152, 169–70
Mystery and Manners. See Flannery O'Connor
Myth, 40–42, 51–52, 102, 222

Narratology, 213–18
Neumann, Erich, 28–30, 32, 113
New Criticism, xiii, 7–12, 112
New York Review of Books, 140
New York Times, 131
Nietzsche, Frederich Wilhelm, 16, 28
Nihilism, ix, 91, 109–10, 173

O'Connor, Flannery

WORKS:
"The Artificial Nigger," xii, 68–72, 75–82, 84, 110–11, 115, 160–61, 199, 221
"The Barber," xi
"The Capture," xii, 19–21

"A Circle in the Fire," xi–xiii, 10, 23, 40, 85–86, 94–96, 110, 158, 196–97, 201–3
"The Comforts of Home," xii, 10, 28, 30–37, 111, 159, 161, 188–90, 194, 196, 206, 211
"The Crop," xi
"The Displaced Person," xii, 28, 40. 43–44, 46–48, 61, 63–68, 86, 93, 108, 110–11, 156, 159–61, 169–70, 201–2, 205, 210
"The Enduring Chill," xii, 3, 11, 28, 30, 36–39, 111, 156, 210
"Enoch and the Gorilla," xi
"Everything That Rises Must Converge," xii, 68–72, 82–84, 110–11, 203, 205
"The Geranium," xii, 3, 16–19, 25, 61
"Good Country People," ix, xii, 3, 28, 46–53, 60, 110–11, 152, 158, 159, 161, 188–90, 196, 199, 207–8, 211
"A Good Man Is Hard to Find," xii, 35, 60, 73, 85–91, 96, 108, 110–11, 124, 196, 199, 204–5, 213–18, 219, 220
"Greenleaf," xii, 28, 30, 40–45, 108–10, 196, 201–2, 205–6, 220–21
"The Heart of the Park," xi
"Judgement Day," xii, 10, 18–19, 68–75, 110
"The Lame Shall Enter First," xii, 3, 21–24, 108, 141, 160–61
"A Late Encounter with the Enemy," xii, 46–48, 56–60, 110–11, 133
"The Life You Save May Be Your Own," xii, 39–40, 85–86, 91–94, 108, 110, 158, 159, 193–94, 207–9, 216, 221
A Memoir of Mary Ann, xiii, 71–72, 122, 138, 142–45
Mystery and Manners, 3–5
"Parker's Back," xiii, 85–86, 100, 103–11, 151, 182–88

"The Partridge Festival," xii, 3, 46–48, 53–56, 108
"The Peeler," xi
"Revelation," 28, 46–48, 59–63, 110, 127, 160, 177–80, 198, 199, 220–21
"The River," xii, 23, 85–86, 96–100, 156, 158, 194
"A Stroke of Good Fortune," xii, 14–15, 31, 156
"A Temple of the Holy Ghost," xii–xiii, 85–86, 100–103, 156, 158, 161, 195–98, 219
"The Train," xi
"The Turkey" (*see* "The Capture")
"A View of the Woods," xii, 21, 23–27, 108, 110, 113, 194–95, 200, 220–23
The Violent Bear It Away, 3, 5, 21, 24, 110, 127, 158, 191–95, 212–13
"Why Do the Heathen Rage?" xi
"Wildcat," xii, 15–16
Wise Blood, 3, 109–10, 194
"A Woman on the Stairs," (*see* "A Stroke of Good Fortune")
"You Can't Be Any Poorer Than Dead," xi

O'Connor, Mrs. Regina Cline, 130, 132, 133

Park, Clara Claiborne, 139
Pascal, Blaise, 13
Paul, Saint, 160
Percy, Walker, 174
Plath, Sylvia, 174
Plato, 30, 90
Poe, Edgar Allan, x, 142, 152, 176–77, 188
Point of view, 9–11
Porter, Katherine Anne, 129, 222
Prescott, Orville. *See New York Times*
Puritan work ethic, 202

Quinn, Sister M. Bernetta, O.S.F., 151–52, 154–56

Rank, Otto, 28–29
Ransom, John Crowe, 7–9
Redemption, 123, 155–56, 168, 212; in "The Artificial Nigger," 80, 115
Richard, Claude, 153, 213–18
Richards, I. A., 7–9, 211–12
Robbs-Grillet, Alain, 222
Roman Catholicism, ix, 3–4, 12–14, 31, 42, 48, 80, 85–109, 122, 133–34, 154–61, 165–68, 176–77
Rubin, Louis D., Jr., 152, 180–82

Sacraments, 156, 219
Sartre, Jean-Paul, 129
Scoptophilia, 188–90
Scott, Nathan A., 15
Scouten, Kenneth, 76
Sewanee Review, 140
Shakespeare, William, 93
Shloss, Carol, 10
Sibley, Celestine. *See Atlanta [Journal and] Constitution*
Simons, John W. *See Commonweal*
Sophocles, 129
Southern regionalism, xi, 18, 29, 47, 56–59, 82–84, 86, 93, 109, 122, 124–25, 127, 130–31, 133–38, 152, 154, 169, 176–82, 197, 199, 209, 214–16, 221–22
Spanish Catholicism, 137
Spivey, Ted. R., 121, 131, 135–38, 141
Stephens, Martha, xiv, 10
Stephens, Wallace, 140
Surrealism, 223

Tate, Allen, 9, 135, 164–68
Teilhard de Chardin, Pierre, 29, 48, 82, 84, 145, 181
Thomas, Saint, 4
Tillich, Paul Johannes, 165
Time, 124, 128, 141
Tolstoy, Leo Nikolaevich, 127
Tragicomedy, x, 87, 103, 110, 122, 177, 185, 221–22
Turgenev, Ivan Sergeevich, 127

Index

Turner, Margaret. *See Atlanta Journal and Constitution*
Twain, Mark, 152, 176, 222

Vande Kieft, Ruth, 10

Walters, Dorothy, 152, 220
Warren, Robert Penn, 7–9
Waugh, Evelyn, 142, 157
Welty, Eudora, 178, 222

West, Nathanael, 179, 222
Westling, Louise, 152, 195–98
Williams, Tennessee, 125
Williams, William Carlos, 140
Winters, Yvor, 7–9, 12
Wolfe, Thomas, 176
Women, xi, 152

Yaddo, 114, 225
Yeats, W. B., 38

About the Author

Suzanne Morrow Paulson is an assistant professor of English at Minot State University in North Dakota. She earned a Ph.D. from the University of Minnesota–Minneapolis in 1984 and has taught American literature and various writing courses at the University of Minnesota–Minneapolis; the College of St. Thomas–St. Paul; the University of Minnesota–Morris; and the University of Illinois–Urbana. She also directed the Writing Center at the Fresno branch of the California State University system. Her B.A. in English was from California State University–Los Angeles. Her current fields of scholarly interest are American literature, the modern short story, and composition theory. She has written on Flannery O'Connor's second novel for *Literature and Psychology* and on other critical responses to O'Connor for the *American Scholar.*

About the Editor

General editor Gordon Weaver earned his B.A. in English at the University of Wisconsin-Milwaukee in 1961; his M.A. in English at the University of Illinois, where he studied as a Woodrow Wilson Fellow, in 1962; and his Ph.D. in English and creative writing at the University of Denver in 1970. He is the author of several novels, including *Count a Lonely Cadence, Give Him a Stone, Circling Byzantium*, and most recently *The Eight Corners of the World* (Vermont: Chelsea Green Publishing Company, 1988). Many of his numerous short stories are collected in *The Entombed Man of Thule, Such Waltzing Was Not Easy, Getting Serious, Morality Play*, and *A World Quite Round*. Recognition of his fiction includes the St. Lawrence Award for Fiction (1973), a National Endowment for the Arts Fellowship (1974), and the O. Henry First Prize (1979). He edited *The American Short Story, 1945–1980: A Critical History*. He is a professor of English at Oklahoma State University and serves as an adjunct member of the faculty of the Vermont College Master of Fine Arts Writing Program. Married, and the father of three daughters, he lives in Stillwater, Oklahoma.